Yankee Rebel

Yankee Rebel

The Civil War Journal of Edmund DeWitt Patterson

Edited by

John G. Barrett

Voices of the Civil War

Peter S. Carmichael, *Series Editor*

THE UNIVERSITY OF TENNESSEE PRESS / Knoxville

THE VOICES OF THE CIVIL WAR series makes available a variety of primary source materials that illuminate issues on the battlefield, the homefront, and the western front, as well as other aspects of this historic era. The series contextualizes the personal accounts within the framework of the latest scholarship and expands established knowledge by offering new perspectives, new materials, and new voices.

This book is printed on acid-free paper.

Library of Congress Cataloging-in-Publication Data

Patterson, Edmund DeWitt, b. 1842.
Yankee rebel: the Civil War journal of Edmund Dewitt Patterson/edited by John G. Barrett; with a new foreword by Nathaniel Cheairs Hughes, Jr.
p. cm.—(Voices of the Civil War)
Originally published: Chapel Hill: University of North Carolina Press, [1966].
Includes bibliographical references and index.

ISBN 1-57233-245-X (cl.: alk. paper)

1. Patterson, Edmund DeWitt, b. 1842—Diaries.
2. United States—History—Civil War, 1861-1865—Personal narratives, Confederate.
3. Alabama—History—Civil War, 1861-1865—Personal narratives, Confederate.
4. Alabama—History—Civil War, 1861-1865—Regimental histories.
5. United States—History—Civil War, 1861-1865—Regimental histories.
6. United States—History—Civil War, 1861-1865—Campaigns.
7. United States—History—Civil War, 1861-1865—Prisoners and prisons.
8. Confederate States of America. Army. Alabama Infantry Regiment, 9th.
9. Prisoners of war—United States—Diaries.
10. Johnson Island Prison.

I. Barrett, John Gilchrist.
II. Title.
III. Series.

E605.P33 2004
973.7'82—dc22 2003024365

CONTENTS

FOREWORD

Nathaniel Cheairs Hughes Jr.

Edmund DeWitt Patterson's diary is a splendid first-hand account of the American Civil War written by a literate soldier blessed with powers of careful observation and clear, compelling prose. The result is a book at once appealing to the young and the forever young, those who will love the heroism, the adventure, the color. These qualities abound. To appreciate the diary properly, however, perhaps one should be over forty. Matching the pride and energy and humor of Patterson's writing are a sadness and a sense of irony. These are the reflective sentences of a man grown old before his time, compelled to make choices that will hurt those he loved, compelled to undergo trials not from self-interest but conscience. Edmund Patterson was an admirable human being. Imagine the degradation of begging on behalf of a friend; imagine a badly wounded man sacrificing his precious water for an enemy soldier, fatally wounded but crying out for water to any who might hear; imagine each day having to take a long probe and press it, topped with a strip of cotton, into the depth of a comrade's shoulder wound, then clumsily but tenderly drawing it out through his breast. It all seemed so useless.

"I wouldn't feel so blue," Patterson entered into his diary, "if Ansel would only get well, but poor fellow he seems to grow worse every day. Last night his pain was so intense that he was perfectly insane. His screams made me shudder, and then when for one brief moment the pains would cease, he would pray God Oh! so earnestly, to let him die. As I sat by his bedside, he feared that I would leave him, and clutched my arm until he left the imprint of his fingers on my arm. There is no use of your doing *that,* Ansel, I would not leave you for anything in this world. . . ."

One agonizes with Patterson, yet grows more confident and comfortable, realizing that the citizen soldier welcomes the reader as a traveling companion, sharing his rations and allowing the reader to peer into his deeply private inner world. It is true, Edmund put the diary aside and refused to revisit the war after it had ended, but he knew the diary was precious and saw to it that it would be preserved, intending, perhaps unconsciously, that others at a later time might enter with safety that desperate world from which he had been delivered, that desperate world that would define him.

A passionate Confederate nationalist, Patterson became so from conviction rather than from birth and family persuasion. Born and raised in Lorain County, Ohio, Patterson came south at age seventeen to sell books. He failed miserably as a salesman and looked about anxiously for other employment. Luckily, the village of Second Creek, just above Waterloo, Alabama, sorely needed a schoolteacher. Inexperienced and uncertified, young Patterson boldly appealed to the directors of the school to allow him to fill the position temporarily. "If I failed to obtain the certificate I would quit the school and charge nothing for my services." Patterson worked hard fulfilling his bargain. At the end of the school year, however, he knew he wanted no more. He would not be a schoolteacher like his father. Instead he chose to make more money as a clerk in a dry goods store in Waterloo. It suited him. Patterson was quite happy with his lot—that is, until the late spring of 1861.

Two years among the people of north Alabama had turned him about. Gone was his boyhood fantasy of adventure out west. "I liked the South," he wrote. "I found nothing existing as I had heard it represented, and I concluded to make my home there. Soon the dark clouds of war arose and grew blacker and blacker. . . . I saw there was no alternative but war, disgrace and everlasting dishonor for the South." Patterson knew he could return home to Ohio and be rewarded with security and the "thorough education" he eagerly wanted. Instead he gave up everything and enlisted "for the war" with his Waterloo friends in Company D (Lauderdale Rifles), Ninth Alabama Infantry.

He was angry. Eighteen sixty-one "will be remembered as the year in which the Southern people, unable longer to bear the tyranny of the North, or rather of Northern fanaticism, determined to exercise those rights guaranteed to them by the constitution and following the example of the colonies, years ago, separated themselves from the old government and set up for themselves another in which there will not be so many conflicting interests."

The nineteen-year-old Patterson inspired confidence. Elected 4th Corporal of the Lauderdale Rifles, from the outset he proved a conscientious and energetic soldier. He admired very much, and studied closely, his regimental commander—Colonel Cadmus M. Wilcox, an experienced professional soldier, a West Pointer and a hero of the Mexican War. Patterson and his friends enthusiastically followed Wilcox off to Virginia on June 3, 1861. Arriving in Winchester, Virginia, weary and footsore from a forced march, the men from Alabama found talk of battle at every hand. When they were issued forty rounds of ammunition, Patterson reflected, "it looks as if someone is to be hurt. . . . These are the first 'Cartridges' that I have ever seen, and is it possible that we are actually to *kill men*? *Human Beings*?" His July 16 diary entry continued, "That these cartridges were made purposely for one poor mortal to shoot at another? Yes, this is war, and how hardened men must become."

Arriving at First Manassas too late to participate in the fighting, Edmund wandered the field in shock. "Here are mangled human bodies on every side, some pierced by a rifle or a musket ball—others almost to fragments by shell—in some places horse and rider have fallen together. Some have a look or expression on their face as mild and calm as if they were only sleeping, others seem to have had a terrible struggle with the monster death and only yielded after having suffered such pain as has caused their faces to assume expressions that are fearful to look upon, their features distorted, the eyeballs glaring, and often with their hands full of mud and grass that they have clutched in their last agony. I noticed one who had striven vainly to staunch the flow of blood from a wound through the body by stuffing mud into the wound. . . . The result of this battle will teach the North a lesson that will not soon be forgotten. It will show to them, and the world, that we are in earnest and that we mean what we say and that in attempting our subjugation [they] have undertaken an herculean task."

Patterson would see combat soon enough. He participated in some of the heaviest fighting at Williamsburg and at Seven Pines. The latter battle cost the army its commander, Joseph E. Johnston, who was badly wounded. This was a terrible misfortune, Edmund believed, and he wondered who might replace the irreplaceable. The Seven Days battles followed. Patterson's superb descriptions of combat at Gaines's Mill, Mechanicsville, White Oak Swamp, and Frayser's Farm so impressed historian Bell I. Wiley that he would assert: "I do not know of any other soldier account which gives a more realistic and vivid representation of what a Civil War battle was like. . . . Its excellence is so outstanding as to set it apart from the general run of published (and unpublished) personal accounts."

Each battle seemed worse than the one before. Finally, on June 30 at Frayser's Farm, the 9th Alabama charged a Federal battery, having to break through and scatter its infantry support. At the height of their success Patterson was struck in the shoulder by a musket ball; another bullet struck his left leg while still another bullet smashed into his other leg, penetrating to the bone where it ranged down and lodged against the kneecap. Patterson crumpled, painfully and dangerously wounded. Wilcox, who now commanded a brigade, pulled back his troops, and Patterson's woes multiplied. He was menaced by a drunken Irishman: "O, you d——d rebel son of a bitch, I'll put *you* out of your misery." Edmund could do nothing to defend himself. "I remember just rolling my eyes heavenward and though my lips did not move, my heart said 'god have mercy on my soul.' And the bayonet was thrust aside by a strong arm." It was a Federal officer. The noble rescuer struck the Irishman with the flat of his sword and drove him off, saving the young Confederate's life. Two Union soldiers, perhaps summoned by the kindly officer in blue, soon came up and "half dragged and half carried him two hundred yards to the rear and laid him among their wounded. There Patterson remained all through the night. "How I long for day. Just that *some* one might see me die. It seems now that it would make but little difference," he would write six weeks later, "but I felt so then. but if the night was dark, it was not so dark as the future. . . . The loss of so much blood had made me very cold, and it seemed to me that I would freeze. I shook until I almost feared that I would shake in pieces. My teeth chattered until they were sore."

A young wounded soldier, "he could not be more than sixteen," took pity upon Edmund and sat with him till daylight, brought him water, covered him with a blanket, and "put my head on his lap. . . . An own brother could not have been more gentle and kind to me." At last the Confederates counterattacked and drove the enemy off. Patterson received medical attention, having the ball in his right leg cut out without benefit of chloroform. "It reminded me of cutting fat pork," Patterson wrote. "It cut so smooth and nice." Even to be touched was excruciatingly painful, but Patterson's wounds were dressed and he began the slow journey to Richmond. He arrived on July 4 and secured quarters in the home of Mrs. Charles Quarles, "an angel minister embodied in woman's delicate form, sent by the Father to relieve the woes of suffering humanity. She never seems to grow weary of well doing."

Weeks passed, and Patterson slowly recuperated. "Doctor Holloway opened my left thigh not long ago. The wound on the under side had healed up too soon, and pus had accumulated until my leg was as big as two ought to have been. While I was reasoning the case with him, and asking him to give me chloroform, he pretended to be examining it and the first thing I knew, had his knife in me and the operation performed 'Before I could say Jack Robinson.'"

Finally Edmund could sit up, and presently he graduated to the front porch. He took great delight in speaking to Confederate

President Davis, who lived nearby and came down the sidewalk each morning. Davis "never passes without speaking, . . . and I like to look upon his face, always so pale and careworn and yet such a pleasant one. *We know each other.* I know him to be our loved President, and he knows me to be a wounded soldier. God Bless him! and may his shadow never grow less." Patterson also saw Vice-President Alexander Stephens: "He comes along in a swinging gait, dressed in black broadcloth, the long tails of his coat reaching nearly to his heels. A ponderous fob chain with a huge seal swinging half way to his knees. An enormous 'Byronical' collar hangs loosely about his neck,—his cravat—a large black silk handkerchief tied in a hard knot and ends hanging down. His general appearance is that his clothes were thrown at him from a distance and remain where they happened to strike." Patterson would watch Stephens preside in the Senate chamber and observed many other Confederate officials. He provides cameos of Clement C. Clay, William L. Yancy, Robert E. Lee, Jeb Stuart, and other well-known civil and military leaders.

By the time of the Maryland Campaign in the fall of 1862, Patterson had not healed sufficiently to rejoin the regiment. Instead he was given sick leave and returned to Waterloo to rest and relax. Thus he missed Sharpsburg (consistently misspelled, as editor John G. Barrett points out), but, as though to compensate, he provided a fine account of travel within the Confederacy and of life behind the lines. When Edmund rejoined the 9th Alabama in late November 1863 he found it shattered from the fighting at Sharpsburg. Indeed, he learned he has been elected lieutenant weeks before to replace an officer and old friend killed in that terrible conflict.

The regiment encamped several miles above Fredericksburg, and soon the action began. As the Yankees threw pontoons across the Rappahannock, Patterson watched as Gen. William Barksdale and "his Mississippians gave them a foretaste of what was in reservation for them on this side, baptizing many of them with blood and water, and offering to bridge the river with their dead bodies if they would come fast enough."

The terrible noise of cannon fire caught his attention:

> Shells above, below, and immediately opposite, meeting, greeting, and bursting over [Fredericksburg], scattering their death warrants everywhere. The light of morning scattered the fog and revealed the height wreathed in smoke, parted every instant by the lightning tongues of those iron throated monsters; while over the city hung a funeral pall . . . of battle smoke. . . . Never before have I ever witnessed a scene of such *terrible* beauty. Or heard music so *grand,* and at the same time so mournfully beautiful. As the mighty choir chanted in thunder tones this grand anthem of praise to the God of War, height answered to height. The hills catching up the echoes, flung them back with scarcely lessened power, and as they died away in the distance far down the lovely valley, new thunders again aroused them and again the woods, the hills and the valleys lent their assistance in keeping up the dread melody. Shells flew shrieking through the air, sounding like a wail of agony from some lost spirit.

Fighting at Chancellorsville proved more dangerous. Just as they were about to be overwhelmed at Salem Church on May 3, 1863, guarding Lee's right flank, the 9th Alabama and Wilcox's brigade were reinforced. "With a wild yell the brigade moved forward at the same time; the whole Yankee line was driven back in confusion, and the day was won." Combined with Lee's bold and successful attack against Joseph Hooker's main body, Chancellorsville proved to be the Army of Northern Virginia's most singular victory. Edmund was elated.

It was not to be so with Gettysburg the following July. Patterson and his men found themselves on the extreme right of the army on the second day. In that savage fighting, primarily conducted against the Irish Brigade of the Army of the Potomac (the third time the 9th Alabama had met them in battle), strong enemy units succeeded in lodging themselves behind Patterson's position. Soon the 9th Alabama was surrounded. In minutes Lieutenant Patterson and about fifty of his regiment were captured.

Twenty months of imprisonment followed. After a short stay at Fort Delaware ("A respectable hog," Edmund declared, "would have turned up his nose in disgust at it"), Patterson was moved with other Confederate officers to Johnson's Island, on Lake Erie, near Sandusky, Ohio. There he would remain until March 1865. Wet, unsanitary conditions prevailed in their sixteen-acre prison. "Of course deaths under such circumstances were frightfully frequent. . . . Men seem to lose their self-respect." Patterson confided to his diary that Confederate soldiers now were called upon to "show they can suffer as well as fight for their country." The situation grew desperate as 1863 turned into 1864. Medicine was in short supply, and the already scanty rations were cut by order of the commandant of the prison. Patterson and his friends were reduced to killing and eating rats, "of which there are thousands." Rat tastes like squirrel, Edmund noted. He spent two winters at Johnson's Island. The wind and cold came through the thin walls of the huts; even his "ink freezes as fast as I write." Men died, men despaired.

Edmund's family, who lived only a few miles away, sent letters pleading with him to take the loyalty oath and thus be released from imprisonment. Patterson resolutely refused.

"Here I am," Patterson entered in his diary, "near the spot where I passed the sunny hours of childhood and the golden dreaming days of youth and under what circumstances—a prisoner of war. I am devoted to a cause that I esteem a just and holy one, and here is a kind father who I believe loves me as he loves his own life,—two sisters whose love for me is as pure as an Angel's love, and my brothers too,—yet all regard me as forever disgraced and dishonored."

Patterson managed to talk with his father once. He "still thinks me wrong and gives me advice which I cannot accept. . . . I can scarcely consider myself a member of the family—we have nothing in common." Finally the family stopped attempting to see him; letters became infrequent.

Patterson was exchanged on March 26, 1865, and set out to rejoin his old regiment. He found only a shadow of the unit that had marched off to Virginia four years earlier. Less than a company in strength, "they have been wasted by the storms of battle and by disease, and even the few remaining look weary and worn. How I love them and how dear the cause for which they contend, made a thousand times dearer by the sacrifice it has cost." Edmund Patterson closed his diary Sunday, April 9, 1865, the day Lee met Grant to discuss terms of surrender.

The diary reverberates in the mind long after the reader has turned the last page. Patterson has shared his life and his thoughts—his insights into the behavior of comrades, their multiple motives, their weaknesses and strengths. To designate it as a "coming of age" journal would be inadequate. This is history upon which one may rely, written by a man who is modest, compassionate, fiercely patriotic, and candid. The reader draws close to the author and agrees happily with Patterson's grandson, who believed "as a small child that if I could have known my grandfather he would have been my best friend." Historian John P. Dyer adds that "more than in any Civil War diary I have seen [young Patterson] has succeeded in putting into words the feeling, the emotional reactions of the soldier to the hours before a battle, during the battle, and as a dangerously wounded and half-frozen man lying on the battlefield wondering if help could come."

This remarkable war journal is enhanced by the skillful editing of John G. Barrett, a highly respected Civil War historian. He corrects Patterson when he is wrong, provides context for small actions in which Patterson finds himself, and identifies places and people hurriedly mentioned by the diarist. He even provides information unknown to Patterson about General John Pope's coat found in the Confederate Capitol Library. The coat, it seems, had been captured by General Stuart the week before. We also learn about Aeolian harps and shin-plasters among dozens of items familiar to Patterson but mysterious to modern readers.

Richard B. Harwell, who knows as much about Confederate lore as anyone, finds Patterson's diary "the finest personal narrative of Confederate experiences since Henry Kyd Douglas's *I Rode with Stonewall.*" Happily, *Yankee Rebel,* long out of print, can now be shared with new generations of readers.

THE MAN WHO WROTE THE DIARY

Edmund DeWitt Patterson, my grandfather, would have called himself a very ordinary man. He displayed no extremes of character, habit, or appearance but was so well endowed with the old-fashioned virtues of honesty, fairness, good judgment, and respect for others that in his later years he was often spoken of as the best loved man in his community.

He was born in Lorain County, Ohio, March 20, 1842. His parents were New Englanders who came to Ohio from Massachusetts and Connecticut in the great westward migration of the early 1800's. While their lives would not be considered particularly hard by the standards of the times, the country where they lived was not long out of the frontier, and survival in both the physical and economic senses was a matter of primary concern. Even so, education held a place of great importance in their lives. Grandfather's father was a farmer during the summer and a school-teacher in the winter, and his mother's family enjoyed local renown for scholarship.

His mother died when he was ten years old and he and his brothers and sisters were separated for a time. In an autobiographical sketch written many years later, Grandfather Patterson wrote: "After my Mother's death I went to live with the family of an uncle [a physician] but spent much time at my Grandfather Brooks'. Though my Father's house had always been a stopping place for Methodist preachers I had never been accustomed to such strict observance of the Sabbath as was required by my grandfather. He would not permit me to whittle on Sunday and I came near to losing one of my most precious treasures, a pocket knife, because in a moment of forgetfulness I took it out of my pocket and began whittling on Sunday."

He attended public schools until he was seventeen at which time he attempted to make his way in the world as a salesman of book and magazine subscriptions. It was this adventure that took him into the South, first to Tennessee and then into northern Alabama. Of this enterprise and his subsequent decision to join the Confederacy he later wrote:

"My three months work as a Book Agent had thoroughly satisfied me that I would never make a success in that line; my employers being of the same opinion were glad to release me as well as to be released from our contract.

"Feeling the sting of my failure to sell books, I determined I would not return home to be laughed at for my wild goose chase in coming South, and began to look about to find something to do. About that time the people on Second Creek just above Waterloo, [Alabama] wanted a teacher for their school. Under the law, the directors had no right to contract with one who had not been first examined by the County Superintendent and given a certificate. I wished to secure the school, the County Superintendent lived in the Eastern end of the County more than forty miles away, and I doubted my ability to stand the required examinations, so learning that the Superintendent would be in that neighborhood in about a month to conduct his examinations, I proposed to the directors of the school that I would teach the school until he came and if I failed to obtain the certificate I would quit the school and charge nothing for my services.

"The proposition was accepted and I began at once. Before the month was out I had reviewed my studies and had no difficulty in passing the required examinations, and my school continued seven and a half months, when a position was offered me as clerk in a store at Waterloo.

"By this time, politics was the all-absorbing topic and persons from the North were looked upon with suspicion, so that I decided to return to Ohio, but before I was ready to start I had a personal difficulty arising out of a political discussion caused by an insinuation that I might be a spy, which caused me to decide to remain.

"The war came on and in May 1861 I enlisted in a company called the Lauderdale Rifles, afterwards Company D, 9th Alabama Infantry. In the organization, I was elected 4th Corporal. We received marching orders on the 28th of May. June 3rd we left Florence, Alabama, for Richmond, and I became a part of the 9th Alabama Regiment, with C. M. Wilcox, afterward a Major General, as First Colonel. We were sent to the front July 14th, 1861."

At the time of Lee's surrender at Appomattox, my grandfather had been returned to Virginia in an exchange of prisoners, and he waited about Richmond with a group of his friends for some time, expecting to be provided transportation home. When it became clear that no such transportation was forthcoming, he and his friends walked home to Alabama, a distance of some six hundred miles.

Upon his return, he was invited by General Edward O'Neal (later governor of Alabama) to live with the O'Neal family and to "read law" in the general's office at Florence. A little later he went to Baltimore, Maryland, and continued his study of law there, returning to Alabama toward the end of 1868. In the following year he married Eleanor Mildred McDougal of Savannah, Tennessee, and entered into the practice of law in partnership with his father-in-law, Archibald G. McDougal. He served as clerk and master of chancery court for twelve years, was elected to the state Senate for one term, then was elected judge of the circuit court. He held this post for eleven years, resigning because of ill health and returning to private practice. He served for several years as president of the Bank of Savannah.

In our family, Grandfather's journal of the Civil War was referred to as The Diary. When the war ended and he returned to Alabama, he preserved the diary but took no interest in it. (Several years later, urged by my grandmother, he reluctantly put it in chronological order.) This disinterest was in keeping with his attitude toward the war. He considered it a tragic mistake and for the rest of his life did not care to discuss it or his experiences in it. He would have no part in any effort to glorify or commemorate the "lost cause" or in the reunions of old soldiers which were frequent and popular during his later years.

Two seemingly contradictory exceptions to his general attitude toward the war were his free admittance that he had been a rebel and had never been reconstructed, and his refusal to be reconciled with his family in Ohio for many years after the war. On this latter point, one difficulty was that his family took the stand that grandfather's action in joining the Confederacy was not only treason to his country and to his family, but also foolish, and he refused to agree. Another point that probably counted at least as heavily as this with my grandfather, was his conviction that his family had knowingly permitted him to suffer near-starvation in prison while they were living in comfort and plenty only a few miles away. By about 1890 a workable truce had been negotiated with his family, and in the years that followed they became good friends again, but it is not certain that he ever completely forgave them for letting him go hungry.

It will be evident to the reader of the journal that throughout the war and during his time in prison, the author read everything he could lay his hand on. His children testify that he read widely and continuously all his life and that his knowledge of a tremendous range of subjects was impressive. One of his daughters, Mrs. H. I. Cecil, relates that when she traveled through Europe with her father a few years before he died, she, "fresh out of college and knowing everything" was constantly amazed at his encyclopedic knowledge of places, history, persons, and tradition. Mrs. Cecil says, "He described events that took place in the Forum, told what Shakespeare or Shelley had said about this or that. . . ." On this tour she also discovered that her father could read French easily though he could not understand spoken French and would not attempt to speak it; his explanation was that he had studied a French textbook while a prisoner at Johnson's Island (some thirty-five years earlier) but unfortunately had only learned to read the language since the textbook did not include any explanation of pronunciation!

My grandfather has always been a very real person to me, although he died several years before I was born. My father and his brothers and sisters never talked for very long among themselves without making some reference to their father. They said he had a remarkable ability for assuming an equal status with anyone he talked to and was a most charming companion to them even when they were young. They usually referred to him as "Judgefather," their memory and feeling for him obviously a pleasant mixture of fondness and a respect that approached awe.

Perhaps the best indication of the power of his personality was the conviction I had as a small child that if I could have known my grandfather he would have been my best friend.

Edmund Brooks Patterson
September, 1966

INTRODUCTION

Edmund DeWitt Patterson was only nineteen when, in May, 1861, he enlisted in the Lauderdale Rifles which became Company D, Ninth Alabama Regiment. At the time he had been living in Alabama less than two years. Yet during this short period, he adapted himself completely to the southern way of life. Furthermore, young Patterson was the only member of his immediate family living in any of the slave states at the outbreak of the war. His father, Hiram; sisters, Sophia and Belle; and brothers, Theodore (Thead), Joseph, and Charles—all staunch Unionists—were in Lorain County, Ohio.

There are many instances of northerners coming South and in time becoming vigorous defenders of the region, but seldom did one so young become so quickly such a strong believer in the southern cause. Patterson never wavered in his convictions, and throughout his journal he expressed the complete southern point of view. A typical entry is the following, dated December 31, 1861: "Another hour and this year will be gone forever. A year fraught with incidents long to be remembered, not only by the Southern people, but by all the world. It will be remembered as the year in which the Southern people, unable longer to bear the tyranny of the North, or rather of Northern fanaticism, determined to exercise those rights guaranteed to them by the constitution and following the example of the colonies, years ago, separated themselves from the old government and set up for themselves another in which there will not be so many conflicting interests. The North, so long accustomed to receive her countless thousands from the South, would not willingly sacrifice her share in the profits accruing from Southern trade, and hence this unholy war, which is being waged against the South and her institutions. . . . The cause of the South is growing brighter and I believe that ere long the Confederate States will be a free and independent government, loved at home, respected abroad."

Patterson was an unusual soldier, not only because of his background and deep loyalty to the South, but also because he could write exceptionally well. His journal has a literary quality that is unusual for a soldier not old enough to vote when he entered the army and whose formal education had not proceeded beyond the public schools of Ohio. Still the young man's training was better than that of most Confederate soldiers. In addition his parents' families were "strong on education." His father Hiram taught school at times and two of his uncles (Hiram's brothers) were physicians. Another uncle, William M. Brooks, founded a school at Tabor, Iowa, which grew to be Tabor College, and served as its president for a number of years. Also several of Patterson's cousins on his mother's side were early graduates of Oberlin College.

Nowhere is the young soldier's literary skill more clearly revealed than in those portions of his journal describing combat. These passages are especially vivid and moving. They describe in graphic detail what a Civil War battle was like. During the Seven Days fighting before Richmond, Patterson wrote: "Up to the crest of the hill we went at a double quick, but when we came into view of the top of the ridge we met such a perfect storm of lead right in our faces that the whole brigade literally staggered backward several paces as though punched by a tornado. The dead lay in heaps, and two minutes in that position would have been utter annihilation. Just for one moment we faltered, then the cry of Major Sorrell, 'Forward Alabamians,—Forward'!, and the cry was taken up by the officers of the different regiments and we swept forward with wild cheers over the crest and down the slope, and though at every step some brave one fell, we did not falter."

Later in the year at Fredericksburg, as he watched the bombardment of the town, Patterson noted how "Battery after battery joined in the dread chorus, until the very hills shook with the thunders of a hundred pieces of artillery, as they poured their concentrated fire into the doomed city. Shells above, below, and immediately opposite, meeting, greeting, and bursting over it, scattered their death warrants everywhere. The light of morning scattered the fog and revealed the height wreathed in smoke, parted every instant by the lightning tongues of those iron throated monsters; while over the city hung a funeral pall, a cloud of battle smoke, in which shells were incessantly bursting, scattering destruction, misery, death among the half frantic women and children who had not heeded the order to leave the city, and now rushed wildly through the streets seeking refuge from the iron storm which raged so pitilessly around them. Never before have I ever witnessed a scene of such *terrible* beauty. Or heard music so *grand,* and at the same time so mournfully beautiful."

Like so many of his comrades, Patterson was unprepared for what he called the "reality of war." He knew nothing about cartridges until they were issued to him in Virginia, and only after a visit to the Bull Run battlefield did he fully realize that he was in the army "to kill men? Human Beings? That these cartridges were made purposely for one poor mortal to shoot at another? Yes, this is war," he lamented, "and how hardened men must become."

This sudden realization that war was a matter of killing did not keep the young Alabamian from becoming a good soldier—in fact an excellent fighting man. Still he never became completely hardened to the realities of war. Thus he records in his journal not only the heroism and glamor of soldiering but also the horror, evil, and cowardice that he observed. He tells, for example, of the desertion of a comrade, the privations and cruelties of prison life, and the cowardice of his colonel.

In many ways the youth was a typical Confederate soldier. He liked the girls, enjoyed his whiskey, and possessed a delightful sense of humor. He loved to visit Inglewood, the home of Dr. Charles Quarles in Louisa County, Virginia, because the doctor was superintendent of the Inglewood Female Institute and there was always "a houseful of girls, or rather young ladies . . . [there] attending school. It is a delightful place." On the other hand, he complained of the weather, the boredom of camp life and picket duty, the monotony of the soldier's diet, and the lack of clothing. He missed his friends and always noted in his journal the letters he received from them. Hungry for news he thought nothing of exchanging newspapers with the enemy pickets.

Equally interesting are his observations on a number of well-known Confederate generals. After Joseph E. Johnston was wounded at Fair Oaks, Patterson did not "know what the army could do without him." Jackson's death prompted this line in his journal: "Never has the army before or since been half so affected as it was by his death." On the march to Gettysburg he observed how the men cheered lustily their "old war horse, Longstreet"; as for Lee, he noted that "The boys never cheer him but pull off their hats and worship." C. M. Wilcox, his brigade commander,[1] was also well liked by the men. This compassionate officer once purposely warned the Federals before shelling their position. As a member of Wilcox's brigade Patterson saw extensive action in the Peninsula Campaign of 1862.

At Williamsburg, on May 5, he was exposed to combat for the first time. Then followed the hard fighting at Fair Oaks and the Seven Days. At Frayser's Farm, the fourth major engagement in the Seven Days Battle, he was severely wounded. Instead of being placed in a hospital to recover, Patterson, at his own request, was taken to Richmond to the home of a friend, Mrs. Quarles, who lived on Twelfth Street. For a month and a half he was not strong enough to keep up with his journal, but on August 15 he was happy to write: "Thank God! able to at last sit propped up in bed with pillows. Since writing in my journal six weeks ago I suffered much, and the doctors say that I have been pretty near the invisible line dividing life and death—separating time from eternity." In lengthy

1. Wilcox's brigade was a part of Longstreet's command up to the reorganization of the Army of Northern Virginia following the Chancellorsville Campaign. At Gettysburg it was attached to A. P. Hill's Third Corps.

entries dated August 30 and 31 he describes the Battle of Frayser's Farm, his wounding, and his experiences afterward. September 12 found him at Inglewood enjoying once again the company of the young ladies in school there. In early October he left these pleasant surroundings on a thirty day furlough to cure, as he put it, "the Alabama fever in . . . [his] head."

Except for the difficulties of travel Patterson had a delightful stay in northern Alabama. His friends in Waterloo (Lauderdale County) and the surrounding country were most happy to see him. He visited part of the time with Mr. Wilson Whitsett with whom he had lived while teaching school at Second Creek, and, doubtless, he stopped by the "C. & J. Higgins" store where he had once worked. But everyone, it seemed, who had a boy in Virginia wished to send a gift or letter or both back by Patterson, which led him to remark: "I have my head full of a thousand or two last messages, tell my boy this, and tell my boy that. . . . I have so many little articles for the boys that I don't know whether I will be able to deliver them to their proper owners."

When he reported to his command near Fredericksburg on November 23, Patterson was surprised to learn that he "had been an officer [a lieutenant] for sometime without knowing it." The men had selected him, as was the general practice in the army, but he later appeared before an examining board to prove his fitness.

In the Battle of Fredericksburg, December, 1862, the Ninth Alabama, on Lee's extreme left, did not see action, but in the Chancellorsville Campaign the following spring, it was engaged both at Marye's Heights and Salem Church. During the interim between these campaigns, Patterson complained bitterly about the drudgery of camp life and picket duty along the Rappahannock. He preferred to fight: "I, for one, wish we could commence fighting and stop only long enough to carry off the wounded and bury the dead, until the issues involved are fought out and settled, *once and forever.*" When Lee started his move north in the summer of 1863, Patterson was happy: "We don't know where we are going but Marse Bob knows, and that is sufficient." The excitement of campaigning ended abruptly, however, at Gettysburg. During the second day's fighting, he was captured and was to remain a prisoner of war until March, 1865. Approximately half of his journal, therefore, is devoted to prison life. All entries following July 16, 1863, seem to have been written on the current dates. But the description of the action on July 2 is undated, and it appears, judging from the writing itself, that this entry, as well as those dated July 3, 4 and 6, were written several days later.[2]

After a short stay at Fort Delaware, Patterson was transferred to Johnson's Island near Sandusky, Ohio. This was far from the worst of the Civil War compounds. The health record was good, and until the last few months of 1864, the food ration was sufficient. The men were given as much freedom as security would permit; they engaged in many recreational activities, were able to obtain reading material, and could receive letters and newspapers from home. With a few exceptions they were not ill treated by their captors.

"Perhaps one of the worst features of prison life . . . ," wrote Patterson, "is that it is so public, that is, it is impossible for one to get away from the crowd, the bustle, and confusion. . . . I like company most all the time, but there are times when I like to be alone, yes, alone."

A few weeks earlier he had "gone forward" at one of the prison prayer meetings, commenting at the time: "If I am not a christian I am determined to become one." It worried him that the "devil . . . [seemed] to be gaining ascendancy over the hearts of a large number confined" with him at Johnson's Island.

Since his birthplace was only a few miles from Sandusky, Patterson's family visited him a number of times. They pleaded with him to take "the oath" and thus gain his freedom, but he steadfastly refused. Following a visit from his father, he had this to say: "Pa still thinks me wrong, and gives me advice which I cannot accept. He urges me to give up the cause of the South which he pronounces a doomed one and one which he is willing and anxious to see put down even though it should take years to accomplish and all the

2. This information was provided the editor by Edmund Brooks Patterson, who possesses the original journal.

treasure and blood both North and South have. I can scarcely consider myself a member of the family—we have nothing in common."

Finally, on March 14, 1865, Patterson and three hundred of his comrades were exchanged and left their "prison home for Dixie." They "thought not of the suffering of the past, of the long weary months of cold and hunger, nor of the dangers that might await . . . [them] in the future. . . ." They thought only of the present. They were once again in their "own land, among friends . . . perfectly happy."

A year's salary and a lengthy furlough awaited Patterson. So it was back to Inglewood, "the scene of many happy hours." His visit was cut short by the rumor that Richmond had been evacuated and that Lee was retreating westward in an effort to join forces with Joseph E. Johnston in North Carolina. As Patterson saw it, he had but one duty and that was to rejoin his command immediately: "I feel sad at leaving here, for I fear it is never to return. I intend to go around the armies if possible, and cross the James River, some where near Lynchburg and join our command. I fear there is terrible fighting in store for us this summer, but the Almighty may care for us as he has in the past." This was the final entry in his journal, dated April 9, 1865. On this fateful Sunday the war in Virginia came to a close. Lee surrendered to Grant at Appomattox.

In preparing this volume for publication, the editor has used a true copy, typed from the original handwritten journal in the possession of Patterson's grandson, Edmund Brooks Patterson of West Newton, Massachusetts. Other than to correct the spelling of certain proper names and places, I have made no corrections in the typescript.

John G. Barrett
The Virginia Military Institute
Lexington, Virginia
September, 1966

Yankee Rebel

· I ·

"Yes, this is war and how hardened men must become"

May 28, 1861, to January 16, 1862

In obedience to a call from the Governor of the State of Alabama[1] for troops to enlist for twelve months in the service of the Confederate States, I. B. Houston organized a company and offered its services to the Governor; his reply was that no more troops could be received for any less time than throughout the war.[2] Learning this, we immediately reorganized and tendered our services for the war[3] were accepted, and received our marching

1. Andrew B. Moore was governor of Alabama, 1857–61.

2. By October 7, 1861, there had been 27,000 enlistments in various military organizations. Several of the commands were enrolled for short terms of three months, six months, or one year. W. L. Fleming, *Civil War and Reconstruction in Alabama* (New York: Peter Smith, 1949—A Micro-offset Edition), p. 79; hereinafter cited as Fleming, *Civil War.*

3. Patterson's regiment, the Ninth Alabama, re-enlisted in 1864 while on duty in Virginia and consequently enjoyed the distinction of having a joint resolution of thanks given it by the Confederate Congress. *The War of the Rebellion: A Compilation of the Official Records of the Union and Confederate*

orders on the 28th day of May, 1861, and on the 3rd day of June left Florence enroute to Richmond, where we arrived on the 7th. Our Company then consisted of the following named officers:

Captain I. B. Houston
1st Lieut. W. C. Reeder
2nd Lieut. James M. Crow
3rd Lieut. W. J. Cannon

And the following named non-commissioned officers and men to wit:

1st Sergeant J. P. Carr
2nd Sergeant F. W. Latham
3rd Sergeant J. W. Turnley
4th Sergeant J. D. Chandler

1st Corporal A. J. Scott
2nd Corporal R. A. Martin
3rd Corporal E. D. Patterson
4th Corporal R. C. Houston

Belsha, J. L.
Bevis, R. F.
Beauchamp, J. E.
Carroll, Jesse
Carroll, G. W.
Carroll, J. E.
Carroll, S. F.
Carroll, F. W.
Cunningham, A. J.
Craig, J. A.
Childress, John
Duncan, J. F.
Dickey, William
Dunham, W. J.
Duncan, James
Duncan, W. E.
Duncan, Robert
Dougherty, A.
Edwards, J. R.
Fielder, T. F.
Fowler, T. J.
Fulmore, J. D.
Fulmore, C. C.
Greenough, T. G.
Harmon, T. W.
Hendrix, Dennis
Higgins, D. B.
Hobbs, B. B.
Harrell, Jack
Iron, A. A.
Iron, Thomas
Iron, James
Jones, Daniel
Lovelace, George
Lansford, G. C.
Martin, Asbury
Matthews, James
Marcella, John
McIntyre, J. L.

Armies (Washington: Government Printing Office, 1880–1901), XXXIII, Ser. I, 1152; hereinafter cited as *O.R.* C. L. Evans, ed., *Confederate Military History* (Atlanta: Confederate Publishing Co., 1899), VII (Alabama, Mississippi), 86.

McKelvey, G. W.	Raby, W. D.	Till, J. G.
McMurray, Joseph	Rayburn, R. W.	Till, E. R.
Munroe, P.	Reeder, P. H.	Towns, J. C.
Newson, A. B.	Rhodes, J. H.	Terrell, P. A.
Orvill, J. W.	Sharp, Charles	Webb, J. W.
Owen, A.	Smith, G. W.	Whitsett, P. H.
Patton, William	Simmonds, John	Williams, A. W.
Phillips, W. G.	Smith, James C.	Whitmore, William
Phillips, John C.	South, L. W.	Whitlow, J. A.
Phillips, John L.	Sunnerhill, E. B.	Wylie, W. J. W.
Pool, E. (Perkins)	Thompson, T. J.	Wylie, Wm. A.
Perkins, J.	Thrasher, A.	Wilson, James W.
		Young, F. M.

On the morning of the 8th of June we marched through the streets of Richmond and camped near the old fair grounds in the western portion of the city.

Sunday 9th. On looking around I find that there is only one Alabama Company here, which is unconnected with a Regiment. This is a company from Mobile, "Beauregard Rifles," under command of Captain Ripley.

July 9th. We have now been here a little more than a month and were yesterday assigned a position in a Regiment, composed of the following named companies:

"Beauregard Rifles"	Company A.	Captain Ripley
Rail Road Guards	Company B.	Captain Williams
Pope Walker Guards	Company C.	Captain Warren
Lauderdale Rifles	Company D.	Captain Houston
Sons of Liberty	Company E.	Captain King
Limestone Troopers	Company F.	Captain Hobbs
Jeff Davis Rangers	Company G.	Captain Hill
Limestone Greys	Company H.	Captain Houston
Calhoun Guards	Company I.	Captain Gillis
Marshall Boys	Company K.	Captain Sheffield

The field officers are as follows:

Col. C. M. Wilcox
Lieut. Col. Same [Samuel] Henry
Major Ed. A. O'Neal
Surgeon L. Anderson
Asst. Surgeon John Hays
Adjutant John Burtwell
A.C.S. Dr. Stevens

July 14th. Today left Richmond enroute we suppose to the "front."

July 15th. Arrived at Manassas this morning, and have remained all day—will start for Strasburg soon.

July 16th. Reached Strasburg, and after drawing and cooking our rations, and drawing forty rounds of ammunition each, set out for Winchester on a "forced march." Arrived this evening weary and footsore, found everybody talking excitedly over the prospects of a battle tomorrow with the troops under General Patterson.[4] We have encamped in a valley about a mile from town, and I begin to feel tonight the reality of war to a certain extent. In the first place, it looks as if someone is to be hurt, by their issuing ammunition to the men. These are the first "Cartridges" that I have ever seen, and is it possible that we are actually to *kill men? Human Beings?* That these cartridges were made purposely for one poor mortal to shoot at another? Yes, this is war, and how hardened men must become. Before I reached Winchester I had to pull off my boots and march bare footed as my boots had blistered my heel—quite a delightful feeling—think I would sell out at half price tonight.

July 19th. "Piedmonte Station."[5] Yesterday while at our camp near Winchester the startling news came over the wires that Gen. Beauregard's army at Manassas had been attacked by a force largely superior to his own,[6] and immediately there was a stir in

4. Major General Robert Patterson.
5. Piedmont, Fauquier County.
6. Action at Blackburn's Ford, Prince William County.

camp and in a few hours Gen. Johnson,[7] at the head of twenty regiments of infantry and some cavalry and artillery, was on the march for Manassas. We have had, thus far, an exceedingly hard march, and heat very oppressive. It was quite a novel sight to see the troops fording the Shenandoah river, though it was by no means a pleasant task, as many of the men were footsore and the bed of the stream exceedingly rocky. As a brigade would reach the bank of the river they would halt, pull off boots, socks and breeches, and fastening them in a bundle on their guns, "fall in" again and cross the river, when the putting on process would begin. Our regiment came nearer being "in uniform" crossing the stream than they ever were before. I had a fine view of the country while crossing the Blue Ridge. Troops are being hurried forward by Rail Road to Manassas as fast as possible.[8] Rations are scarce, the wagons having gone on without waiting for the troops, and there would be much suffering were it not for the liberality of the citizens of this section. One family in particular, Mrs. Dixon and her daughters, have been untiring in their efforts to provide for the wants of the soldiers, and this while Mr. Dixon, the husband and father, holds a position in the Federal army,—though a brother of these young ladies is in our army, and is now (Miss Annie tells me) at Manassas.

July 23. "Bull Run." We left Piedmonte yesterday morning and reached this place in the evening. We should have been here on the 21st, in time to have participated in the battle but through the carelessness or treachery of an engineer a train of cars was run off the tracks. He is now under guard at Piedmonte, and his case will be inquired into. On the day on which we reached this place the rain poured down in torrents, and when we camped for the night it was in mud and water, several inches deep, and near the bloodiest part of the battlefield. All night long the rain continued to pour down upon us, and here we stood on the banks of the muddy, ill-

7. General Joseph E. Johnston. Throughout his journal Patterson misspelled Johnston's name.

8. The movement of Johnston's troops by rail to Manassas is significant in military history as the first use of a railroad to achieve strategic mobility.

looking stream, and shook and shivered with cold, although in midsummer.

I have just returned from a walk over the battlefield. I made an attempt to go over it some hours ago, and the smell of the blood made me sick, and I had to turn back, but this time I succeeded, and may God grant that I may never see another. I have often read descriptions of battlefields, but never, until now, realized all the horrors that the word expresses. Here are mangled human bodies on every side, some pierced by a rifle or a musket ball—others almost torn to fragments by shell—in some places horse and rider have fallen together. Some have a look or expression on their face as mild and calm as if they were only sleeping, others seem to have had a terrible struggle with the monster death and only yielded after having suffered such pain as has caused their faces to assume expressions that are fearful to look upon, their features distorted, the eyeballs glaring, and often with their hands full of mud and grass that they have clutched in their last agony. I noticed one who had striven vainly to staunch the flow of blood from a wound through the body by stuffing mud into the wound. This was probably while the battle was raging, and no one near to attend to him. Another clutched in his hand a portion of a pack of cards, while the remainder of them lay scattered around him. But why attempt to describe in detail the particulars of this sickening scene? Many a poor fellow who left his home a few weeks or few months ago full of hope for the future now lies sleeping on this battefield never more to be disturbed by the rattle of musketry . . . or the roar of artillery. The result of this battle will teach the North a lesson that will not soon be forgotten. It will show to them, and the world, that we are in earnest and that we mean what we say and that in attempting our subjugation [they] have undertaken an herculean task. It seems to me that this battle has been a complete victory.

July 30th. Sickness has been continually on the increase since we arrived at this place and seems to be growing worse. Today my friend Geo. C. Lansford died. He is the only one of our little band that has died, but, oh, if this continues, many, many of our company will be gone.

July 31st. Today with heavy hearts we buried our friend and comrade. He sleeps his last long sleep beneath the shady boughs of a walnut tree, on the green grassy hillside, another martyr to truth. The hard marching, exposure and unhealthy location is beginning to have its effect on the men and our sick are more numerous than the well ones.

"Broad Run." August 8th, 1861. We came over here today from Manassas or Bull Run and it's well we did, for we were losing men every day over there. Another comrade has left us, 2nd Sgt. Frank Latham, whom everybody in the company loved, was sent from our former camp sick with the measles; today comes the news that he died on the 3rd inst., at Orange Court House.

August 17th, 1861. Our camp here at Broad Run is a most delightful place, and we have it in fine condition, cool shady groves and what is more important than all, good water. Col. Wilcox is drilling us daily and we are becoming more and more accustomed to the hardships of a soldier's life and better prepared to do battle for our Country. Two more of our company gone, Dunham and Smith, both died in the vicinity of Orange Court House.

October the 22nd. More than two months have passed by since I wrote anything in my journal. I have been very sick, and when the boys left me here they gathered around my bunk and told me goodbye, thinking it was the last time they would see me, but I am glad to disappoint them. I am not dead, nor do I intend to die as long as I can keep from it. The regiment broke camp here and moved to Centerville on the 21st of September, and camped on the ground occupied by the enemy previous to the battle of Manassas, where they remained until the 16th inst. when they moved to "Cub-Run" doing picket duty and drilling. I came up today from our Broad Run camp where I have been very sick, and though not yet very stout, think I will be able to do my share of the duty.

"Rocky Run." Nov. 20th '61. We came up here on the 14th inst. and commenced fortifying, and the camp of the army around

Centerville is now one of the strongest positions in the country. In addition to the hard work on the fortifications we have been doing pickett duty on the Old Braddock Road, out in the direction of Leesburg. Before we left "Cub-Run," our old Col. (C. M. Wilcox) [9] was appointed Brigadier General and assigned to the command of our brigade, which consists of the 8th, 9th, and 10th Ala. Regiments, and the 19th Mississippi and 38th Va. Regiments. We are now known as the 5th Brigade, 2nd division, Army of the Potomac.[10] The promotion of Wilcox has left us with Henry for Col., E. A. O'Neal for Lieut. Col., and J. H. J. Williams for Major. We all hated to give up Wilcox, but are glad to know that he is still in command of us and will be near us in the hour of danger. The men of the brigade put the most implicit confidence in him.

Mount Jackson, Va. Dec. 20th, '61. Here I am up in this beautiful valley of the Shenandoah, and a "sick man" too, though now most well. On the 9th inst., as we were out on pickett, I was taken quite sick and had to be sent to camp in a wagon, and on the next morning, in company with some others, they started me to this place, and here I have been ever since, but am feeling quite well today and think I will be able to rejoin my command in a few days. Newton Martin also of "Co. D." is here with me and improving.

Dec. 25th. Christmas has come again and with it a house full of ladies with loads of delicacies of all kinds for us—They are certainly very kind and untiring in their efforts to ameliorate the condition of the sick. But my friends and I wish to have a good "egg-nog" and we would not care if they would leave for a little while. I have a suspicious looking jug stowed away under my bunk,

9. Colonel Cadmus M. Wilcox, a native of North Carolina and graduate of West Point, grew up in Tennessee. He resigned from the U.S. Army in June, 1861, and became colonel of the Ninth Alabama. He was promoted to brigadier general in October, 1861, and to major general after the Gettysburg Campaign.

10. The Confederate Army of the Potomac was organized on the eve of the Battle of First Manassas. This name remained until Lee replaced Johnston as commander of the troops opposing McClellan before Richmond. In an order issued June 1, 1862, Lee unofficially bestowed the name Army of Northern Virginia upon his troops.

with plenty of the one thing needful in it, and the eggs and sugar are near at hand.

Dec. 30th. Have just returned from a little tramp out in the country with my friend, Paul Lewis. This country is perfectly lovely —lofty hills and beautiful valleys, and the Shenandoah, like a silvery serpent, winding among the hills and through these lovely valleys.

Dec. 31st, '61. Another hour and this year will be gone forever. A year fraught with incidents long to be remembered, not only by the Southern people, but by all the world. It will be remembered as the year in which the Southern people, unable longer to bear the tyranny of the North, or rather of Northern fanaticism, determined to exercise those rights guaranteed to them by the constitution and, following the example of the colonies, years ago, separated themselves from the old government and set up for themselves another in which there will not be so many conflicting interests.[11] The North, so long accustomed to receive her countless thousands from the South, would not willingly sacrifice her share in the profits accruing from Southern trade,[12] and hence this unholy war, which is being waged against the South and her institutions. What a grand spectacle does the South present to the world—all communications with the surrounding nations cut off, forced to rely entirely upon her own resources, still she has in the field today an army of nearly three hundred thousand men,[13] all well equipped

11. Patterson is repeating an argument used by many southerners.

12. Thomas P. Kettell in his book, *Southern Wealth and Northern Profits* (New York, 1860), presented the thesis that the weakness of the southern economy could not be attributed to slavery. He pointed out that the South created the major portion of the nations' wealth by furnishing the bulk of the exports but the North profited from this wealth through an unjust monopoly on the processes of trade.

13. The *Official Records* do not contain "any return of the total present and absent in the Confederate armies at any time." However, Livermore in his *Numbers and Losses* estimates the number of the Confederates under arms in January, 1862, at 351,418. Thomas L. Livermore, *Numbers and Losses in the Civil War* (Bloomington: Indiana University Press, 1957), pp. 41–43; hereinafter cited as Livermore, *Numbers and Loses.* This little volume was first published in 1900.

and bidding defiance to the grand armies of the North who would fain desolate our fields and march in triumph to our beautiful capitol. The cause of the South is growing brighter and I believe that ere long the Confederate States will be a free and independent government, loved at home, respected abroad. Yes, the old year with its battles, its bloodshed, its sorrows and tears is gone. The moments yet to come are pure and stainless—the deeds to be performed unrecorded. I hope that the year 1862 will witness the termination of this war and that when twelve months more have passed away the dark war-cloud, now hanging over us, will have rolled away and the sun of peace once more shine upon our now dark and bloody land.

Jan. 3rd, 1862. I came down from Mt. Jackson yesterday, and found all the boys at work putting up "winter quarters." Capt. W. Reeder is in command of the company and a nice gentleman he is, and a splendid officer. I hope that he may not be compelled to leave on account of sickness, though I am afraid that his health will not permit him to remain with us.

Jan. 16th. Sickness and death are doing their work. Since the 1st several members of our company have died. Our pickett duty is very hard.

· II ·

"I suppose that we will have to fight before we reach Richmond"

March 7, 1862, to June 17, 1862

March 7th, '62. Some weeks have passed since I last wrote in this journal—these weeks have been spent in going through the same routine of duties day after day, but now there is a prospect for change. Orders came down from Headquarters this morning for us to cook up what rations we had on hand, and be ready to move tomorrow morning. Whether this is to be a forward or retrogade movement none of us know, and we don't care, for anything is better than this hum-drum sort of life.

New Baltimore, Va.[1] ***March 9th.*** Yesterday the grand army of the Potomac was put in motion—we marched out from camps and bivouacked in a pleasant little grove three miles this side of our winter quarters. This morning we passed through Gainsville and

1. New Baltimore, Fauquier County.

marched during the day quite slowly, and are camped here for the night.

Culpepper C.H. March 13th. We moved from New Baltimore on the morning of the 10th and passed through Warrenton, crossed The Rappahannock river at the springs. We are waiting here, I understand, to allow the artillery and the trains to get in advance, and the sick are being sent forward to Richmond.

Orange Court House, March 20th, 1862. We reached this place yesterday and there seems to be no prospect of our leaving here today. It is quite a pleasant place and I would not object to camping here some time. Just twenty years ago today a very important event happened at "our house." I am not sure that any strange phenomena in the heavens foretold so important an event, nor that the sun rose any earlier on that day or shone any brighter than other days, but I am sure (for I was there at that time) that on that day in the County of Lorain, in the State of Ohio, I, Edmund Dewitt Patterson, was born into the world. Twenty years old—how time flies. A few years ago I was so happy. The future seemed to me all bright and joyous and no clouds darkened my pathway; then I was at home, enjoying the comforts of a happy home; now I am a soldier in the army of the Confederate States, and "I am become a stranger unto my brethren, and an alien unto my mother's children." But I am engaged in the glorious cause of liberty and justice, fighting for the rights of man—fighting for all that we of the South hold dear.

March 22nd. Have just returned from a visit to the tomb of Madison. Last year I visited that of Monroe.[2]

Richmond, Va. March 25th, '62. Back again to the same old camping ground that we left last July. We left Orange Court House yesterday evening and I suppose have not reached our destination.

2. Monroe died in New York in 1831, but his remains were moved to Richmond in 1858. Madison died at "Montpellier" (now "Montpelier") in 1836 and was buried there.

Rumors are flying thick and fast—some say that we are going to Goldsborough, North Carolina,[3] others to Yorktown, and others that we are to remain here. I suppose time will tell. Friend Ansel carried me around this morning and introduced me to his friends, Mrs. Quarles and family, on 12th Street. Had a pleasant time—am glad to have made such acquaintances. Mrs. Q. made us promise that in case we were wounded we would come to her house. I hope that we may not have an opportunity of accepting this invitation.

Weldon, N.C.[4] *March 27th, '62.* We left Richmond yesterday on the Str. Northampton and came as far as "City Point" [5] where we took the cars and came to this place. We have been here in this little grove by the side of the R.R. nearly all day and it is now said, though I don't know by what authority, that we are going back to Petersburg.

Lebanon Church, Va.[6] *April 1st, '62.* Who would not be a soldier? Since writing in my journal at Weldon, "I have seen the elephant." After remaining at the above mentioned place one day we returned to Petersburg, and that night were marched aboard of a barge to be taken down the river. As we were going aboard, Lieut. Ben Taylor walked overboard, but was rescued with no damage done farther than a good ducking. We were soon under way and proceeded to City Point where we stopped some time—then on down the James. During our trip down the river we had our choice

3. Federal strategy in 1862 called for General A. E. Burnside to take Roanoke Island and from there push into the interior of North Carolina by way of Goldsboro. By following this route, Confederate communications south of Richmond could be cut. Also, Federal troops would be in position for a flank movement when General George McClellan drove the Confederates out of Richmond. By March 25 Burnside had captured Roanoke Island and New Bern and had Fort Macon under siege.

4. Weldon was an important railroad junction in northeastern North Carolina. It was on the mainline south from Richmond.

5. City Point (present city of Hopewell).

6. Lebanon Church (York County), which is often confused with Slash Church, "is about one-half mile south of Peake's Turnout on the C & O. Slash Church is a mile away on the old State Road from Richmond to Hanover C.H." D. S. Freeman, *Lee's Lieutenants* (New York: Charles Scribner's Sons, 1942), II, 219n.; hereinafter cited as Freeman, *Lee's Leiutenants.*

—either to remain down in the hold which was close and dark, or to expose ouselves to a cold drizzling rain. I preferred the latter, and "weathered the storm." We arrived at Kings Wharf [7] last night just at dark and the rain still falling very cold, were notified that it was important that we should go to Lebanon Church before camping. Then commenced a march that beggars description. The night was so dark that it was absolutely impossible to see anything and we relied entirely on the sense of hearing and feeling. And the mud and water was literally knee deep, and the men would run against each other, strike their faces against another's back or gun without seeing anything. Some fell in mud holes and had to be dragged out, and our regiment became scattered for a mile, and all along the road you could hear, "This way Co. D.," "Here is your Company A," "Close up Company C," &c., &c. I continued the march about five miles when I ran into a clump of bushes, and winding myself up in my wet blankets as well as I could remained there until daylight, keeping the bushes under me as much as possible to keep from drowning. As soon as it was light enough for me to see how to do, I took up my line of march and found men scattered along the road. I had gone about a mile farther when on the top of a little hill I saw my old friend and messmate Tom Harmon, his overcoat spread down on the ground and he, barefooted, standing on it—to keep his feet from the cold and freezing ground. "Halloa," says I, "where are your shoes?" (Tom) "Oh, Pat," said he, "I left them last night down in the hollow yonder," (pointing to the foot of the hill), "I tried to find them but they are too deep." For him to walk barefooted was out of the question, so we stood there some time trying to devise a way to provide another pair. Soon an old darkey came along who had an extra pair, and Tom gave him his new overcoat for the pair he had on, which were just five sizes too large for him, No. 10's and Tom wearing 5's, but we were all pleased with the trade and went on our way rejoicing, reaching camp a little after daylight, and found upon enquiring the Col. and nine men of the regiment reached the Church the night before.

7. Kings Wharf (King's Mill Wharf) was slightly below the mouth of College Creek which flows into the James south of Williamsburg.

Lee's Mills,[8] ***April 4th, '62.*** This morning we were called out by the "Long Roll" and have been traveling most of the day, seemingly with no other view than to show ourselves to the enemy at as many different points of the line as possible. I am pretty tired and am anxious that folks should quit this kind of foolishness, and go home. There are about a thousand and one negroes at work fortifying this place, and it would seem that there is danger ahead. The yanks are in plain view, and make us quite careful about having our heads exposed above the breastworks. I think from their actions that they would just as willingly shoot one of us as we would one of them. I suppose it is right, and when a fellow's time comes, down he goes. "Every bullet has its billet."

Wimis Mill,[9] ***April 15th.*** Rain and mud in abundance and the only articles except sickness that we have a sufficiency of. It's quite pleasant after having worked an hour in the rain and mud building a shelter and floor of poplar bark, and starting a fire,—about nine o'clock—dark—rainy—gloomy, to be ordered to "fall in" and go down to Fort Magruder [10] when you know that the mud and water is not more than a foot and a half deep and as for "falling in," it's no trouble at all to "fall in" at least half a dozen times before getting there—the trouble is in getting out.

April 19th. We are having a little peace today, for the first time in three or four days. On the 16th at our regular dinner hour, our mess were gathered around a camp kettle filled with "pea soup" up in one of the cabins that had been built by the 2nd Florida for winter quarters—Jim Crowe, Tom Harmon, Ansel Newson, Choctaw, Joe Murray, John and myself, each with a spoon and all eating

8. Lee's Mill or Lee's Mills (City of Newport News) was on the Warwick River. It was part of the Yorktown defenses.

9. Wimis Mill is not mentioned in the reports of either General Wilcox or Colonel Samuel Henry. Patterson evidently meant Wynn's Mill which was near the center of the Confederate line at Yorktown.

10. Fort Magruder was the center and strongest part of the Confederate defensive line east of Williamsburg on the Yorktown road. In view of subsequent entries in Patterson's journal (see below pp. 18–23) and the reports of General Wilcox and Colonel S. Henry, the move to Fort Magruder did not take place at this time, or if it did, the command was back at Yorktown by May 3.

out of the kettle and enjoying it hugely—when "all at once a shell burst over our house," and we thought perhaps that there was going to be a general attack, but heard nothing more for about half a minute. Then a shell came through our little cabin, cutting a log out of each side of it, passing just over our heads and ruining our soup with mud and splinters. It was just as well that it did, for we all lost our appetites and found ouselves safe in the "bomb proofs" *quicker*—and from that time until today they haven't given us fifteen minutes rest at any one time. The result of this three days shelling has been one man killed, our commisary, two men wounded, one of whom was Charlie Sharp of my company, and a whole brigade pretty badly scared. If our friends across the field knew to what inconvenience they are putting us, they would certainly stop.

Williamsburg, May 4th. We evacuated Yorktown and our whole line of defense there this morning before daylight,[11] and have marched leisurely along during the day—we are camping tonight though in line of battle, just out west of town in these old fields. There has been some fighting in the rear this evening and some prisoners few, and it is plain that the Yankees are following us up, and I suppose that we will have to fight before we reach Richmond.

Burnt Ordinary,[12] May 6th 1862. Yesterday was a day never to be forgotten by me.[13] Early in the morning we heard heavy firing

11. On April 5 McClellan's advance was stopped at Yorktown. After a two day reconnaissance of the Yorktown line, the Federal commander decided that the Confederate defenses were too strong to be forced. So he sent for heavy guns to take the place by regular siege. The major assault was to begin on the morning of May 5. In the meantime the Confederate forces at Yorktown under Major General John B. Magruder had been reinforced by those around Richmond under Joseph E. Johnston. The idea of making a stand at Yorktown, however, did not appeal to Johnston and on the night of May 3 he evacuated his position and fell back on Richmond.

12. Burnt Ordinary, James City County.

13. In this entry Patterson describes the Battle of Williamsburg (May 5, 1862). Longstreet's division formed the rear-guard of the Confederate army as it moved on Williamsburg after evacuating Yorktown. General Longstreet, under orders to delay the Federal advance long enough for the Confederate trains to

not more than a mile and a half from town, and could see from the smoke that our artillery was replying gallantly to that of the enemy. I was not much surprised when we were ordered to "fall in" and were marched back through the streets of Williamsburg. Women were to be seen everywhere, some with water for the soldiers, others offering to take care of blankets, while others still, who had relatives in the army, wept and wrung their hands in agony. We marched hurriedly through the town and in the direction of the firing. After getting out of town we stopped a few minutes in the wheat field and were ordered to load our pieces. In front of us and to our right the artillery thundered forth death,—the day dark and gloomy and the rain falling steadily. The smoke settled down over the hills and valleys and added to the general gloom. I can never forget my thoughts as I stood there and looked around, though they were *feelings* rather than thoughts, for they were undefinable. It was the first time that I had ever been called upon to face death. I felt that in a few moments some of us standing here, vainly trying to jest and appear careless, would be in eternity. Would it be this friend, or that one, or myself? I did not feel at all afraid—the feeling called *fear* did not enter my breast, but it was a painful nervous anxiety, a longing for action, anything to occupy my attention—nerves relaxed and a dull feeling about the chest that made breathing painful. All the energies of my soul seemed concentrated in the one desire for action. We were not kept long in suspense for very soon orders came for us to go forward, to the right of the road; we advanced to the edge of the woods, where we joined our right to the left of the 19th Mississippi regiment, and then changed directions, and advanced in a course at right angles to the one pursued in entering the woods. Our line of battle was soon formed; our brigade on the extreme left of that part of the line and our regiment the extreme left of the brigade; our left was supported or protected by a

---

get well on their way to Richmond, took post on May 4 along the strong line of defenses Magruder had constructed across the peninsula before Williamsburg (see above p. 17, n. 10). Early the next morning the enemy moved against the Confederate position precipitating the daylong Battle of Williamsburg. Patterson's regiment, the Ninth Alabama, was involved in some of the heaviest fighting.

battery which was engaged with a battery of the enemy's about three fourths of a mile in our front. The woods on our right were so dense that they completely hid from us the operations of the remainder of the brigade, with the exception of the 19th Mississippi, which was the next regiment to us. The place over which we had to pass was what in boyhood days I would have called "slashing."

It had been heavily timbered land, and all had been cut down, letting it fall in every direction, and it formed an almost insurmountable barrier. But we advanced slowly, climbing over logs, stumps, through tangled undergrowth, etc., when the crack of a rifle and the falling of a man announced to us that we were in range of the enemy's sharpshooters. Just as the firing began a mounted officer whom I did not know, but who was, I afterwards learned, Gen'l. Anderson[14] of South Carolina, rode up and said, *"Go forward men, straight forward, don't halt at all."* We continued advancing as fast as we could under the circumstances, though it was impossible to preserve anything like a well formed line, and the Yankees being stationed and posted behind the logs had much the advantage of us, for we had to expose ourselves continually in getting over the logs, while we could but seldom get a shot at them. Among the first wounded in the regiment was June Bynum of my company. He had his gun to his face, and the moment he fired a ball struck him in the arm between the wrist and the elbow, passed through shattering the ulna, and then passed through the fleshy part of the arm near the shoulder. "D—n you," he said, "you have wounded me, but I finished one of you." In moving forward, our left companies were in a more exposed condition and suffered more than the right of the regiment. There was an open space between our regiment and the 19th Mississippi, and I was sent down to the right to ask Col. Mott to move his regiment a little farther to the left, but found that regiment, like our own, without much of a line, and Col. Mott dead. We remedied the difficulty as well as we could, and still advanced

14. Brigadier General R. H. Anderson stated in his official report: "That part of Pryor's brigade which was not required to hold the redoubts was ordered to co-operate with General Wilcox, and I left Fort Magruder to direct the operations on the right." *O.R.*, XI, Ser. I, Pt. I, 580.

driving the Yankees before us for about one half a mile,—then there was a cry from some one, "They are flanking us on the left." And Col. Henry, cowardly, or at least foolishly ordered the regiment to fall back to the ravine, which was nearly a half a mile in our rear.[15] The five left companies obeyed the command, as perhaps we ought to have done, but we could see that we were leaving the 19th Mississippi exposed to a cross fire; besides the Yankees themselves were ready to run, and in fact were giving way at the time. We saw a battery in our front, and it was determined that we should charge it. Companies A., D., I., C., and a few men from Co. H. together with Co. E. of the 19th Mississippi, under command of Lieut. "Jump Jones" charged forward at a double quick, drove the Yankees straight beyond it to the woods, and took possession of it. Just then a shell burst among us, from our own battery, as they had mistaken us for a party of Yankees, but Jones of the 19th Mississippi had their flag, and Jim Crowe took ours and they each mounted a piece of artillery and soon showed them that we were not proper subjects for them to work on.

About this time Col. Wilcox[16] came up and complimented us and was loudly cheered. Col. Henry and the remaining companies of the regiment came up, and forming our line again we moved forward to the edge of the woods where we soon became engaged and fired until our ammunition gave out; then we had to lie still, for had we started back we must have gone through an open field, exposed to the enemy's fire; where we were we were protected by logs and hidden by undergrowth. We remained here for some time, and until the 2nd Florida came to relieve us, which was at 4 o'clock in the evening. They came up in good style, and were to take our places, and we to get out as best we could. But when the command was given to our regiment the Florida regiment misunderstood it for all, and they started too; then commenced a scene of wild confusion; both regiments broke in perfect disorder and went running through the field to the rear. I shall never forget the impres-

15. In his report Longstreet complimented Colonel Henry and a number of other officers for the "marked skill and fearlessness" with which they discharged their duties. *O.R.,* XI, Ser. I, Pt. I, 567.

16. It should be General not Colonel Wilcox.

sion made upon me by Col. Ward of the 2nd Fla. He was a brave, gallant man. He rode among his men and cried, "Floridians, Oh, Floridians, is this the way you meet the enemies of your country?", and fell from his horse dead on the field of honor, his heart pierced by a bullet.

The men were now panic stricken, and there was no such thing as stopping them until we had reached some place of protection, for some were falling at every step. After running back a mile or more we reached a ravine, and there stopped and reformed. Wilcox complimented us on the endurance and bravery that we had manifested. As soon as the Florida regiment was formed it moved right forward in the face of the now jubilant enemy, driving them back and taking the position we had just given up. Just as we came down in the ravine I noticed an officer very richly dressed, riding a beautiful and gaily caparisoned horse, coming in full speed toward us, carrying in his hand a slouch hat, in which was a long magnificent plume—he was the very picture of a cavalier, and his appearance made me think of Murat.[17] He rode up, saluted Gen'l. Wilcox and the troops, spoke some cheering words to the Floridians as they started forward, then turned and rode in the direction of a body of cavalry. I did not know until he was gone that this was Gen'l. Stuart.[18] We had done our share of fighting for the day, and as soon as the men could be collected together we marched off the field through town and camped near the same place that we occupied night before last. We lay down on the wet and muddy ground, weary and torn; thus closed *our* first battle.

Owing to the nature of the ground over which we fought, our loss was not so heavy as I thought. Sixty seven killed and wounded.[19] Among them were quite a large number of officers. In my company the only man killed was Pony Summerhill. He was a

17. Joachim Murat, French marshal under Napoleon.

18. Brigadier General James Ewell Brown "Jeb" Stuart's cavalry had engaged the enemy on May 4 in a rear guard action. Stuart covered the rear of the Confederate columns as they withdrew from Yorktown.

19. The Federal losses at Williamsburg were 2,283. Hooker's division alone lost 1,575. Longstreet lost 1,565. M. F. Steele, *American Campaigns* (Washington: U.S. Infantry Association, 1922), I, 198; hereinafter cited as Steele, *Campaigns*.

good soldier and a particular friend of mine. At the time the Col. ordered the next regiment to fall back, Capt. Murphey of Co. A. from Mobile sprang ahead of the line and mounting a log, waved his sword and shouted to his men to follow him unless they loved that coward better. Just then a ball struck him in the left wrist, shattering it terribly, and immediately afterwards one passed through his body, going directly through a large gold watch which he had in the watch pocket of his pants. He was carried off the field to the hospital in town; some who saw him this morning think he cannot possibly recover. Capt. Gillis is wounded through the arm but is marching along with us. Several of the boys had narrow escapes; Jack Harrel had the hammer of his gun shot away while his gun was at his face, in the act of firing. Joe McMurray had his so badly bent that he could not use it any more, as also did John Chandler. "Wesley" and myself were together most of the time during the day.

The artillery is arranged as though an attack is anticipated, and we seem in no hurry to leave. The 17th Virginia hung a man this morning, whom they caught yesterday. He had deserted from the regiment only a few days before and unfortunately one of his old company detected him.

Chickahominy River. May 9th, 1862. Reached this place this morning and I understand that we are to camp for some time. The rations have joined us, and I am glad enough, for I am tired of stealing corn from the horses when I know that they can't well do without it. C. F. has returned to the regiment after having been absent nearly a month on detached service. Those of our wounded who came with us from Williamsburg have gone to Richmond.

May 23rd, 1862. Nearly all the officers of the regiment have gone to Richmond today to attend the funeral of Capt. Gillis, who died yesterday. He was a good man, brave, kind, and true, and loved by all who knew him. He leaves a young wife back in our dear old Lauderdale, married only one week before starting to Virginia. God pity her. I fear that there will be thousands in like condition before the war is over. He is to be buried at Oakwood cemetery.

May 26th. Richmond. Yesterday we changed our camp and are now bivouacking just North of the city. I like the situation better for I can go into the city so often and see my lady friends on 12th Street.

June 2nd. Since writing in my journal we have had another little brush with the enemy and a heavy battle has been fought.[20] On the 31st of May we marched down the Chickahominy River swamp and were under artillery fire some time, being moved about on the battle field—held in reserve. Col. Moore's regiment, the 11th Alabama, was hotly engaged and lost very heavily. He, himself, was dangerously wounded. They will probably want Lieut. Col. Hale back, but we can't spare him. He has been in command of our regiment since Col. Henry was put under arrest and charges preferred against him for his conduct at Williamsburg. *Our* Lieut. Col. O'Neal whom we all liked has accepted the Colonelcy of the 26th Alabama, and Capt. Reeder of my company, the major-ship of the same regiment. Only one member of my company wounded on the 31st,—Jack Harrell.

About dark we marched down through the thickest part of the battlefield—through the camps of Gen'l. Casey's Division.[21] Here were dead and dying on all sides, they were so completely surprised —many were killed at dinner, some in their tents, and I saw others who had fallen in the fire where they were cooking. The wounded on every hand are imploring assistance; on every side too, in the darkness, could be heard piteous voices calling out Water! Water! I

20. The Battle of Fair Oaks or Seven Pines (May 31 and June 1, 1862). In this battle General Johnston planned to take advantage of the isolated position of the Federal Fourth Corps at Fair Oaks and Seven Pines south of the Chickahominy and destroy it.

21. Brigadier General Silas Casey commanded the Third Division of Erasmus K. Keye's Fourth Corps at Fair Oaks. His division bore the brunt of the first Confederate attack by A. P. Hill's troops. Even though Casey's position was overrun, he was promoted to major general because of the stout defense he put up on May 31.

gave all I had in my canteen, and only wished that I had time to attend to them better.

At last came the order to halt and rest for the night, and the men commenced to arrange for the night, though the Yankees were lying so thickly on the ground that in the darkness many of the boys, taking them for members of the regiment, laid down beside them, and did not know until morning that their bedfellows were dead men, and when they did discover it, the only remark was, "I *thought* that he slept mighty still."

Water, though plentiful enough in the swamp, was scarce enough in the regiment, and none of the company having any in their canteens, Capt. Crow set about getting some. It was quite dark, and he moved a little to one side and throwing his cape partly over his face and changing his voice, began moaning piteously and soon attracted attention—several of the boys drew near and commenced questioning him. He told them that he was Major of the 12th Massachusetts regiment, was severely wounded through the body, and wanted water. Several ran to get it, and one gave him a drink of whiskey. After filling his canteen, and fixing him comfortably, *he became quite easy,* and all went to sleep; but when those who had been so kind to the wounded Yankee went to see how he fared in the morning, they found that they had been sold.

I awoke quite early yesterday morning, and everything seemed very quiet. I went over the field seeing what I could see. Here were Sutler's tents, filled with luxuries—oranges, lemons, oysters, pineapples, sardines, in fact almost everything that I could think of. My first business was to eat just as much as I possibly could, and that was no small amount, for I had been living "on hard tack" several days. I then picked out a lot of stationery, paper, envelopes, ink, pens, and enough to fill one haversack; then I found a lot of puff bosomed linen shirts and laid in a half dozen, together with some white gloves and other little extras enough to fill another haversack. Then I filled another with nuts and candies and still another with cheese. With this load, I wandered around picking up some canteens to carry back to the boys. Then adding to my load such articles as a sword, an overcoat, etc., while walking around, I came by a little clump of trees and saw a fellow sitting leaning against one of them. He asked me for a book that I had in my hand, that I had picked up—I found that he was from South Carolina, his leg was broken, and he told me that he was tired of sitting there with nothing to amuse him. So I gave him the book, and as I left he told me that he hoped that the ambulance would be around after him soon. He had been sitting there since the evening before.

I now wended my way toward the regiment—I had gone up to the left of the line—and as I was passing down the line about fifty yards in rear of Pryor's brigade [22] I heard some one say or give the command to Forward guide, Center March, and could hear and see Pryor's men getting ready for action. I quickened my pace, and before I had gone twenty steps the Yankees opened fire on them and the balls whistled around me in a perfect shower. I had about two hundred yards to go before reaching my regiment, and by the time I reached it I had thrown away all my plunder. And was just in time, for the regiment was moving to form a connection with the right of Pryor's brigade. I was soon in my place and busy watching out for an advance on our part of the line.

Pretty soon we could hear them coming through the thick undergrowth, and when they first came in sight we were prepared for them. We gave them a volley which killed a great many and they took the back track, only giving us one volley which did not do much damage, wounding only fifteen men in the regiment and killing none. Col. Hall's horse was killed under him, but he was not injured by the fall.

This was the only fighting that we did during the day, though on other portions of the line the battle raged furiously, and we were scared all day by shells bursting among us. They marched me around so much that I lost all my ill-gotten spoils, and when we arrived here back in camp again I found myself as poor as when I started out, but powerful glad that I did not leave *myself* down in those swamps as many a poor fellow has done.

22. Brigadier General Roger A. Pryor commanded the Fifth Brigade of Longstreet's division. Longstreet at Fair Oaks commanded the Confederate right wing and his mistakes were the primary reason for the failure of the operation.

Well, it has been a big battle and both sides, I've no doubt, gained a decided victory, "so called." It is reported that Gen'l. Johnson is dangerously wounded, and not expected to recover. I don't know what the army could do without him.[23]

June 17th, 1862. Yesterday, Company "F" and our company went down the Charles city road on pickett. While down there, Capt. Crow, who was commanding the two companies, received orders to take a few men and go down the road and try and ascertain what force there was in our front. We went down some distance, keeping deployed as skirmishers, when we came to the swamp. We halted, and Dolph Owen and Ansel Newson were sent forward to scout; they advanced a short distance when they discovered a large force at no great distance, so they concealed themselves in the bushes to watch the movements. Soon three of them started directly toward them. They waited for them to get in good range, and Newson brought down one of them. The other two ran back to the reserve, and soon the whole command, about two hundred, were under arms and coming. Ansel and Dolph had to come back in a hurry, and we all had to go up the road much faster than we went down. They were too smart to follow us far; they might have found more than they were looking for if they had.

23. General J. E. Johnston, in command of the forces opposing McClellan, was severely wounded on May 31 and G. W. Smith, the next in rank, assumed command of the Confederate army. Then on June 1 General Lee, in compliance with orders from President Davis, assumed command. His army soon became known as the Army of Northern Virginia (see above p. 10, n. 10). Johnston did not return to duty until November, 1862, at which time he was put in command of the Department of the West.

· III ·

"Up to the crest of the hill we went at the double quick"

June 28, 1862, to August 29, 1862

On the Battlefield, Gaine's Mill.*[1] *June 28th, 1862. On the night of the 25th, just as we were preparing to go to bed, we were called out by the "long roll" and marched down to the battlefield of Seven Pines, where there was some fighting going on.[2] The night was very dark, and we moved pretty close to the enemy's line without being seen. After remaining in line of battle for an hour or more we marched straight back to camp and all lay down, thinking that it was only a false alarm; but before daylight we were again aroused by the long roll and marched around towards the

1. The Battle of Gaines's Mill was fought on June 27. Patterson misspelled the name of the battle throughout his account.

2. The Battle of Oak Grove (June 25) was also known as Henrico, King's School House, and the Orchards. According to Clifford Dowdey this engagement was small and local and did not mark the opening round in the Seven Days Battles. Clifford Dowdey *The Seven Days* (Boston: Little Brown and Co., 1964), pp. 159–347. (See also below p. 29, n. 3.)

Northern part of the city. By the time we reached the road leading to Hanover Court House we could hear very heavy firing, both artillery and musketry, across the river. Here we were halted and spent the whole evening listening to the most terrific fire and watching the lines of smoke as they showed us the situation of the two contending lines.[3]

It is a feeling that cannot be described that takes possession of one, when the battle is raging and you know that every moment some one of your fellow soldiers is dying. The most wicked man in the army cannot help praying to the God of battle that He will shield and protect our soldiers. The same restless, feverish feeling that one experiences before going into battle is felt. The breath comes thick and short, and it is only when there is a momentary lull in the fearful storm that you draw a long breath. And no matter what the danger, you feel a desire to rush to their assistance. While you watch the progress of the conflict you become weary, and great drops of perspiration will stand upon your forehead.

During the evening[4] our lines had been forcing their lines back, little by little, but paying dearly for every foot of ground gained. The sun set as clear and beautiful as though no scenes of bloodshed and misery were being enacted by the light of its mild beams. Ah, that same sun has looked down on many such scenes. As the dimness of eve closed over the conflict there was a lull in the storm for a few moments, and I thought that the fearful day's work was ended. But it was only the dead calm that preceeds the tempest. The contending forces were just catching their breath for the fearful

3. In the Battle of Mechanicsville (June 26, 1862) Lee planned to strike McClellan while his army was astride the Chickahominy. This engagement marked the opening round in The Seven Days' Battle around Richmond. The fighting, though, lasted only six days, from June 26 to July 1. "An attempt has been made to count McClellan's limited action of June 25 on the Williamsburg Road as the seventh day, but the series of battles was recognized by the participants as the execution of Lee's General Orders No. 75. In Lee's orders to his troops after the battles, his reference to the Seven Days read, 'The battle, beginning on the afternoon of June 26th, above Mechanicsville. . . .' While this established Mechanicsville as the opening action, Malvern Hill, the last battle, was not the last day. July 2 was the day McClellan ended his retreat at the river and could constitute a seventh day in the completion of Lee's counteroffensive." *Ibid.*, p. 347.

4. "Afternoon" might have been a better word to use here.

struggle—darkness had shrouded the scene, a funeral pall for the heroic dead—and both lines ceased firing as if by mutual consent. But suddenly a wild yell, that sounded as if all the demons of hell had broken loose, went up from our lines, answered by cheers of defiance from the enemy, and as our line moved forward through the darkness and gloom that had gathered over the scene we could catch glimpses of them occasionally, as the fierce flames of the red artillery would wrap them in their lurid embrace.[5] The sheeted fire from long lines of infantry showed us what a wide swath Death must be cutting. The earth trembled as these iron-throated monsters, with their dread voices of power, belched forth death. Every ray of that changeful light that cast such an unearthly glare over the scene was a death warrant.

The struggle so fearful could not last, and as we held our breath to watch it a long-pent-up vindictive yell of triumph announced that our boys had carried the works. The enemy was retreating, and the day's work was done, and the troops slept upon the field so nobly won—thus ended the battle of Mechanicsville.[6]

No sooner had the firing ceased when we were marched down the road and across the river, over to the battlefield, where we lay down with our guns by our side, and our cartridge boxes for pillows. We were all sleepy and tired and soon forgot the troubles of a soldier's life. About daylight the next morning we were awakened rather suddenly by a storm of shell bursting around us, and above us. I suppose the Yankees thought we were sleeping too late. In two minutes we were up and in line ready for anything.[7] The 19th

5. Late in the afternoon A. P. Hill sent two brigades against the Federal right in a gallant but suicidal attack. Small-arms fire continued until 9:00 P.M. and artillery for another hour or more.

6. Mechanicsville was anything but a Confederate victory. In fact, tactically it was a failure from beginning to end. Nevertheless, on the night of June 26 McClellan decided to move his base from White House on the Pamunkey to the James.

7. The remainder of this entry is devoted to the fighting at Gaines's Mill on June 27. After his failure the previous day to destroy Fitz-John Porter's Corps, Lee pressed toward Gaines's Mill and Boatswain Swamp where the Federals had established a new defensive position. Lee's strategy called for A. P. Hill to strike the enemy center, Longstreet the left, and D. H. Hill and "Stonewall" Jackson the right. Jackson, however, for the second straight day performed poorly. He was very late getting into position. All the while A. P. Hill was fiercely engaged in battle. The major assault on the Federal line did not occur until dusk.

Mississippi was thrown forward to ascertain the strength of the enemy. But they quietly withdrew. A line of battle was soon formed with the right resting on the Chickahominy, and the left extending a mile and a half North. Our brigade about the center of the line, we moved forward slowly, over the hills and valleys and through the woods, keeping the line intact and presenting a beautiful appearance, as we advanced with banners rippling in the morning breeze. We continued our advance down the North bank of the river three or four miles and until we were in about a half mile of this place, where we halted until we could see the bayonets of Jackson's troops gleaming in the sunshine,[8] then forward again.[9]

The enemy had massed a large force on the side hill where we are resting now, and it is naturally one of the strongest places that could be found, and they had improved it by building two sets of breastworks on the side hill so that those in the rear lines could fire over the heads of the front ones. Thus, they could pour a double infantry fire into us, while on the crest of the hill above these lines the artillery was posted. In twenty feet of the lower line of work is a deep gully or ravine, six or eight feet deep and the same in width, and as I look at it now, I can't see why this front line alone did not remain firm. Had our regiment (the "Bloody Ninth" as it is now called by the rest of the Brigade) been behind this line, we would have filled that ditch with any troops in the world who tried to cross it. And so might the Yankees have done if they had fought like men, but I have no fault to find on that score—they fought "plenty well" enough for me.

Immediately on arriving in front of this position, Gen'l. Pryor attempted to gain a position where he could operate to advantage against the enemy, but at each advance he was met with so deadly a fire that he had to abandon the idea. Several times his troops advanced in face of this double fire but each time were driven back under cover of the hill, with heavy loss. This had occupied the time until about five o'clock in the evening, and about this time orders

8. "Stonewall" Jackson not only was late getting into position but also he allowed his brigades to arrive on the battlefield at different locations and at different times.

9. Longstreet's division, to which the Ninth Alabama was attached, did not fully engage the Federal left flank until late in the afternoon.

reached Gen'l. Wilcox to move his brigade to the front. We immediately moved forward and halted under cover of the hill to reform the line, and here we had a chance to form an estimate of the magnitude of the undertaking before us. Immediately in front of us was a high hill, and until we reached the crest of it we were pretty well protected from the enemy infantry's fire. The order was given; "Forward Guide, Center March, Charge Bayonets."

Up to the crest of the hill we went at a double quick, but when we came into view on the top of the ridge we met such a perfect storm of lead right in our faces that the whole brigade literally *staggered* backward several paces as though pushed by a tornado. The dead lay in heaps, and two minutes in that position would have been utter annihilation. Just for one moment we faltered, then the cry of Major Sorrell, "Forward Alabamians,—Forward!", and the cry was taken up by the officers of the different regiments and we swept forward with wild cheers over the crest and down the slope, and though at every step some brave one fell, we did not falter.

This deep ravine or ditch took us as completely by surprise as the sunken road or cut did the old Guards at Waterloo. Just as we reached it we poured a volley into the front lines of the Yankees, and then some of the more active cleared it at a bound; others jumped in and scrambled up the opposite side. Immediately in front of me was a log or piece of timber thrown across. I crossed on it as did many others.

By the time we had gotten across, the front line, broken by our fire, frightened by our screams which sounded like forty thousand wild cats, had reached their second line and thrown them into confusion, and they, panicstricken, left their works and crowded to the top of the hill, thus preventing their artillery from firing into us, and then commenced a scene that only the pen of an Abbot [10] or a Victor Hugo could describe. The assaulting column consisted of six brigades, ours occupying the extreme right of the line, and each brigade had been successful. And the enemy, completely routed at every point, now lost all order and every man only thought of

10. Possibly Patterson was referring to John S. C. Abbott (1805–77), clergyman and historian, who wrote on Napoleon.

saving himself. They threw down their arms and ran in one grand mass, out of the woods and down the valley beyond. In vain their officers tried to rally them; they could not stand the terrible fire poured into them. We ran over their artillery, killing the gunners at their guns, and as this confused mass of fugitives fled down the long open valley we kept close to them and shot them down by the hundreds and thousands. We were so close to them that pistol did as much good as guns, and we could not miss them for they were at least twenty deep, and very few of them offering to fire a shot. Ah, we paid dearly for this occasion, but they paid still more dearly, for their dead and dying lay so thick as almost to block our pursuit.

By the time we had gone half a mile we were as much confused as the Yankees, for no one had paid any attention to company or regiment, but each had devoted his entire attention to loading and firing as fast as possible. At this critical juncture a large body of the enemy's cavalry appeared on the field, bearing down upon us.[11] Here we were in an open field, not a single regiment that could claim its individuality—some running one way and some another; but on came the vast body of cavalry, making an appearance well calculated to create a panic in troops situated as we were. But there was no time for consideration and the men, completely exhausted, saw at a glance that it would be impossible to reach the works before the cavalry would be upon them, and that their only safety lay in standing firm and giving them as warm a reception as possible. Quickly we closed our ranks and presented a pretty good front to the enemy, not such a line as would have stood an infantry charge, but plenty strong to resist cavalry. When the head of their columns had gotten within about fifty yards of us we gave them a well directed and murderous fire that emptied many a saddle, and sent them flying in the opposite direction; and taught them a lesson that when infantry are fighting they should keep out of the way. On the same principle that a *boy* should not meddle when men are fighting.

The sun had set looking through the dust and smoke and fire of

11. This Federal cavalry was under the command of Brigadier General Philip St. George Cooke, a Virginian and father-in-law of "Jeb" Stuart.

the battlefield, of a blood red color. We had won a complete victory, and now the scattered remnants of the various regiments and brigades that had been engaged had nothing to do except care for the wounded and to concentrate, that is, each man to find his proper command.[12] Our brigade were concentrating in the rear of the field, and as I started back over the ground that had been the scene of the terrible slaughter I found myself with two other members of the company, Newson and Pool,—as we walked slowly up the steep hill we were congratulating each other on our escape when so many had fallen. A few shots were being fired by some Yankees in a skirt of woods about eight hundred yards distant, but we did not mind them at all. But just before reaching the brow of the hill, while talking and feeling perfectly safe, I heard the peculiar sound that a bullet makes when it strikes a man (and which does not resemble any other sound either in nature or art) and my friend Perkins Pool fell across my feet dead. I bent over him and spoke to him, but he died so instantaneously that not a muscle of his face changed—the same pleasant expression that he always wore. The ball had struck him in his right side just under the arm, and, passing through, came out under the left arm and lodged in his vest. I picked it up and threw it away. Ansel and I went on to where the regiment was being collected together, finding four Yankees in the woods; we took them along with us and turned them over to the provost guard.

I did not know how tired I was until the excitement of the battle was over. I was almost too weak to stand, and my cheeks as hollow as though emaciated by a long spell of sickness. I dropped down under a bush and slept such a sleep as comes only to a tired soldier after a battle. When I awoke this morning the sun was shining upon me through the branches. I was so stiff and sore that I had to make several attempts before I could rise. When I got up and fully awoke I found a barrel of whiskey near. It was set upon its end, and the head knocked out, and all helping themselves. I took a tin cup

12. Lee was victorious at Gaines's Mill but the price of victory was high. He suffered eight thousand casualties.

about half full and drank it down, which helped me a great deal. Gen'l. Wilcox had secured the whiskey for us, knowing that it would be beneficial.

After eating a hearty breakfast of "hard tack" and bacon, I started out with several others to look up our dead and have them decently buried. Of our little company four were killed; Daniel Jones, Perkins Pool, Clayborne Thrasher and Moses Perkins. Poor Jones was shot through the lungs just as we reached the crest of the hill, and did not die until this morning. Clayborne was cut almost entirely in two by a cannon ball. It struck him just above the hips in his side and his head and feet fell together. In addition to the killed I find that quite a number of the boys were wounded. Capt. Jim Crow was wounded by a cannon ball while carrying the colors of the regiment, though his wound is slight. Lieut. Wilson was shot through the hand just as he raised his repeater to fire the last barrel, Marion Young shot through the ankle, John Beauchamp in shoulder, and several others slightly wounded. I was struck on the shin by a "spent ball" which made a black and blue spot, and had my hat knocked off by the explosion of a shell, besides having the strap of my haversack cut from around my neck.

There were many instances of personal daring, and where all did so nobly it is hard to pick out any particular one. Capt. Crow during the fight had a hand to hand fight with a big stout six footer who refused to surrender to him. He finally succeeded in getting him down on the ground but the Yankee was too powerful for him and was about to rise again when Lefevre ran up and stuck a bayonet through him.

I find that several of my friends in the glorious old Fourth were killed yesterday; Tommy Westmoreland, and Billy Oakley, Capt. Armstead also. Billy was carrying the colors of the regiment as it moved forward in the charge and Capt. A. patted him on the shoulder, saying "Go it, my Billy." The same ball killed them both, passing through Billy to Capt. A. Two more brave men never fell together. Major Williams is commanding now and I hope may continue to do so, for he is a splendid man, and we all like him.

Darbytown Road, June 29th, 1862.[13] This morning bright and early we left the Gains Mill battlefield and marched in the direction of Richmond, crossing the Chickahominy at Long Bridge,[14] marched close by our camps and turned down this road. It has been an awful hot day. Once on the march I became so much overheated that I could scarcely get my breath, and felt that I would faint, but happily I had a canteen of water and stretching myself on my back in the shade of a tree, I unbuttoned my shirt and poured the canteen of water in my bosom, which soon relieved me.

It is certainly passing strange how careless men become. *Now,* the boys are chatting away as gaily as though on a pleasure excursion, and one would not think that only two days had passed since they witnessed such terrible scenes, and saw their comrades fall by their sides. We certainly must be a hardened set of wretches. We laugh and play cards, and make arrangements and calculations for the future although we know that it cannot be many days before we go into battle again, and we know that some of us will fall. Will it be this one on my left, my best friend? Will I be among the number? Oh! it's well we don't know, though death finds most of its victims unprepared. One would think that a life of danger would influence men to prepare for death, but it has a directly contrary influence. I know that I am growing worse every day of my life, but still, I never go into battle without a silent prayer for protection. But some always come out alive; and I have a firm but blind belief that I will live through the war—perhaps it's only a hope.

13. After Gaines's Mill, Lee was not certain of McClellan's intentions. As a result he did practically nothing with his army on June 28. However, by the morning of June 29 he was convinced that McClellan was making for the James; so he put his troops in motion at once hoping to cut off the Federal retreat. Generals Magruder and Huger were to move forward on the Williamsburg and Charles City roads; Longstreet and A. P. Hill were to cross the Chickahominy at New Bridge and hurry southeast to the Darbytown Road, following it to the Long Bridge Road. This move, Lee hoped, would put them in a position to strike the Federal flank. Jackson, with his own and D. H. Hill's troops, was to press directly upon McClellan's rear. During the afternoon of June 29 Magruder engaged the enemy at Savage's Station but all of his attacks were repulsed.

14. Patterson crossed the river at New Bridge rather than Long Bridge.

Richmond, Va. August 15th, 1862. Thank God! able to at last sit propped up in bed with pillows. Since writing in my journal six weeks ago I have suffered much, and the doctors say that I have been pretty near the invisible line dividing life and death—separating time from eternity.[15] I am thankful that I did not pass over for I was not and am not prepared for the journey; and I have a particular aversion to becoming one of the subjects of Pluto and his lovely wife, Proserpine. It may be glorious to die on the battlefield with the cry of victory ringing in one's ears, but if *less glorious,* it is certainly more agreeable to live.

August 16th. I was able this morning, with the assistance of a crutch and a little extra lifting, to get to the front door and feel the fresh morning breeze once more. I think that if I am careful I will soon be able to walk about in the city; and I believe I could now if I had two good arms, for one leg needs a crutch as much as the other—but they are much better than *no* legs. I am staying at the home of Mrs. Quarles on 12th Street, and if she were my own mother she could not treat me more tenderly. All that nursing and patient watching and care could do, she has done; and I believe that next to God, I owe my life to her. She is an angel minister embodied in woman's delicate form, sent by the Father to relieve the woes of suffering humanity. She never seems to grow weary of well doing; and in addition to the care and attention bestowed on Ansel and me, she goes daily to the hospitals, now so crowded with mutilated forms, and there amid the dead and dying fulfils woman's highest, holiest mission on earth—to soothe through suffering, to nurse the sick, to purify and redeem. It matters not that the object of her care be unknown to her; she knows them to be soldiers and that they received their wounds in upholding the banner of our Sunny South, and whether she smooths the pillow of a pale sufferer from South Carolina or binds up the wound of one whose home is on the plains

15. Patterson was severely wounded in the Battle of Frayser's Farm (June 30, 1862). This explains why there are no entries in his journal between June 29 and August 15, 1862. (See below pp. 45–60.)

of Texas, whether writing a letter for one whose good right arm was left on the battlefield to his loved ones in Alabama, preparing some little luxury to tempt the appetite or cool the parched lips of that fair haired boy, who tosses restlessly on his hard couch and longs for the familiar faces of his own home amid the orange groves of Florida, she does it all for the South. And there are many others like her, not only here at the capitol but all over Virginia and, in fact, all over the South the ladies are devoting themselves to the work. It should cause the blush of shame to mantle the cheek of any man who, in this hour of trial, hesitates to do his duty, but the man who would falter now would be lost to all sense of shame.

Aug. 19th. Day by day I am becoming stronger, and the life blood once more courses through my veins healthfully. I was able this morning to perform quite a feat in "pedestrianism." I walked down to Broad Street, nearly a square and a half, but had not our chaplain, Dr. Whitton, been with me I don't know when I would have gotten back for he had to carry me, but then he is big enough and stout enough to carry two or three such little fellows as I am. I don't think I'll venture out again soon.

Ansel was, for a time, getting well faster than I was, but is not now near so well. His foot is nearly healed, but his other wound is bad. Dr. Holloway opened the wound in his shoulder and tried to reach the ball, but it slipped deeper and lower as soon as he touched it. He then decided to open his breast and take it from there, and attempted to put him under the influence of chloroform, but the condition of his lung from the effect of the ball would not bear it. So he had to stand the operation without it. It was an exceedingly painful one, and as I lay on my bed and watched it I could feel sharp twinges of pain in my own wounds, for I have felt the surgeon's knife myself. Before the Doctor could get his forceps on the ball it slipped still lower, so that it was impossible to reach it and dangerous to attempt it, so the ball will have to remain as it is. It may kill him and it may not. Noble boy! how I love him. Dr. Holloway is a good man, as well as an excellent surgeon. Although he has charge of the general, No. 2, a large four story building crowded from cellar to roof with wounded,[16] and is on the medical examining board,[17] so that he is almost constantly at work, still he finds time to come up here, eight or ten squares, every day to see Ansel and me. Cousin Frank [18] came to see me whenever he could, but he is now in Mississippi, sick with the typhoid fever.

Doctor H. opened my left thigh not long ago. The wound on the under side had healed up too soon, and pus had accumulated until my leg was as big as two ought to have been. While I was reasoning the case with him, and asking him to give me chloroform, he pretended to be examining it and the first thing I knew, had his knife in me and the operation performed "Before I could say Jack Robinson."

August 21st, 1862. My appetite must have been sleeping during the last month or so, for until recently I have not cared much for the "inner man." But now I feel that I could eat a mule and a cart load of vegetables, and yet the Dr. (what tyrants these doctors are) won't let me eat more than would make a light *snack* between meals for a sickly Mississippi mosquito. And there is no danger of my disobeying his orders, for he puts on a wise look and shakes his head knowingly, and intimates awful consequences that would follow any violation of his laws. But he lets me have little luxuries, and Mrs. Q., dear, good soul, never gets tired of fixing up delicacies for Ansel and me. And it is difficult to get anything nice now, but she will have it if it is in the city. Day after day, during all the long hot weary days of July, she or Miss Mary Lew or Miss Lillie sat by our bedsides and with fan in one hand and book in another tried to amuse and make us comfortable. I can never repay

16. Early in the war Richmond became the medical center of the Confederacy. A special committee of the Confederate House of Representatives reported in April, 1862, that there were twenty Confederate and State hospitals in the city. Still, these were insufficient to care for the wounded of Fair Oaks and the Seven Days. H. H. Cunningham, *Doctors in Gray* (Baton Rouge: Louisiana State University Press, 1958), pp. 45–50.

17. See below p. 40.

18. Cousin Frank Patterson was a first cousin of Edward DeWitt Patterson and the only relative he had in the South. Cousin Frank was a surgeon with the Twentieth Georgia Regiment but it appears that he lived in Mississippi. (See below p. 56.)

their kindness, but will ever pray that their reward may be in proportion to their goodness, and that if any of them ever need a friend they may find such ones as I have.

Since I have been able to do so, I like to sit out on the porch, my left arm in a sling and my legs propped up with cushions and chairs, and see what is going on in the street, and I confess that one reason for liking to sit out there is that I like to speak to President Davis. He lives nearly opposite [19] and always crosses to this side of the street to go down to the office, and whether going down in the morning or returning in the evening, he never passes without speaking, and I like to look upon his face, always so pale and careworn and yet such a pleasant one. *We know each other.* I know him to be our loved President, and he knows me to be a wounded soldier. "God Bless him! and may his shadow never grow less."

Ansel and I cannot complain of any want of attention from our army friends for before they left this place, Capt. Crow, Billie Cannon, Chandler, Dr. Minor, Dr. Whitten, Hays, Jones, Joe McMurray, and in fact a host of others came to see us.

August 25th, 1862. Well! I have been before the August examining board, that board of medical men who say just how long a fellow must be in getting well, and they have looked upon so many mutilated forms that I suppose they can tell about how long it will be before a man can be made of some use. They give me forty five days in which to recover, at the end of which time I am expected to be well and ready to undergo more shooting. We shall see.

Bromwell [20] has been gone for some time on one of his "raids."

19. The Confederate White House was located at the corner of Clay and Twelfth streets.

20. The editor was unable to identify Bromwell. Since Mrs. Quarles ran a boarding house, he could have been taking his meals with her and there met Patterson. See also R. C. Todd, *Confederate Finance* (Athens: University of Georgia Press, 1954), p. 202 n.19.

During the war the Confederate Treasury found it exceedingly difficult to manufacture notes. Agents were sent abroad to procure skilled workmen, machinery, and materials while financial inducements were offered to individual contractors in the South. Major Benjamin F. Ficklin was sent to England to

The government employs him as secret envoy. He has now gone to Baltimore, Philadelphia and New York on business connected with the Treasury Department. Hope he may come through all right, but it is risky business. He has been so kind to Ansel and me. From our first arrival here until he left for the North he has not, or rather did not, fail to dress our wounds three times a day, taking the time from his duties at the Treasury Department. Young and so brave—long may he wave.

August 27, 1862. Eh! bien, Ansel has been before the "board." They gave him sixty days in which to get well, but it's my opinion that if he lives sixty years he will never entirely recover. Poor fellow, I feel so sorry for him, when I have to "fix" his wound. Every day I have to take a long probe, and press into the wound in the shoulder a strip of cotton cloth to the depth of the wound, and then introducing the probe from the breast draw the end out there, so that he is "roweled" pretty deep. This has to be done to prevent the wounds closing up which would produce speedy death, by not allowing the pus to escape. He bears it like a hero—that he is. My love and admiration for him has increased every day since we fought each other last winter in the dark cheerless woods in front of our pickett line on the "Braddock Road." There we gained each other's respect, and respect has ripened into love by common danger and common suffering, until now I love him as a brother, and he does me the same.

Senator Oldham of Texas[21] boards here and I go to Congress with him.[22] He makes a speech occasionally, while I do not, and

employ engravers, lithographers and printers as well as to purchase steel dies, presses, inks, bank-note paper, and other materials needed in the production of notes. Agents were also sent to the North for similar purposes and Bromwell could have been on this type of assignment. *Ibid.*, pp. 90–94.

21. Senator William S. Oldham was a champion of state rights. While a member of the Confederate Congress, 1861–65, he opposed both conscription and the suspension of the writ of habeas corpus.

22. During the life of the Confederacy there were three congresses. The original Convention in Montgomery became the Provisional Congress (February 4, 1861, to February 17, 1862). The first body elected by the people was called the First Congress. It met on February 18, 1862, and adjourned February 17, 1864. The Second Congress, actually the third and last to meet, held two sessions, adjourning on March 18, 1865.

they never ask for my vote as they do for his. But if I cannot do any good, I certainly cannot do any harm, and it is a much pleasanter way of passing the time to come here and study our great men than to be loafing about the streets.

First there is a little man, but with an intellect bigger than his body, Alex. H. Stephens, Vice President of our Confederacy, and by virtue of his office, speaker or president of the senate.[23] He comes in with a careless, swinging gait, dressed in black broadcloth, the long tails of his coat reaching nearly to his heels. A ponderous fob chain with a huge seal swinging half way to his knees. An enormous "Byronical" collar hangs loosely about his neck—his cravat—a large black silk handkerchief tied in a hard knot and ends hanging down. His general appearance is that his clothes were thrown at him from a distance and remain where they happened to strike. He doesn't appear to be anything extraordinary until he takes his seat on the little throne and commences business. Then the whole man changes. The change in his eyes and the expression of his face makes him appear an altogether different man from the one seen a few minutes since walking so leisurely and carelessly into the Senate chamber.

Immediately on the right of the speaker's stand sits the "Eagle orator of Tennessee"—Gustavus C. Henry. Looks much as he did in 1860, when I heard him on the great issues then before the Country. Then, his silvery notes of eloquence echoed up and down the hills and valleys of Tennessee and North Alabama, and his cry was "Save our glorious Union," and the multitudes who flocked to hear him echoed back the strain. Quite a change has come over the spirit of his dreams since then—in those days he was particularly severe on that calm dignified looking man who now sits on his right, Alabama's gifted son, William L. Yancey. Now they work hand in hand for the same great cause, and they differed two years ago only as to the means.[24]

23. Patterson was lucky to get a glimpse of Stephens. He was a bitter critic of the administration and at one period he stayed away from Richmond for a year and a half.

24. Gustavus Adolphus (not Gustavus C.) Henry supported the Davis program in the Confederate Senate whereas Yancey, the ardent secessionist, did

Some of the greatest minds of the South are in our Senate Chamber, where they ought to be. There is Judge Phelan of Mississippi,[25] Burnett of Kentucky,[26] Clay of Ala., the youngest looking man of his age that I have ever seen.[27] Preston of Va.[28] too, is a great man, and Oldham of Texas and Wigfall his colleague,[29] though he generally looks as if he had taken one too many drinks. He is a smart man for all that, though.

August 29th. I have found another place to spend my leisure hours, viz: in the state library, which is in the capitol building. There, besides books of all kinds, I find a good many trophies of war. Various kinds of shells, thrown from those water monsters, the "Monitors." [30] There is also Gen'l. Pope's coat which he forgot in his great hurry when Stuart called on him.[31] Stretched overhead is a tremendous flag, the "glorious old flag" so called, one presented to Gen'l. McClellan by the ladies of New York City to be hoisted over our capitol. His troops left Gain's Mill in such a hurry that they forgot it and instead of floating over the capitol, it hangs in the capitol. I suppose that does just as well though. There are a great

not. W. B. Yearns, *The Confederate Congress* (Athens: University of Georgia Press, 1960), pp. 236–44; hereinafter cited as Yearns, *Congress.*

25. Senator James Phelan is reputed to have once lectured General Lee over breakfast and even planned a military campaign for him. *Ibid.,* p. 20.

26. The State of Kentucky, even though it remained in the Union, also had representation in the Confederate Congress. Senator Henry Cornelius Burnett opposed secession until the firing on Fort Sumter. *Ibid.,* p. 238.

27. Senator Clement Claiborne Clay was born in 1816.

28. Senator William Ballard Preston died of a heart attack November 16, 1862.

29. Senator Louis Trezevant Wigfall first served as a brigadier general in the Confederate army before resigning his commission February, 1862, to accept a Senate seat.

30. "Generic term for a shallow-draught warship mounting one or two large guns and especially designed for bombarding. The name was coined by John Ericsson, their inventor. . . ." M. M. Boatner, *The Civil War Dictionary* (New York: David McKay, 1959), p. 559; hereinafter referred to as Boatner, *Dictionary.*

31. Major General John Pope's coat had been captured by Stuart only a few days before (August 22). According to a member of Stuart's staff the uniform was put on display "for many days . . . in the window of one of the stores on Main Street, in Richmond. . . ." H. B. McClellan, *Life and Campaigns of Major J. E. B. Stuart* (Boston: Houghton, Mifflin and Company, 1885), p. 95.

many curiosities scattered about over the rooms, things that may give a body some very slight idea of war or a battle, but one knows in reality nothing at all about it until he has participated in it. It's like the game of "draw poker," you may sit and look on all day and still know little or nothing of the game; but just "take a hand" yourself and before you have played long you will *learn* it, and pay for it too.

· IV ·

"We moved down the road until we came to a strip of woods on Mr. Frazier's farm"

August 30, 1862, to September 19, 1862

August 30th. Two months have passed since I "went up," and before I leave this place grown dear by being the scene of so much suffering, relieved by such patient labor and care, I must pick up the scattered threads and unite the past with the present. Let me see, where did I leave off with my journal, so many weeks ago? I was down on the Darbytown Road, and I wrote last on the 29th day of June.[1] Ah, I didn't know what was coming or I would not have been so gay, and I don't think I would have sat up half the night playing cards.

Well, on the morning of the 30th of June we moved on down the road, stopping quite frequently, awaiting further developments of the enemy, I suppose. Just before we reached the scene of our fu-

1. See above p. 36.

ture struggle, President Davis and Gen'l. Longstreet passed us. The President looked every inch a soldier and we manifested our love for him in the usual way by the most deafening cheers, and each felt a new stimulus to sustain the hard earned reputation of our Brigade, in the fact that we would fight under the immediate eye of our President. At least such were my feelings. We always like to see Longstreet about too. He always knows what he is about, and has won the name of the old "war horse."

We moved down the road until we came to a strip of woods on Mr. Frazier's farm, near "White Oak Swamp," and there filed to the left and halted in the woods.[2] But we had not been there long before shells came flying into us thick and fast cutting off great limbs of the trees—cutting down bushes and tearing up the dirt around us in a manner that was anything but pleasant. The battery was hardly half a mile in front of us, though hidden from sight by a thicket. Instead of moving back to get out of range of the unpleasant neighbors (as I would have suggested had I been consulted), we were ordered to take the battery. It was immediately in front of our regiment, and paid us *very marked* attention.

Capt. King, who was in command of the regiment, ordered us forward. We jumped over the fence dividing or separating the woods from a wheat field, and formed under a heavy fire of grape and canister. It was very evident that it would not do to advance under such a fire and such a distance in line of battle. So Capt. King gave the command: *By the right of Companies to the front! Batallion! Right Face! Double quick march!* We obeyed the command with a right good will and soon lessened the distance between

2. In this and the following entry Patterson describes the Battle of Frayser's Farm (not Frazier's Farm), June 30, 1862. He was wounded in this engagement, also known as White Oak Swamp, Glendale, Charles City, New Market Crossroads, Nelson's Farm, and Turkey Bend. After Savage's Station (see above p. 36, n. 13) McClellan concentrated his forces behind White Oak Swamp Creek and on a line through Malvern Hill to block Lee's pursuit while his supply trains continued their movement to Harrison's Landing on the James. Lee planned to strike the Federal line with his entire forces but poor staff work prevented this. Most of the fighting was done by Longstreet and A. P. Hill. The battle was desperate and lasted until well after dark but "no strategical advantage was gained by the Confederates nor did they inflict a greater loss of men than they suffered." Steele, *Campaigns,* I, 208.

us and the battery. The fire was fearful, but a little thicket intervening between them and us prevented them from taking aim accurately, and most of the damage was to the rocks and ground between the companies. Among others wounded while advancing in this manner was Lieut. Cannon, who bumped his head against a grape shot about the size of a hen egg that was flying through the air. This left the Company without a commissioned leader to command it, Capt. Crow and Lieut. Wilson having been wounded three days before and Chandler being in command of the regimental ambulance corps. Lieut. Patton of Co. G. was assigned to command us and nobly did his duty.

We advanced in this manner until just before we reached the edge of the thicket, and within three hundred yards of the battery the command was given "By Company into line, March!" And the movement executed at a double quick threw us into line of battle without retarding our progress. We moved forward as fast as possible through the tangled thickets and emerged into the open field beyond with line somewhat broken, and formed ourselves within two hundred yards of the enemy's guns, and not so much as a cornstalk or bush between us. As might have been expected, the moment the line came out from under cover of the thicket we were met by a murderous fire from the artillery. The smoke had settled over the little open field, between the thicket and the woods in the skirts of which the battery was posted, and the sudden flashes of flame from six pieces of artillery lighted up the scene, and while it gave us the idea of a young hell on earth it showed us solid masses of infantry who seemed to spring up as if by magic from the woods in the rear of, and on each side of the battery, like the fruit of the Dragon's teeth armed for the conflict.

We had not seen them until now, and when we saw them standing there we knew that the death angel had his eye on many of *us*. We saw him plume his wings and felt his breath. *It was do or die,* probably both. And with a cry that sounded more like a wail of maddened despair than a cheer, we rushed forward. A fearful and blinding flash of fire from thousands of muskets literally scorched our faces, and lighted for one instant the object of its fury. Just as the lightning's scathing finger pointing, it dazzles its victim when too late for escape. Oh, it was *fearful,* I cannot recall it without a shudder. Twelve brave men of my little company fell under that first volley. Again and again the death dealing artillery executed the death warrant and sounded the knell of departing heroes.

Straight forward, into that flame, into the jaws of death, we pressed. Those of us left standing poured a volley at a distance of not more than ten paces into the faces of the gunners. They fell across their guns and under the wheels, whole teams of horses hitched to the caissons fell dead in their harness. Others, wounded, plunging about in their mad agony, trampled under foot the wounded. Caissons exploded and scattered fragments of human bodies in every direction—head here, an arm there, and a leg yonder. Under foot the blood stood in pools. The clash of arms, the sulphurous smoke and fire, the almost unearthly moans of the wounded horses, pleading in their unknown language for mercy at man's hand, the shriek of the wounded, the groans of the dying, the shouts of officers and men, the steam from the hot blood—incense to the God of war—combined to make a *hell.* To feel the warm blood of your slaughtered comrades, the one you loved best, spurted in your face, or bespattered with his brains, feel him clutching at you in his death agony as he falls across your feet, . . . Ah! it is fearful, but it is a true picture.

The fighting continued. The artillery was silent, but only became so when the silence of death reigned over the hearts of the brave men, yes, *brave* men, who had worked it, and fought it in our very teeth. The few scattered men of our line, thinking that reinforcements were close behind them, would not yield the field. The Yankee line pressed forward, guns were clubbed and bayonets used. Right at the muzzle of one I fell, after having seen nearly three fourths of the company fall. The first ball that struck me was so close that the musket's breath was hot on my face. I had my gun at my face in the act of shooting, "but the fellow got the go on me," and I fell forward across my gun, my left arm, useless, under me. The ball had struck me high up on the shoulder, and as I was leaning forward, and that arm extended at the time, the ball passed under my shoulder blade, and out much lower down than it entered. I did not at the moment feel any pain, only a numbness all over my body. I felt as if some one had given me an awful jar, and fell as limber as a drunken man. I could not even tell where I was hit.

But I was not left to pursue my meditation long without interruption, for no sooner had I become conscious that I was a wounded soldier unable to get up without assistance, than I felt a decided assistance, for a ball fairly lifted me from the ground. Passing partly under me, it struck me in my left thigh, passing through that in a "slantingdicular" direction into my right, about half way between my knee and my body, and striking the bone, ranged downward and lodged against my kneecap. I suppose from the looks of the wound since that one ball did it all, though there may have been two. I did not feel the wound in my right leg for some time after that in my left was given—no, rather received—and only discovered it from the pool of blood that was under me. I was completely helpless, a fit subject for the good Samaritan. I could not move my left arm or either leg.

The storm still raged in all its fury around and above me—men ran over me, balls knocked dirt in my eyes, cut through my hair, and I did not know at what moment a bullet might make my "quietus" for me. Gradually our men were pushed back; I saw but could not join them. The Yankee line moved forward, and the great flag of some Pennsylvania regiment dragged across my face as I lay in the dust. Had it been our flag I would have kissed it; as it was, I did nothing but get as close to the ground as possible. I think I must have spread out like a "spreading adder"; if I didn't it was not my fault.

Just as the line had passed over me, a drunken Irishman, attracted by the brightness of my uniform which was new, turned aside and with the most fiendish look brought his gun to bear on me and started towards me, with the words, "O, you d—d rebel son of a bitch, I'll put *you* out of your misery." By his emphasis on the *you* I knew he meant *me.* The glistening bayonet was within a few feet of my breast, no time for reasoning the case, no time for prayers, expostulations' entreaties. I remember just rolling my eyes heavenward and though my lips did not move, my heart said "God have mercy on my soul." And the bayonet was thrust aside by a strong arm. I was saved by a Federal officer, a Captain or Lieut. He struck the fellow with the side of his sword, and in language more forcible than pious, gave him to understand it would not be conducive to his health to attempt such a thing again. Whether that officer fell that day or the next, or whether he still lives, I know not. I do not even know his name or regiment, but think the regiment that passed over me was the 8th Penn. Reserves. I would like to thank him for his little act of duty, for while it was of little consequence to anyone else, it was a matter of vital importance to me.

Almost before I realized that I was still on this side of the "pass of shadows," I was called to the stern realities of my condition by feeling and seeing myself picked up by two bold "soger boys" [3] and half dragged and half carried to the rear. One caught me under my right arm and the other under my left, and although the torture was excruciating and although I begged and demanded by turns that they should lay me down, they did not halt until they had me about two hundred yards in rear of the lines of battle, where they stopped for a moment behind a big tree. But it was only for a moment, then they hurried me forward again. Perhaps they liked an opportunity of getting a little farther from the front themselves, or maybe they feared that I would get hurt if they did not carry me back. At any rate, they did not stop until we had reached a little open field about a quarter of a mile from where we started. Here were thousands of their own wounded, and they set me among them, leaning me up against the chimney of a little house around which their wounded were lying.

Aug. 31. I continue my story.

While I was being hurried so unceremoniously to the rear, I heard the battle raging more fiercely than ever, and could tell by the sound that our boys were driving the enemy back toward us. And sure enough, in a few minutes the Yankee line had been driven back to the edge of the field in which I lay with the Yankee wounded. They had driven our line across the field to the thicket

3. Slang for soldier.

where, other troops coming up, Gen. Wilcox, more noted for bravery than piety, rallied the scattered men of our brigade by the cry of, "Give 'em hell, my brave Alabamians!" And though *that* was not theirs to give, they came as near obeying his orders literally as they could, by sending many of them where they could get it for themselves. Back over the same bloody ground they drove them, and the fresh troops who had so opportunely made their appearance took position beyond the battery we had captured.

It was now quite dark, but several of our batteries had secured positions where they could keep up the fire on the Yankee line. And while the shell fell thick and fast among the enemy, they came altogether too close to me for comfort. I thought it would be just my luck to be knocked on the head with a shot from one of my own men. This night work is more fearful than the day. The fire from artillery and infantry is so heavy that it pushes the gates of death open, and at the same time lights up the way down to them; and then when a fellows blood is oozing out of him in five or six different places at once, it makes the ground so slippery under him that he is in danger of slipping down through the open gates at almost any moment. By ten o'clock the firing had ceased, "And thousands had sunk on the ground overpowered, the weary to sleep and the wounded to die."

I still remained in the position in which I had been placed by my two worthies, my right shoulder resting against the chimney, supporting the weight of my body, my left arm hanging in front of me, and my legs so stiff and sore that I had no control over them,—mixed up with the arms and legs of other wounded miserables. Some time before I had given my brand new handkerchief to a yankee to make me a sling of it, in which to support my arm, but I suppose that he thought that "To the victor belongs the spoils," for while three or four others were expatiating on the enormity of the sin of rebellion and telling me how thankful I ought to be that I still had space and opportunity for repentance, and adding the gratuitious insult of suggesting that perhaps I was forced into the army, the unmitigated cuss who had undertaken to manufacture the sling disappeared, and with him my handkerchief. The weight of my arm made my shoulder much more painful than it would have been otherwise, but I was afraid to move even had I been able, for fear of increasing the flow of blood, and I felt that I had but little to spare. I thought that before daylight again dawned over the earth I would be in the presence of Him who made me, and for once in my life I looked death calmly in the face. I thought of more things in *one hour* than I could write down in a year. I thought of a home far away in the North-land, and of those dear ones there who will never know how much I loved them, and I wondered if my fate would ever be known to them. I had a horror of dying alone, with:

"No voice well known through many a day,
To speak the last—the parting word;
Which—when all other sounds decay,
Is still like distant music heard."

I was afraid that none of my regiment would ever find me, and that with the unknown dead, who lay scattered around me, I would be buried in one common ground, where no one but the resurrection Angel could ever find me. To meet death under any circumstances must be terrible, but to die there in the darkness of night, without being noticed by friend or foe—the thought was terrible. How I longed for day. Just that *some* one might see me die. It seems now that it would make but little difference, but I felt so then. But if the night was dark, it was not so dark as the future. Ah, a cloud, "dark as the frown of hell," hung over it, and if ever an earnest prayer was sent heavenward by mortal, mine was one that night, but I had but little faith. I could not help thinking that had I escaped without being wounded, I would not have thought of praying. I would have been *glad,* and would have called that gratitude, and that would have been the extent of my devotional feelings. I found some comfort though, that my mother's prayers offered up to heaven long years ago, in my behalf, would be answered. I had more faith in them than my own. Thank God for such a mother! To her influence, and to the memory of her, I owe whatever of good there is remaining in me. How many times, when just about to commit some sin, have I been restrained by the hallowed memories of those far-away innocent days, when I knelt at my mother's knee. Would that I had always listened to these spirit whispers coming over life's restless waters from the "beautiful long ago." But I am digressing.

The loss of so much blood had made me very cold, and it seemed to me that I would freeze. I shook until I almost feared that I would shake in pieces. My teeth chattered until they were sore. If I had not known it to be impossible, I would have really believed that I would freeze to death before morning. My limbs were as cold as ice, and still I wanted water. That had been my first want after being wounded, and I believe the universal experience of wounded men will attest that their first want is water. I don't know what had become of my canteen, perhaps it had gone after my handkerchief. The Yankees had given me water repeatedly, but now all who were not in line of battle were either attending their own wounded or were asleep, and I began to think that I must die from several causes at once: thirst, cold, loss of blood and pain, either of which seemed sufficient to kill me.

But my repeated request for water at last attracted the attention of a youthful soldier who was lying but a short distance from me. He brought me a cup of water, and began asking me questions. Where was I wounded? If I was suffering much? Etc.,—then without saying anything in reply, he left me but soon returned bringing me a blanket, which he put under me, and sitting down on a part of it, he gently changed my position and put my head on his lap. From that time until daylight he did not leave me, except to bring me water—holding my head and doing all that he could to alleviate my sufferings. His voice was as mild and soft as a woman's and his smooth boyish face as he bent over me showed plainly that he could not be more than sixteen years of age. An own brother could not have been more gentle and kind to me. He belonged to some Pennsylvania Regiment, and told me his name and where his home was, but I forgot it all in the intense pain of those terrible hours. I hope that he may never be in the condition that I was then, but should he be so unfortunate, I hope that he may find some one as kind as he was to me, or as kind as I would like to be to him, if he should fall into my hands.

About midnight I heard the command whispered along down the line to get up and move as quietly as possible—the line of battle was within ten feet of me—and I never heard men move more quietly in my life. I did not know whether they were falling back, or were going to make a night attack.[4] This was a fresh line that had relieved the other about dark, and they left with decidedly less noise than they made when they came up; then they cheered extensively, and a one-armed General (Gen'l. Sumner,[5] they said) made a speech and said that Heintzleman's division[6] had Gen'l. Longstreet's command surrounded and etc., and then rode out under fire on horseback, which convinced me that if his name was Sumner, he was certainly no relative of the hero of Massachusetts.[7] Only a pickett line and a few stragglers who had gone to sleep among the wounded remained, and a little while before daylight they left, and with them my good Samaritan.

I busied myself in the gray light of dawn looking about me to see how my companions were faring. A little distance from me was a Lieut. who seemed to be in a particularly bad humor, his leg being shattered, terribly, below the knee, but it did not interfere with his "cussing" powers. He cursed the surgeons of the army in a body, and swore that there was not at the time of the battle nor had there been since, a surgeon within five miles of the place, (which was probably true, as not one of their wounded had been attended to), and to wind up with, he wished the army, surgeons and all, in hell

4. During the night the entire Federal army withdrew unmolested to Malvern Hill.

5. Edwin Vose Sumner, native of Massachusetts and commander of McClellan's Second Corps, was the oldest active corps commander in the Civil War. He was a tough old man with white hair and beard and a tremendous booming voice. But he had not lost an arm. The one-armed general referred to by Patterson was probably division commander Philip Kearny who had lost his left arm during the Mexican War.

6. Major General Samuel P. Heintzelman commanded the Federal Third Corps. During the Battle of Frayser's Farm, Heintzelman's divisions did engage Longstreet in some fierce fighting, but never was the Confederate general surrounded.

7. Senator Charles Sumner of Massachusetts became a "hero" after the Brooks-Sumner affair of 1856.

for having left him there helpless, to fall into the hands of the rebels whom he seemed to think beings of a different nation from his own, who would dash his brains out against a rock and eat him for breakfast like some old one-eyed cyclops. Poor fellow, they didn't eat him but he had to lose his leg, which was amputated during the day and he was attended to as well as he could be under the circumstances.

While gazing around and feeling particularly glad that I had not been called away during the night, I heard some one say, "The Rebels are coming." I turned my head in the direction indicated and saw that sure enough our boys were advancing.[8] I had thought that I loved our soldiers before, but never had I loved them as then, and never do I expect to feel such a thrill of joy through every nerve as I felt then. That line of skirmishers made me feel that friends were at hand, and then I knew that with them our cause was advancing. This kindred of a common cause—common hope—common fears, and common suffering—is it not sometimes stronger than the ties of nature? But they came on through the fields and woods, picking up Yankees by the scores, a great many worn out by fatigue had lain down at night under the bushes in fence corners and everywhere else in squads of from three to a dozen, and slept so soundly that they awoke only after repeated shakes. It would have been quite laughable under other circumstances, to see them get up and rub their eyes in utter amazement to find themselves prisoners. Some of them seemed to hardly realize that they were not dreaming, or that they were not being duped by their own men, but it was no use grumbling and they submitted with a very good grace. The line passed and was soon lost to sight in the woods beyond and it was some time before the line of battle advanced.

At last I saw the long line of bayonets gleaming in the sunshine as they advanced, banners waving proudly and pointing forward. I did not know what troops they were, but as the Col. of the regiment that passed through the little field rode near me, in passing, I called

8. After failing at White Oak Swamp to hit the Federal army with a co-ordinated blow, Lee made his final attempt, and failed again at Malvern Hill on July 1. This was the last of the Seven Days' Battles.

out to him, "Col., what regiment is this?" "The 20th Georgia," said he. I almost forgot my wounds in the joy that his answer gave me. It was the regiment of which Cousin Frank was surgeon, and I did not know that it was in ten miles of that place. How strange! Frank. The only relative that I have in the Confederacy, and that his regiment, of a hundred and fifty, should be the one to pass me. Said I, "Col., where is your surgeon, Dr. Patterson?" "He is back on the battlefield looking for the body of a cousin of his who was killed yesterday," he replied. "No," said I, "he wasn't killed, but was most; I am that cousin." The Col. then sent a man to look for him and he passed on.

It was nine or ten o'clock when he found Frank, for he had gone from the battlefield (after his fruitless search) to my regiment to see if they had heard anything of me. Some of them who had seen me fall told him that I was certainly dead, or at least mortally wounded, but at last the man found him and directed him where I was to be found. I soon saw him come riding up looking anxious and he eagerly bent over me to see the extent of my wounds. He found me almost played out and low spirited enough, but he showed his excellent judgment by *forcing* some brandy down my throat. He then went into the house and tried to get permission from the woman who lived there to bring me in and put me on a bed; she said "No," that no soldiers of either army could come in there—that her husband was "neutral"—in neither army—and was not going to be, but that the Yankees had carried him off with them and left her alone with two or three little children. At last, however, she consented that I should be brought in and laid on the floor near the door. I was very glad for it was beginning to rain.

After *forcing* another drink down me, Frank commenced cutting my clothes off to get at my wounds. I was so sore that he had to cut them all to pieces and work some time to get them off, for they had been completely saturated with blood and had now become dry, and per consequence, stuck fast. At last he found that the ball was still in my right leg, a fact which I had not discovered, so he took out his knife and told me that he must cut it out. I felt that I was hacked up enough already, and I could feel my wounds throb, and sharp twinges of pain run from one to another, and I wanted him to give me chloroform so that I would not suffer any more, but Frank said that it wasn't best and that it would soon be over and would not be very painful, so I must "grin and bear it." I did both. I watched him while he laid open the flesh and it reminded me of cutting fat pork, it cut so smooth and nice, and it hurt my wounds equally as bad as the place where he was cutting. "Sympathy," he said. After washing my wounds and doing all that he could, he spread a tent fly over me and hastened on to rejoin his regiment, who was going on into a fight, but he did not forget to leave me a bottle filled with corn juice, and the contents of which I managed to force down without assistance. I looked at the great big ball, as big as the end of my thumb, and an inch long,[9] which had been the cause of part of my sufferings, and determined that I would preserve it, and in the next battle send it back to the side it came from, but I left it there, forgot it when I was carried away.

Some time during the evening two of my company found me, Joe McMurray and Andrew Cunningham, and I knew that I was all right then for there are not two better boys in the world than Joe and Andrew, and though they could not stay with me all night, they promised to return again in the morning, to have me moved from the place.

While lying there, I had abundant time and opportunity to study the character of my hostess, and I found her a perfect she-devil. There was a poor crippled Yankee lying just outside the door, and he asked her to make him a cup of coffee. She said she would do so if he would pay her for it. She made the coffee and then would not give it to him until he had given her the money. He gave her a one dollar gold piece to take out what the coffee was worth, and she quietly put the money into her pocket, handed him the coffee and walked back into the house, saying that would pay her very well for her trouble. I was mad enough to have "wrung her neck" had I been able. The idea of a woman doing such a thing, and in Virginia

9. Although a tremendous variety of small arms were used during the Civil War, the principal weapon on both sides was the 58-caliber Springfield rifle musket firing the Minié bullet. Boatner, *Dictionary,* p. 766.

too. She went stamping across the floor, screaming some time at her children, some time at some poor wounded Yankee, and occasionally turning her attention to me when she could see no one else to quarrel with, abusing me for bleeding on her floor. What a relief it must have been to her husband to be carried off by the Yankees.

On the morning of the 2nd of July, Joe and Andrew came and brought with them their haversacks, blankets, etc., and told me that what remained of the regiment had gone back to camp, and that they had permission to remain with me as long as it was necessary. They brought with them a large side of bacon which they had found in the Yankee Commissary's camp. This they gave to the aforesaid hostess, as they had enough without it. This so pleased her that when she was done with breakfast she kindly asked me if I would not drink a cup of coffee. I took some, which was the first thing I had eaten or drank since the battle, with the exception of the whiskey and brandy Frank had given me.

The boys then told me the fate of our company. Of the 28 men that went into battle seven only were left, and the proportion was nearly as great in the other companies of the regiment. Six had been killed on the field, and fifteen wounded, some of them mortally. Of my mess, Joe only remained of eight. Ansel Newson had been shot through the foot and shoulder, Tom Harmon twice through the thigh, John Craig through the body and hip—mortally, Ed Till in the side with two ribs broken, John McMurray through the thigh, Billy Dickey killed, myself used up, and Joe alone unhurt. My dear friend, Wesley Turnley, young, noble, generous, brave—my most intimate friend, one that I loved almost to idolatry, he too had fallen; but I knew that, for he had fallen by my side before I was wounded. Two balls had stuck him in the forehead and one I think in the breast. Jim Mattews, John C. Phillips, John L. Phillips, and John Childress also were killed. It is strange how one can hear the human voice amid the roar and confusion of the battlefield, but when John Childress fell, shot through, he said, "I am killed, tell Ma and Pa goodbye for me," and I heard it as distinctly as if everything had been still.[10]

10. Confederate losses at Frayser's Farm were 3,615. *Ibid.*, p. 916.

After giving me the history of the regiment, telling over the long list of killed and wounded, Joe set out to look for a surgeon, to try to get an ambulance to move me away from that place. At last he found one, the surgeon of the 45th N.C., who had some of his wounded about half a mile from where I was in some little pens and stables. He sent an ambulance down to move me up there, where he could attend to me with his men. I was so sore that I could not bear to have my body touched anywhere. So Joe and Andrew with two others took hold of the corners of my blanket and lifted me into the ambulance in that way. Before leaving, I told Joe to take my pocket book and pay the lady for the trouble I had caused her, which he did, but his indignation was considerably aroused when in reply to his question how much she considered it worth she said five dollars. I, too, thought it was rather dear for one day's lodging without rations, but Joe paid her, and as the ambulance drove off she said, to Joe, "Tell that gentleman that I hope that he may get well soon."

Arrived at our destination, the boys lifted me out and carried me in among the other wounded, and laid me down on a rail floor. It was a "shuck pen." The Doctor came around to see me, and I found him a capital fellow. He laughed and talked so cheerfully that he made me feel better almost immediately, then he gave me a good strong "mint julep" which helped me amazingly. Joe and Andrew gave me their blankets to go under me, and busied themselves generally making me comfortable that day and the next. On the morning of the 4th the Doctor came in and asked me if I thought I could stand a trip to Richmond. I told him yes. Soon the ambulance came around and they put me in and packed blankets around and under me, and then a member of the 3rd Alabama was put in with me. He was shot through the body, and if possible was suffering more intensely than myself. We then started on the road for Richmond, Andrew and Joe accompanying the ambulance as far as the regimental camp, where it stopped, and all the boys came out to the road to see me.

By the time we reached Richmond I had not sense enough to tell the driver where I wanted to go, but I remembered the name, and where the 3rd Alabama man stopped I got a negro boy to go with us and show the driver which house I wanted to go to. As the ambulance stopped before the door, Mrs. Q.[11] and others came out, knowing that it was some friend. At first they thought I was dead, lying there so white and still, wrapped in a piece of tent cloth, but when I opened my eyes and they saw that life still remained, they made instant preparation to carry me in. The bottom of my bed in the ambulance was a litter, and I was carried in on that and gently placed on a bed soft as down. Mrs. Q. saw that the ride had been almost too much for me and that I was very low, and so she fixed up a strong milk punch which revived me considerably. The old family physician was sent for, and he gave me large quantities of morphine and left some to be given during the night. I was unconscious or in dream-land most of the night, but awoke in the morning feeling somewhat refreshed and found Mrs. Q. sitting by my bedside. On the 4th of July 1861, I was in Richmond carousing around generally, and on the 4th 1862 I made my entry into the city more dead than alive, while most of those who were with me on that day in 1861 now sleep "neath Virginia soil." Perhaps by the next 4th I may be with them. In a few days after my arrival, Mrs. Q. found Ansel in one of the hospitals and had him conveyed here, where we have been ever since, but will soon go to Gordonsville.

Inglewood Va.[12] ***Sept. 12, 1862.*** I thought when Ansel and I left Richmond that one could not meet twice in a life time such friends as we had left there, but I was mistaken. They are the same here. The Doctor[13] is superintendent of the "Inglewood Female Institute"[14] and there is a houseful of girls, or rather young ladies, here attending school. It is a delightful place. The house stands on an eminence commanding a fine view of the surrounding country.

11. Mrs. Quarles (see above p. 15).

12. Inglewood was the Louisa County home of Reverend Charles Quarles.

13. Reverend Charles Quarles was also a physician, but when he was ordained a minister in 1854, he gave up his practice. Malcom Harris, *History of Louisa County, Virginia* (Richmond: Dietz Press, 1936), p. 210; hereinafter cited as Harris, *Louisa County.*

14. It was not unusual for ministers, as an additional means of livelihood, to conduct boarding schools at their homes. *Ibid.,* p. 226.

One would never think from the looks of the country around Gordonsville that out here, three miles from it, could be found such a country as extends from here six or eight miles down through the "Green Springs Neighborhood."[15] It is such a delightful home place. Yes, that is the word. It is *home.* I felt so very soon after my arrival, and have been feeling so ever since.

We found Mrs. Quarles and Miss Nannie at home, and they gave us a most cordial welcome. Newson had enjoyed their hospitality before, and I was welcomed as a friend of his and as a soldier. The Doctor and Miss Sallie came home in the evening, and gave us the same true Virginia welcome that the others had extended to us on our arrival. I think the Doctor's wife just such a woman as Mrs. Q. in Richmond. And Miss Nannie and Miss Sallie—well, it's no use saying anything about them, they are just the dearest little creatures in the world. I have been over to Bellemonte—two miles from here to the Captain's (Mr. Jno. Quarles, a brother of the Doctor's).[16] He has two daughters too, Miss Jennie and Miss Sue. He has three sons in service, two in the Stonewall Brigade[17] and one in the Western department, and there are two others who *will* be in the service if the war lasts until they are old enough.

September 13th, 1862. It's mighty pleasant after enjoying a good dinner to walk out on the piazza and find a good easy rocking chair placed there for me. To have my pipe filled and brought to me, filled with the best old Virginia tobacco, and by the hand of a fair gentle Virginia maiden. Ah! I could not be induced to give up the weed, not I, as I lean back in my cushioned chair and rock slowly to and fro watching the smoke curling gracefully above my head, hearing the merry laugh of my fair physician. I am "Constrained" to exclaim "Who wouldn't be a soldier and a wounded one

15. This section of Louisa County is still referred to as the "Green Springs Neighborhood."

16. Patterson was not consistent in the way he spelled Bellemonte, the home of John R. Quarles. Sometimes he spelled it Belle Monte (see below p. 65).

17. The Stonewall Brigade was one of the most famous fighting units in the Confederate army. It was organized and trained by "Stonewall" Jackson. When Jackson moved to higher command, he had his old brigade transferred to his unit.

too." The wounds in my body are doing very well, but I feel as if Cupid had been shooting some of his arrows in my direction, and it is said that they make more dangerous wounds than bullets. *Nous Verrons.*

September 14, 1862. As I was going over to Belle Monte this evening with my facetious friend, McKellough, from the Palmetto State, I saw a solitary horseman approaching. I did not recognize him until he spoke and who should it be but Cousin Frank. When he started to Mississippi he left his horse at Richmond, and now on his way to rejoin his command, he was taking the most pleasant way over the country on horseback. He looks a little thin but says that he is quite well. Of course he had to stop at Inglewood. He is downstairs now, with Miss Alice Hunter. She is playing the piano, and they are singing something about a "poor gypsy maid." Ansel is suffering terribly and can rest only when under the influence of morphine or laudanum.

Sept. 16th. I wish I was well enough to go with Cousin Frank and rejoin my command, though I would hate to leave Ansel as sick as he is. I would like so much to be with the boys in Maryland. I can hear nothing from them. Frank seems more like a brother than a cousin. We being the only ones of our family South, and probably the only ones whose sympathies are on this side, we feel a stronger attachment for each other than we otherwise would feel.

I wouldn't feel so blue if Ansel would only get well, but poor fellow, he seems to grow worse every day. Last night his pain was so intense that he was perfectly insane. His screams make me shudder, and then when for one brief moment the pains would cease, he would pray God Oh! so earnestly, to let him die. As I sat by his bedside, he feared that I would leave him, and clutched my arm until he left the imprint of his fingers on my arm. There is no use of your doing *that,* Ansel, I would not leave you for anything in *this* world. I gave him doses of laudanum last night that it seems to me would have killed anyone else, but he has taken so much that it seems to have lost its effect upon him. Although the Doctor said give him twenty drops at a dose, I gave him sixty, and repeated the dose frequently through the night and he begged for more. He is easier today, but I am afraid it is only temporary. And must he die? Noble boy,—it is too hard to see him, just in the vigor of early manhood, lying there so helpless, and to think that those deep bright eyes that speak whole volumes of truth must soon be closed in death; that the generous heart that throbs within that breast must cease to beat; that the tall, graceful, manly form that lies here before me must soon moulder back to mother earth. If the invisible reaper cuts him down, truly "death loves a shining mark." But I don't believe, I will not believe that he is to die this time.

September 14, 1862. As I was going over to Belle Monte this rapidly. The Doctor thinks him out of danger. He is able to sit up and the inflamation has left his shoulder, and now, if he doesn't catch cold, I think he will be all right again soon. I have been down in the parlor hearing Miss Alice and Miss Sallie sing "Norma." They sing well together. I have also had a tremendious romp with them. They have whipped and beaten me until I am sore, and all because I wouldn't peel their peaches for them, and I had to do it at last. That's the way it always ends. A woman will have her way and a man might as well submit with a good grace, and get some credit for it, as to wait until he is taught that although his *sex* call themselves the "Lords of Creation," still they must recognize the woman's right to rule. I think it mighty pleasant to be the "Prisoner at the bar," and be sentenced by one of these fair creatures. Bless the ladies, I wouldn't live in a world where they didn't raise them.

· V ·

"I have got the Alabama fever in my head"

September 22, 1862, to November 15, 1862

September 22nd, 1862. Have been to Gordonsville and while there the train came in from Culpepper bringing in quite a number of wounded from the battle that had been fought at Sharpsburg, Maryland. The reports are very conflicting in regard to it, and it is impossible to get any correct idea of it.[1] Among the wounded I found one of my men, Steve Greenough. He tells me that our regiment lost heavily, but as he was wounded and left the field early, and has not seen any of the boys since, he couldn't tell me much. He thinks Wilson is dead, he fell into the hands of the Yankees. Dolph Owen is also wounded. The entire regiment num-

1. Sharpsburg was the Confederate name for the Battle of Antietam (September 17, 1862). In some ways this engagement was a defeat for both armies. Even though McClellan stopped Lee's invasion of the North, he failed to win the smashing victory that many thought to be within his grasp. On the other hand this battle is considered by some to be the turning point of the war. It showed that Lee was not invincible, gave Lincoln the opportunity he needed to issue his Emancipation Proclamation (September 22, 1862), and influenced British thinking (negatively) on the question of recognizing the Confederacy.

bered only one hundred and thirty men in the battle, and ours was a fair sample of the army. Two thirds of the men able for duty were on this side the Potomac barefooted. He tells of hard times the boys had and I don't doubt it, living for days on green corn and apples don't improve the health of an army. Greenough is wounded in the wrist with a piece of shell, will be well in two or three weeks. I wish I could be with the boys. I am actually getting home-sick to see them again.

Sept. 29th, 1862. Newson having no particular need of my attention, being able to help himself, I left him this morning and came down here, partly to see the folks, and partly to enquire after any of the boys who might be here wounded. I have already found out my good friend, Tom Harmon. He went down at the same bloody day that came so near finishing me. I have got the Alabama fever in my head and think I will go back to Gordonsville tomorrow and try and persuade Ansel into the notion of going. Tom has just gotten back from Dalton where he has spent one furlough and has now come here to get another, as he is not able for duty. I hope we may all get off together.

October 2nd, 1862. Inglewood, Va. Today at noon we bid goodbye to all these people who have tried in every way to make this a pleasant home and well have they succeeded; never can I forget their kindness and if I ever pass through this country again, I am certain to revisit Inglewood, Belle Monte and these other places, as that I will be welcome when I come again. In Alabama, among friends of other days, I will not forget this happy home and the kindness of all the inmates. Oh, how I hope that they may never feel the desolating hand of war laid heavily upon them. But I can't write this morning—I am too much excited with the prospect of seeing old Lauderdale [2] again.

Richmond, Va. October 3/62. Tom has been stirring himself and is "armed and equipped as the law directs" with a thirty day

2. Lauderdale County, Alabama (see above p. xvii).

furlough. Ansel and I will get ours renewed when we reach Alabama.

We were all very much delighted and surprised this morning to see Bromwell come walking in, looking as natural as life, with the exception of some "new fashioned clothes" which show that he has been on a raid. He had a hard time, was in many close places and proved himself a splendid pilot to work himself out of the tangled web of difficulties that hedged him in on every side. It is quite laughable to hear him tell of his arrest at Winchester, how he managed his escape—of his midnight ride to Strasbourg with the Yankees pursuing him so closely that he could hear the clatter of their horses' hoofs, but he says it wasn't so laughable then.[3] However, he came through all right after spending several weeks in various Northern cities, and having a good time generally. He is a trump. I shall always love him for his attention to Ansel and me.

Crutchfield Home. Chattanooga, Tenn. October 7th, P.M. Leaving the good old capital about sundown on the 5th, we arrived here this evening "in good order and well conditioned," and found that we cannot get away until daylight tomorrow morning. We have taken a room, but find that it is held by other occupants who have a prior claim. We were willing to share it with them, but they are satisfied with nothing less than undivided possession. In these war times, "might makes right," and we determined to fight for it. But no sooner had we entered than they commenced an unprovoked attack on us. The fight has been raging for some time, and although *I* am whipped and have retired, Ansel and Tom still continue the unequal contest and are performing prodigious valor.

3. Winchester was in Federal hands from March 12 to September 2, 1862, at which time Brigadier General Julius White, acting under orders from General Halleck, evacuated the town. The following day, September 3, the Confederate troops moved in. On October 3 (the date of the above entry) Lee, following the Antietam Campaign, was encamped in the area. Thus Bromwell's arrest at Winchester and his "midnight ride to Strasbourg" had to take place sometime between March and September. It could have occurred around August 23. On this date Confederate cavalry captured and burned a train headed from Harper's Ferry to Winchester and also cut telegraph wires. General White reported: "What mounted men I can command are in pursuit of the enemy." *O.R.*, XII, Sec. I, Pt. III, 652.

Although the enemy have the advantage both in position and number, Tom and Ansel are still "unterrified" and their repeated assaults have covered themselves with "glo"—bedbugs and fleas, I mean. (confound this pen, I must look for another).

Later. The enemy have been compelled to retire within their works, into their inaccessible retreats where it is impossible to follow them, and the boys have retreated from the blood stained field and are fixing to go into camp in the open field. We are trying to get some oil to pour around our quarters, and so form a fortified enclosure camp where we will be safe from a night attack. ("Blast" this pen, it is worse than the other). The accumulated dust of ages has settled on all within the room, and I would not imagine that it has been inhabited for years were it not the sheets attest that bloody warfare has been waged here in days gone by. Suppose that a fellow should be devoured by these "varmints," the only notice taken of it would be in the morning papers under the head of "missing" or "mysterious disappearance." But I must risk a sleep for I am worn out, and though I expect to dream of being shipwrecked and cast away on some island, and dream of being eaten up by cannibals, and wake to find that it was not a dream.

Winchester, Tennessee. October 8th, 1862. 9 P.M. Perhaps it was the fumes of indigestion, perhaps the want of something to digest, or perhaps 'twas something else that caused me to dream last night of cannibals, (Surgeons, no disrespect intended), and Hydra-headed monsters. But after exhausting all the anathemas in the vocabulary, at least all that I felt privileged to use, I was glad when the blessed daylight dawned. Talk not to me of the quietude—the calm repose—the loveliness of night. "I can't see it." It is all very nice for a fellow to be with his sweetheart on a moonlight night. But it's being with his sweetheart that makes it so nice—the night has nothing to do with it. Ugh! In a close room in a strange hotel—in a strange town, and the last of the inch of tallow candle (given me to go to bed by) exhausted, no bell to ring for a servant, and no servant to *come* if there had been a bell. If I attempted to find my way down three or four flights of stairs to terra-firma, in danger of running into some room where I had no business, and having my head broken by some indignant husband, or have some young lady scream fire! Thieves! Murder! (strong accent on the last syllable) —while indulging in these reflections, to feel all at once a "chintz" on the back of my neck, one at each heel, one under each toe, six under each arm, four on each elbow, and a hundred and one on that place "where mothers smite their young." How can a fellow scratch all over at once? Oh, for daylight. I suppose I must have felt as old Ajax did when, contending with Hector for the body of Patroclus, he exclaimed, "Father of heaven and earth, deliver thou Acha's host from darkness; clear the skies: Give day; and since thy sovereign will is such, Destruction with it, but Oh, give us day." [4]

Day came at last and with it a summons to get aboard the train, and I left Chattanooga with a determination never to see it again. We soon reached the river and found no bridge, so we all hands dismounted and went aboard a flat boat which was in waiting to convey us across the chute to an island, and found about half a dozen boys with canoes and "dugouts" ready to convey passengers to the opposite bank for the trifling sum of twenty five cents. Tom, Ansel and myself took passage in one, preferring that to waiting half an hour for the steam boat which was to ferry us over. As soon as our frail bark landed, we hurried up the bank and secured seats in the train that was waiting there, and then had time to look around and see Bridgeport,[5] the "port" still remained but "nary" bridge.

Soon under headway again, nothing of material interest happened until we reached the tunnel when the car we were in, being a little too wide for the tunnel, or the tunnel a little too narrow for the car, it rubbed and tore off some of the siding, demolished some windows, and scared me almost into fits. I thought the whole tunnel

4. Patterson was quoting from the *Iliad,* Book XVII: "Zeus, O Father, deliver the sons of Achaia from Darkness; Bring out a clear bright sky vouchsafe our eyes to see clearly. Only in light let us die, since such, it seems, is thy pleasure." W. B. Smith and W. M. Miller, *The Iliad of Homer. A Line for Line Translation in Dactylic Hexameters* (New York: Macmillian Company, 1944), p. 381.

5. Bridgeport, Alabama (on the west bank of the Tennessee River) was on the Nashville and Chattanooga Railroad. This line ran in a southwesterly direction out of Chattanooga to Stevenson, Alabama. There it turned north into Tennessee proceeding to Nashville.

was tumbling in, but it wasn't. And with very little delay we soon reached Decherd Station.[6] A drizzling rain had been falling for an hour or two, and it was as cold as all out doors. But while shivering away so extensively, I had been talking with a jolly old farmer, and had succeeded in getting on the blind side of him. As soon as the cars stopped, Ansel and Tom, with the rest of the passengers, made a rush for the eating house to get a warm dinner. But my elderly companion "gave me the knowing wink" and we walked to a little house about fifty yards from the depot where the old man found an acquaintance who immediately produced some "Old Peach Brandy." A good drink of it warmed us up and I joined the boys at the eating house, in time to get my dinner and take the first hack for this place.

Secured this room and then went in search of some conveyance to take us to Florence. There's another man in our party going to Florence, a merchant from Lynchburg, Mr. Morgan, an elegant gentleman, I think. I think we have made arrangements with Mr. Burroughs to carry all four of us down, that is if he doesn't get sick of his bargain, before morning.

Florence, Alabama. October 11, 1862. Back to the starting point once more. Not two years have passed since our company started for Virginia, with high hopes, lofty ambitions. Today nearly one third of its members are sleeping the "sleep that knows no waking." Such is life and such is death.

On the morning of the 9th Mr. Burroughs drove around to the Hotel and Mr. M., Ansel, Tom and myself not being encumbered with unnecessary baggage were soon seated and the horses moving at a break neck pace out of the pleasant town of Winchester. The rain soon began falling and we were rather cool. Someone said that it would be absolutely necessary to have either overcoats, undershirts or some substitute for them. We could not get the articles needed, but found a good substitute at a little town called Salem. We stopped the first night at Mr. Murphey's, in the neighborhood

6. Decherd, Tennessee, was a rail junction on the Nashville and Chattanooga line. The Winchester and Alabama Railroad ran west from Decherd to Fayetteville, Tennessee.

of "Cross Roads." And last night at Mr. Sloss' just the other side of Elk River, and arrived here this evening and were duly welcomed by Mr. Crow and family. Ansel and Tom will stay at Tom's house; I mean to spend a day or two in town and then down in the country to my old "stamping ground." Col. O'Neal is at home; I went around to Col. Rutherford's in Richmond, where Col. O. was staying, to come home with him, but he had gone.

Oct. 12th, 1862. Those who have relatives in our regiment or in the 4th are very anxious to hear from Virginia. And the mail communications are so very bad that we are the bearers of bad news to many of them. The fate of some of the boys who were killed on the day that I was wounded was unknown by their friends until our arrival. Newson, Tom and I have been up to see Col. O'Neal. He was delighted to see us. Introduced us as "his boys." He is still confined to his bed, and it will be some time before he forgets "South Mountain." [7] I went to Dr. Stewart this morning and got him to examine my wounds and extend my furlough which was out the day I landed in Winchester. Dr. Stewart thinks it will be at least a month before I will be fit for duty.

Gravelly Springs. October 13th, 1862. This morning I hired a horse and buggy and came down here among my old Ante Bellum friends. I drove up to Mr. Chandler's and by the time I was out of the buggy, Mrs. C. came running from the house to meet me, mistaking me for her nephew, Jim Chandler, whom she was expecting home from Bragg's army.[8] She discovered her mistake just in time to prevent her "hugging the wrong man." But although disappointed they were all wonderfully glad to see me, for I had good news of another nephew, John Chandler, and Mrs. Chandler's brother, Billie Cannon, who are Lieutenants in my company. I have been over to Mr. Cannon's and assured them that though Billie has

7. The Battle of South Mountain was fought September 14, 1862. It was part of the Antietam Campaign.

8. Braxton Bragg, appointed full general in the Confederate army in April, 1862, commanded the Army of Tennessee.

been twice wounded during the campaign still he is all right and with the command.

At Mr. Whitsett's.[9] *October 14th, 1862.* Being too poor to keep a hired conveyance I sent the horse and buggy back from Gravelly Springs, and this morning having signified my intention of coming down here, Mr. C. sent me down and offered me a horse to ride while I remain at home. About two miles from Waterloo[10] I met Major Witherspoon and he turned back and we rode on together. I took dinner with him—made hasty calls on my good friend Dr. Sullivan, Mr. McCorkle, Rawlings, Reynolds, Cunningham and Mrs. McMurray's and then out here. Quite a change has come over the spirit of my dream, since I boarded here, and taught school in the little log school house across the creek. I have seen hard times since those days but I believe I'd rather be a soldier than to teach school again.[11]

At Uncle Wiley Edward's.[12] *"On Cypress." Oct. 20, '62.* I was wonderfully surprised to find, on getting up this morning, an inch of snow on the ground. It is something that has not occurred before "in the memory of the oldest inhabitants," that is so early in the season. The snow did not last long after sun rise and now it is warm and pleasant. After spending several days among my Waterloo friends, giving them news and messages, Mr. Whitsett kindly informed me that there was a horse in the stable and a boy ready to catch him and saddle him at any and all times that I should feel like visiting my friends in other parts of the country. So on the 18th I went up to the creek into the edge of Tennessee, calling at various places on the road, and finally stopping at Mr. Garner's for the night. Had a pleasant time, as I always do there.

Yesterday I came over here, only ten miles, found Uncle Wiley

9. See above p. xvii.
10. See above p. vi.
11. See above p. vi.
12. "Uncle Wylie" was the Reverend Wylie B. Edwards, father of Patterson's friend James R. Edwards of Company D. He was uncle by courtesy and affection only—not a blood relation.

and his wife[13] gone, but the servant said that Miss Josie was at home, just tell her that a gentleman wishes to get dinner for himself and horse. I seated myself and awaited Cousin Ella Joe's[14] movements very patiently. At last I heard her coming. She stepped to the door and said: "Your dinner—Oh, Cousin Ed, how do you do? Where did you come from—why didn't you tell me. How is my darling Bud Jim," etc., etc. It was a pleasant meeting and I wasn't so hungry as I thought I was. I had a thousand questions to answer about myself, and Jim, and then when the old folks came, had to repeat them. I've some mighty good friends, more and better ones than I deserve.

Florence, Alabama. October 23rd, 1862. After leaving Uncle Wylie's I called at Mr. Thomas' and dined at Mrs. Buroughs, then called at Mr. Reeder's and afterwards went to Mr. Power's. Found Tom at home, his regiment being camped over at Tuscumbia. Miss Sallie and Mollie were at home and our mutual friends Pope Lansford and Tom Brown. So we had a most magnificent time. About midnight we retired, Tom, Pope and I occupying one room. We were soon sleeping soundly and unfortunately continued to sleep until about daylight when we all awoke about the same time, almost strangled with smoke. Springing out of bed, we threw open the doors and windows, and soon found out what was the matter. In going to bed, as there was no fire in the stove, one of the boys had thrown his clothes across the top of it, and the negro boy coming in before daylight, had built a big fire and gone out without having a light in the room and without disturbing any of us, and it was the burning of these clothes that had caused such a scatteration among us. It was quite a relief to me when some one examined the burning fragments and pronounced them Pope's. As it was rather early we all crawled in again, and amused ourselves at Pope's expense. He was so much taller than the rest of us that we knew he would look like a fright dressed up in any clothes that Tom could

13. This was the Reverend Mr. Edward's second wife. His first wife, a McDougal, had died before the war. Her niece married E. D. Patterson, so in a roundabout way Uncle Wylie eventually became Patterson's uncle by marriage.

14. Cousin Ella Joe and Miss Josie, mentioned in this entry, are in all probability the same person.

procure for him. After having our laugh out, the rest of us determined to get up and see what we could do for Pope. I commenced pulling over the clothes, but did not find mine. At last I saw something that I recognized as a small part of my brand new $20 breeches just bought before I left Richmond. I was like the little boy the calf run over, "Nothing to say." This change in the tune set the boys going again, and they didn't stop till breakfast was announced, when we had to send down word to the ladies that they must wait a few minutes. Tom soon found a suit of broadcloth that fitted me exactly and I was all right again.

After breakfast we all rode into town and had a "gay time" winding up by Tom Powers having a fight with Hunt Kirkman. About sundown the boys went home and I remained in town and let Tom Harmon have my horse to go to Russellville to see his sister. When he comes back Ansel and I are going down in the country. In the meantime I have been to see Capt. Crow's sweetheart.

Uncle Wiley's. Oct. 25th '62. Yesterday evening Ansel and I started out to Mr. Powers' and got lost. After riding hard for four or five hours to go seven miles, we found the place about nine o'clock. We were tired and our horses more so. But we soon forgot our troubles and were as happy as two little pigs in the sunshine. This morning Ansel felt quite unwell and was afraid to continue the trip we had started on, so he returned to Florence. We had agreed to start back to Virginia next week and I am getting almost crazy to get back among the boys again. I must call at Capt. Boggs' tomorrow and see "Sissie." And then at Gravelly Springs to notify them to have their letters ready, then to Waterloo and begin my final adieux. A soldier is always nearly crazy to get away from the army on furloughs but as a general thing they are more anxious to get back. There is a feeling of love—a strong attachment for those with whom one has shared common dangers, that is never felt for any one else, or under any other circumstances.

Waterloo, Ala. Oct. 31, '62. I begin to wish that communication was more direct between this country and Virginia. I have about a half bushel of letters and socks enough to supply a good sized army, but I have to refuse almost everything but letters. The "cantankerous" Yankees have so destroyed railroads that we are a hundred miles from any place, and what provisions they could not carry away with them they destroyed, and the citizens will have a hard time I fear, this coming winter.[15] But their hearts are all right and they really love to make sacrifices for a soldier. Mr. Whitsett has presented me with a fine heavy overcoat which will be extremely comfortable when those cold winds from the North come sweeping across the old fields of Northern Virginia. I have so many little articles for the boys that I don't know whether I will ever be able to deliver them to their proper owners. I wish I could carry more, but I am afraid to attempt it, while communications are so difficult. I have been down to Capt. W. and told them goodbye and received some things for Phil, among other things some money which may prove serviceable to me, as I fear that I will run short of funds before I land safely in the camps of the old 9th Alabama.

Wilson Whitsett's. Nov. 1st 1862. This is my last night here, and it seems like leaving home again, they have been so uniformly kind to me. I have spoken my goodbye to all my Waterloo friends, and Mrs. Till's folks, and have my head full of a thousand or two last messages, tell my boy this, and tell my boy that, etc. And some whose boys went with me a few months ago, now wipe the tears from their eyes as they remember that they have no longer any boy to send a message to. Still they are proud of them.

Uncle Wylie's. Nov. 2, '62. I have added largely to my store of letters and think I'll have to divide when I get to Florence. Cousin Ella has been telling me a thousand things to tell "Dear Bud

15. The Confederate defeats at Forts Henry and Donelson and at Shiloh in the winter and early spring of 1862 left the counties of north Alabama open to the Federals. Huntsville fell to a Union force under General Q. M. Mitchell on April 11, 1862. Decatur, Athens, Tuscumbia, and other towns of the Tennessee Valley were occupied in a few days. By summer the Federals controlled a large part of the Memphis and Charleston Railroad which ran through North Alabama. The fighting in this region was almost entirely in the nature of skirmishes but it was continual.

Jim." And I have promised faithfully not to forget, but I am afraid I will. I am really glad that I have no sister or near relative here to tell goodbye. I don't think I could stand it at all. It is as much as I can do to keep my upper lip from twitching and my eyes dry telling *friends* goodbye, especially after Uncle Wylie has been talking so good to me. I do believe that he is one of the best men in the world. He is just what all preachers *should be.* Never was there a truer christian, a better neighbor, a more faithful friend, a purer man in all the world and then to think men professing to wage a war for the restoration of the Union, in a civilized land, to apply the torch to his barn, to sweep everything except the roof that now shelters me, and then to hunt him as a wild beast and compel him to lie in the woods, and then because they could not find the old gray haired man, take their *manly* revenge on his wife and daughter, cursing and abusing and threatening to blow their brains out if they did not reveal his hiding place. All this they have done. And why? that is the question Cousin Ella asked——— "Just because he is the damnedest old gray-headed rebel in all this country." And these are the *"Union Savers."* And talk of the "old flag." Perhaps they may save the union, but I pray God that they may not, and may the hand that writes these lines be paralyzed before I attempt to uphold a government that sanctions this kind of war fare. I care not for myself, I care not for my fellow comrades in arms—but O, I do hope and pray that our women and children may be spared.

Florence, Alabama. November 4th, '62. Our arrangements are concluded and everything is in readiness to start. I came in from Uncle Wylie's day before yesterday, and found the boys in good spirits. Some officers from the Western Army[16] have come home on a furlough and we will go back in the stage, at least a part of the way, as far as Huntsville. Mr. Addison Carroll goes out with us to see his son who is a member of our company. Mrs. Brown, Tom Harmon's sister, has just presented Ansel and me with a pair of fine heavy overshirts. They are nice and "oncommonly" acceptable, but I am sorry that she had to cut up a couple of fine dresses to make

16. The Army of Tennessee under General Bragg.

them. But thus it is, everything in the dry goods line as in the eating line, is literally played out. One more night's sleep at home, an early rising, a few loving goodbyes and last messages and we will be en route for Virginia.

Huntsville, Ala. Nov. 6th 1862. We arrived here this evening only to find that the R.R. has not been repaired and that we are as far from any starting point as when we left Florence. Whenever I leave any particular place to go on a journey, I cannot help thinking of the *possibility* that I may never return, and in these war times possibilities shift themselves over to the opposite side of the question, and probabilities take their place. Today has been awfully cold, and I am decidedly of the opinion that there are modes of travelling preferable to staging. Fourteen miles from here we bought half a gallon of whiskey and six of us managed to finish it about the time we reached town, and without any one being unpleasantly affected by it. My friend, Jim Chandler, has just arrived enroute for home, and I have cautioned him about reporting the proceedings of "our party."

The only chance we can see to get away from this place is to stick to the stage, and to go to Gadsden, on the Coosa.[17] Wisdome (our stage man) lives there and is in such a hurry to get home that he won't take us in any other direction. We don't much like this trip over "Sand Mountain,"[18] but unless we can procure some conveyance tomorrow morning to take us to Stevenson[19] we will have to take it.

Guntersville, Ala. Nov. 8th 1862. We have stopped here for dinner and to let the horses rest after the drive this morning. Here is the home of Col. Henry, against whom our officers preferred charges for cowardice at the battle of Williamsburg. He is still suspended from rank and pay. The citizens here say that he is a brave man, and were very mad when I intimated that I would have

17. The Coosa River.

18. This reference to "Sand Mountain" could mean overland transportation.

19. Both the Memphis and Charleston and the Nashville and Chattanooga railroads served Stevenson, Alabama (see also above p. 68 n. 5).

to disbelieve my eyes, if I thought so. I thought it prudent to drop the subject lest I have an opportunity to display my bravery.

Two companies of our regiment are from this county, and Capt. Rayburn of our regiment lived here. The Yankees have never been in this place but have come up on the opposite bank of the river a few weeks ago and without a moment's warning opened with their artillery. They did not hurt any soldiers, for the reason that there were not any here, but they did what gave them equally as much pleasure, that is, shattered some few dwelling houses and killed Capt. Rayburn's mother, a helpless old woman who could not escape out of the range of their shells as fast as the others. Is it any wonder that our boyish Captain is so brave? And this is the war? "For the restoration of the Union." Yes, we ought to return to the fold and receive remission of our sins, through the mercy of the sanctified cut-throats of New England who uphold this warfare in the name of our blessed Savior. I can't see it in that light, no doubt it is because I am so blinded by my own wickedness. Oh, how miserable would I be, if the dear ones of my own home were exposed thus to the fury of an invading army.

Gadsden, Ala. Nov. 10th 1862. We reached this place last night after a most tiresome ride over the roughest road imaginable. I am heartily glad that we are to change our mode of travel, though we will have to wait here a day or two for the boat. It seems that there is only one running now-a-days. This is a kind of a one horse town, built all on one street, but I think from the number of business houses that it must have been quite a flourishing little town before the war. There are some old citizens here waiting for the boat. They are going out to visit relatives in the army. Brown of C.A. 10th Alabama is also here with clothing to take to his regiment.

Choice Hotel, Rome, Ga. Nov. 14. I don't see the reason for the name of our hotel as there is no other chance for a fellow to take his choice in this town. It has been so long since we left Gadsden that I have forgotten when it was. "To the best of my recollection" it was day before yesterday evening. Our boat did not profess to be fast, as might have been known by the terms, which were so much for the ride, "meals extra." The river was very shallow but the "Alfarata" could run wherever a duck could swim, (almost). A few miles from here we found a place that was a little too swift and we had to fasten a cable to a big tree above the shoals, and draw the boat over by windlass. Our freight was principally pumpkins, and in fact the only produce of the country seems to be corn, shucks, chickens and pumpkins.

At one of the landings we were informed that we could walk across the neck of it if we wished, while the boat went around the bend, and that by going across we would pass immediately by a "still house." It is needless to say that most of the boat crew went across. Of course no one would ever have accused me of being in the crowd. We arrived here this evening just in time to see the train move off. But were informed that there would be another train tomorrow. Well, there is some comfort in that. Ansel, Tom and I have been to the transportation office and secured the necessary papers.

Kingston, Ga. Nov. 15, '62. Arrived at noon just about five minutes too late to make connection with the Dalton train.[20] We have been on a "high horse" all evening, and none of us would be proud of our doings, if our quiet, staid friends could hear a full report. Late this evening the prospect was fine for a "row." I was cutting up and "mine host" got mad, and then Brown insisted that it would be well to whip him a little; but we "compromised." We will get away tonight a little after midnight. Mr. Carroll (Old Uncle Add) is sustaining the honors of a military hero admirably. We introduced him as General Carroll of the Virginia army, and Tom, Ansel and I are members of his staff. We only have to drop a few hints as to his daring bravery, and suggest his great eccentricity, as a cover to any defects of Military knowledge or appearance that may

20. The Rome Railroad ran to Kingston and the Western and Atlantic from Kingston to Dalton.

be noticed. And the deception works like a charm. An old lady here thinks it very strange that none of us know her son, who, she says, is in Mr. Jackson's command. (Stonewall). His is a pretty big company, but the old lady don't understand the organization of an army.

· VI ·

"Another great battle has been fought"

November 18, 1862, to December 31, 1862

Richmond, Va. Nov. 18, 1862. Back again to the capitol of this great state and of our young Republic. We arrived this morning before daylight, and I have spent a portion of the day with my friends on 12th street and part of it visiting some of the hospitals to see if some of our men were here. Mr. Carroll is anxious to proceed immediately to the army, and the voice of duty as well as inclination bids me do the same. I would like to spend more time here but I must wait until another drawing takes place in the great lottery in which we have invested. Perhaps I may draw another prize though I don't want one quite so large as fell to my shore on the 30th of June. Tom left us at Burkesville and has gone via Petersburg to see some relations. Ansel will remain here for the present as he is totally unfit for service. Mr. Carroll and I will go up on the 6 A.M. train tomorrow to Culpepper C.H. where, as we have just learned, our command is encamped.

This evening I went to the Passport office to procure the necessary papers but was directed to Sergt. Crow's office. (What soldier in the army of Northern Virginia does not know where that is?) I went down, but as there was a big crowd around the door, could not get in immediately. As I stood outside waiting my time, I noticed that none came back but that as soon as they received their papers that they went upstairs. I began to "smell a rat" and as I had no notion of remaining cooped up there until tomorrow morning, when I had other and pleasanter ways of passing the time, I thanked my stars that I was still outside and left. The services of friend Bromwell were called into requisition. His acquaintance with the officers of the various departments made it an easy matter for him to procure a passport for himself to go to Culpepper, and as I liked his name as well as mine, I shall be known to the inspector of the passports tomorrow as Bromwell.[1] I go forth with the blessing and accompanied by the prayers of the best woman in the world. I only wish I were more worthy of the motherly kindness she has shown me.

Inglewood Va. Nov. 20th '62. I thought when I left Richmond that I would be compelled to forego the pleasure of a visit here until some future time. But when Mr. Carroll and I reached

1. Patterson very wisely did not attempt to travel without a passport. The ubiquitous and efficient provost guards would arrest anyone traveling without proper papers. E. Merton Coulter has this to say about the system of provost marshals:

"Almost as galling as the suspension of the writ (of habeas corpus) was the system of provost marshals. Originally employed to protect property and preserve order in the vicinity of armies, to arrest stragglers and deserters, and to guard armories, they exercised no authority over civilians, but their functions were soon greatly extended. They traveled on trains, loitered around railroad stations, occupied seats on stage lines, and took positions anywhere they could intercept travelers—to catch spies and traitors. Anyone not able to show a passport was liable to be taken in charge and held until his identity could be established. Great numbers of able-bodied men were thus employed.

"An outcry against them soon arose because of their interference with the customary liberties of travel and their harassment of 'the loyal people of the Confederacy.' The requirement that all travelers must secure passports led to great inconvenience, for passport offices were open only at certain hours of the day. Often soldiers on furlough lost days in reaching home on account of missing trains while awaiting passports. People did not like to be shouted at every time they got on a train, 'Show your passport,' and hear it repeated when they got off. Some of these provost marshals became little tyrants, and their conduct led to great bitterness in the communities where they operated." E. Merton Coulter, *The Confederate States of America 1861–1865.* (Baton Rouge: Louisiana State University Press, 1950), p. 395.

Gordonsville, we learned that all the troops had left Culpepper, and are moving in the direction of Fredericksburg, and an order has been received to stop all soldiers returning to the army at Gordonsville. Mr. Carroll took the train for Hanover Junction and as I couldn't get a passport to accompany him, I deposited my baggage in town and walked out here. Everything seems natural but would seem more so if Newson were with me. The institute is in session, and I found myself domiciled under the same roof with between thirty and forty young ladies. It is better than soldiering to stay here. But a shadow falls across the sunlight of the present, caused by the reflection that I must leave so soon, perhaps tomorrow. Oh, if I only had a thirty day wound now. I would not take anything for it. But the Doctor's retiring bell has rung and that's a sign that it's time for honest people to go to bed.

In the woods, four miles from Orange C.H., Va. Nov. 21st '62. Soldier life has commenced. When I left Inglewood this morning and told them goodbye, I wasn't certain whether I would get off today or whether I would return and pass the night there, but I'm pretty certain now. When I reached Gordonsville I found that all of the soldiers there, who like myself were on their way to the army, were going to start today, it having been definitely ascertained that the army is at Fredericksburg. So I joined the crowd. We came up to the Courthouse this evening, and after trying in vain to make some kind of organization, we all came to the conclusion that every man was plenty old enough and ugly enough to take care of himself. "Texas," "Florida," and I have formed a kind of mutual liking, and we have acknowledged a community of interest in the commissary stores of the party. We have just finished supper and have a big fire blazing cheerfully and in a few minutes I will, for the first time in several months, spread my blankets on the ground and "go to bed right." "Texas," spare the contents of that canteen until morning!

Camp 9th Ala. Vols. Near Fredericksburg. Nov. 23rd, 1862. It is a strange and indefinable feeling that one has when after a long absence, he once more grasps the hands of his old comrades in arms. It is a mixture of hope and regret, pain and pleasure, sadness and gladness. I miss some faces which used to be familiar. Some of them are absent for a time recovering from their wounds, others have received their final discharge, and now sleep where the roar of battle can never disturb their slumbers.

After some trouble I at last found the boys encamped in this little hollow, about a mile and a half from town. As soon as I came near enough for the boys to recognize me, my ears were saluted by the cries of, "How are you Ed!" "How are you Pat!" "How are you Lieutenant," etc. The latter salutation would have been more gratifying had the words not confirmed the death of one of the truest friends I had in the army. Wilson had been killed at Sharpsburg,[2] and the boys had elected me to fill the vacancy occasioned by his death, so I found that I had been an officer for some time without knowing it.[3] But I learn that I will have to stand an examination before a board of officers organized for the purpose of testing the fitness of those who are elected for the position which they are expected to occupy. I am not much afraid of an examination, and I think it an excellent arrangement.

If any one who has a friend or relative in the company could have seen the faces and heard the remarks of the boys as I distributed the letters I had brought, I am sure that such a one would not fail to embrace the next opportunity of sending a letter. Letters from home or the immediate neighborhood of home have more to do with keeping up the spirits and morale of the army than is generally supposed. When each individual member of a company or regiment feels that his labors are appreciated by his friends and neighbors at home, he asks no other recognition of his services and is cheerful and contented, and the spirit becomes general and animates the command as a body. Give the boys letters written in a cheerful hopeful spirit and they are more conducive to health than

2. Sharpsburg was the Confederate name for the Battle of Antietam.

3. There were both advantages and disadvantages in allowing the men to select their officers but the latter greatly outweighed the advantages, for a person who could win election did not necessarily possess military skill. Patterson, however, seems to have been a capable leader.

medicine and more potent to prevent desertion than the articles of war "which pronounces the sentence of death."

Mr. Carroll says that he can't stay long, that these horrible lice will eat him up. He says that they are so thick that he is afraid to go to sleep, for fear that in an unguarded moment he might snore, and these vermin would think it was the dinner gong and eat him up. A soldier a few days since was going home on a furlough, and being fresh from the camps of course had abundant cause to scratch. A citizen sitting near him on the cars noticed it and said: "What is the matter? Have you fleas on you?" "Fleas," said the indignant soldier, "D—n you, do you think I am a brute? I'm no d—n dog, I'm human, they are lice, sir!" I feel very clean and comfortable now, but in a few days will be scratching away, and looking as seedy as any of the boys. I wish these Yankees would all go back up North and stay there, so that we could leave and go home and attend to our business. The Yankees here suit me very well though; they are peaceably disposed. Their pickets occupy one bank of the river, and ours the other, and we have no shooting. I hope they will continue their good behavior.

Camp near Bank's Ford.*[4] *Dec. 1st 1862. I am again on duty and have settled down into the regular daily routine of camp life, as naturally as though I had not been absent. My examination passed satisfactorily, and I am now a Lt. de facto. My duties are not much increased, but I feel a greater responsibility than when I occupied a lower position. I feel that it is my duty now to pay more particular attention to the interests and wants of my company, to see that they are as comfortable as possible under the existing circumstances. Our present camp is pleasanter than where I found the boys. We are not so crowded and wood and water is more convenient. It is evident that our command is to remain on the front lines this winter and do picket duty. At present our brigade has to keep up the entire picket line from Scott's dam to the dam at Dr. Taylor's.[5] It requires a

4. Banks's Ford was on the Rappahannock River several miles above Fredericksburg. It was located at the first sharp bend in the river west of the town.

5. In 1862 there was a dam on the Rappahannock just below Beck's Island a short distance above Fredericksburg where the canal running into the city

regiment on duty at a time, so we come on every fifth day. I don't mind it at all except in bad weather.

On Picket near Dr. Taylor's. Dec. 11th 1862. I retract all I said about these Yankees being friendly, for though those immediately across the river are peacable enough, they have been pouring shell into Fredericksburg ever since before daylight this morning. I expect we will have a big fight tomorrow. I had nothing to do today except to watch, from this hill, the bombardment of the city. I hope they won't "bombard" me tomorrow.

In line of battle. Dec. 12th 1862. Here we are, about to get into it sure enough and in the worst place imaginable, supporting a battery which expects to do hot work. The Yankees are in and below the city.[6] We are on the extreme left of our line of battle, and [the] left of our brigade resting on the river. Should the infantry attempt to assail our position on these hills they might start ten thousand at the foot of them, and not one would reach the top. It would be like murder to kill them in such a place.[7] I believe Capt.

---

originated. Approximately one quarter of a mile south of the dam and behind or west of General Wilcox's line was located the Taylor home. Scott's Dam was located near Banks's Ford.

6. When Major General A. E. Burnside assumed command of the Army of the Potomac on November 7, 1862, he proposed to move his forces to the east side of the Rappahannock at Fredericksburg, cross the river at this point, and then follow the railroad to Richmond. When Lee learned of this plan, he decided to move Longstreet's and Jackson's corps to Fredericksburg and to use the excellent defensive terrain on the west (south) bank of the Rappahannock to contest the Federal crossing.

"Although his strategy had been delayed so long as to lose whatever merit it may have originally possessed," General Burnside, on December 9, decided to attack the Confederate line. To prepare for this assault he posted his artillery along the bluffs on the Falmouth side of the river and had pontoon bridges thrown across the icy stream. By December 12 his Sixth Corps had crossed the Rappahannock and were in position to attack on the morning of December 13. Boatner, *Dictionary,* p. 313.

In a subsequent entry Patterson describes the shelling of Fredericksburg referred to in his entry of December 11 (see below pp. 87–88).

7. Lee's position on the day of the battle was along the irregular edge of a ridge that extended from the Rappahannock at Beck's Island southward some seven miles to Hamilton's Crossing, where the Richmond, Fredericksburg and Potomac Railroad crossed one of the roads leading into Fredericksburg. The disposition of the Confederate troops revealed Lee's keen tactical sense and

Lane with his battery alone could drive back any assaulting column that should attempt this part of the line.[8]

In camp, Dec. 15th, '62. Another great battle has been fought. The Yankees numbered their dead by the thousands, where we numbered ours by hundreds, and they are now on the opposite bank of the river, and will not soon care to repeat their attempt.[9] On the evening of the 10th a detachment of three companies of our regiment under command of Crowe was sent on picket. I went in command of my company, and as one company was to be held in reserve, of course Jim chose ours. After we had visited the various posts and found everything quiet, we returned to the reserve, on the hill near the dam, and sat there for hours, relating incidents of the war and talking of old times and playing cards by the light of our little chunk fire. About two o'clock we stretched ourselves out before the fire thinking to have a little nap, but had not been sleeping long before we were aroused by the report of a signal gun.[10] Before the echo had died in the distance we were up and ready for anything. Having lain down with my sword and pistol buckled around me, I only had to raise up and shake myself and my

---

appreciation of the military uses of terrain. Longstreet's corps, holding the north end of the line, occupied a frontage of five miles while Jackson at the south end, with approximately the same number of men, was in position in depth within the space of only two miles. Lee could divide his troops in this way because Longstreet's position was so strong defensively. There was little danger of a Federal flanking movement on the left because of the Rappahannock. Also Marye's Heights at the north end of the line was practically impregnable. (Taylor's and Marye's hills are together known as Marye's Heights and extend approximately two miles).

8. Captain John Lane.

9. Federals losses in killed and wounded were 12,700 out of an estimated 106,000 engaged. Confederate casualties numbered 5,300 out of a 72,500 man force. Boatner, *Dictionary,* p. 313. Patterson in this entry gives a description of the Battle of Fredericksburg, December 13, 1862, as well as the preliminary skirmishing that occured on December 11 and 12.

10. Federal engineers were scheduled to start laying the pontoon bridges across the Rappahannock at daybreak on December 11, but the noise made in moving the bulky equipment into position reached the ears of Confederate pickets in Fredericksburg while it was still dark. Major General Lafayette McLaws of Longstreet's corps, in command of the Fredericksburg sector, was convinced by 4:30 A.M. that the long-awaited attack was about to commence. Thus he ordered two guns to fire a prearranged warning signal.

toilet was made. I ran down to the edge of the water to see if I could learn anything by the use of my eyes and ears, but it was so dark that I could see nothing, and I could hear nothing but the dam roaring—No, the roaring of the dam. The sound of another gun broke the stillness and published to every command in the Yankee army the order to get under arms. Gen'l. Lee must have known the hour, if not the very moment they were to attack, and our signal gun pealed the first note, and by the time theirs fired our army was under arms, and the different commands ready to move at once to the respective position in line of battle. I heard the rattling of drums, and sound of bugles, and then the rumble of artillery getting into position. It was still dark, and such a dense fog hung over river and valley that earth and sky were alike invisible.

It lacked just twenty minutes till six when the storm burst forth in all its fury. Commencing opposite us the fire swept forth along the crest of the hill, forming a semicircle around Fredericksburg.[11] Battery after battery joined in the dread chorus, until the very hills shook with the thunders of a hundred pieces of artillery, as they poured their concentrated fire into the doomed city. Shells above, below, and immediately opposite, meeting, greeting, and bursting over it, scattered their death warrants everywhere. The light of morning scattered the fog and revealed the height wreathed in smoke, parted every instant by the lightning tongues of those iron throated monsters; while over the city hung a funeral pall, a cloud of battle smoke, in which shells were incessantly bursting, scattering destruction, misery, death among the half frantic women and children who had not heeded the order to leave the city, and now rushed wildly through the streets seeking refuge from the iron storm which raged so pitilessly around them. Never before have I ever witnessed a scene of such *terrible* beauty. Or heard music so *grand,* and at the same time so mournfully beautiful. As the mighty

11. The town of Fredericksburg at the time of the battle extended from the river bank to the west perhaps a quarter of a mile in the direction of Marye's Heights. The generally open terrain between the western limits of the town and the Confederate position on the heights was bisected by a canal and a neighboring drainage ditch that carried off its waste water. Thus there was not much room for maneuvering in the region.

choir chanted in thunder tones this grand anthem of praise to the God of War, height answered to height. The hills, catching up the echoes, flung them back with scarcely lessened power, and as they died away in the distance far down the lovely valley, new thunders again aroused them, and again the woods, the hills and the valleys lent their assistance in keeping up the dread melody. Shells flew shrieking through the air, sounding like a wail of agony from some lost spirit. They seemed demons rushing from various directions to hold their mad revelry over the beautiful city. But amid all the storm could be heard a low, melancholy minor breathing, a low, sad, plaintive miserere. But why attempt a description of that which is indescribable. Words are too barren, they are powerless to convey to the mind a picture that can in any way compare with the reality. One must see the flashes of fire, and hear the thunder, see the effect of the missiles, and hear the wild cheers from those heights as the flames from burning houses showed how well their shots had been directed. One must see and hear all this before one can appreciate it. Then it makes a picture that time can never efface.

The firing continued nearly the entire day, but after repeated attempts they succeeded in effecting a crossing but not until Barkdale and his Mississippians had given them a foretaste of what was in reservation for them on this side, baptizing many of them with water and blood, and offering to bridge the river with their dead bodies if they would come fast enough.[12] I thought it strange that after they had effected a landing on this side our batteries did not

12. When General McLaws arrived on November 25, he was ordered to occupy Fredericksburg with part of his command. Accordingly Brigadier General William Barksdale's (not Barkdale as Patterson spelled it) Mississippi Brigade of sixteen hundred men was assigned the mission. It was Barksdale's job to pick off the Federal engineers when they should try to lay pontoon bridges across the river. On December 11 he posted his men in cellars and behind fences along the river bank and for hours frustrated Burnside's efforts to bridge the Rappahannock. He withdrew only after Federal detachments managed to cross the river in boats and flank his position. The heavy shelling of the town did not drive him back. One student of the battle has said: "It was not until 7:00 P.M., after darkness had fallen, that Barksdale concluded his mission had been accomplished, and his men had done all that could reasonably be expected of them. This is something of an understatement in face of the fact that 1,600 Confederates had stalled the entire Army of the Potomac for a full day and quite possibly ruined the chances for a Union victory which would have been achieved under

open on them,[13] but the sequel proved that they were only waiting. On the 12th they crossed troops in large numbers, at and below the city, but seemed in no hurry to bring on a general engagement, although they made an unsuccessful charge on Jackson's corps, down near the crossing.[14] About night our brigade moved a little to the right and went to work with a right good will when we found that we would be exposed.

On the morning of the 13th, we could see from the commotion in the enemy's camp that they were preparing for something. Their batteries soon opened on our lines, and we had to hug the works as closely as possible. Each man seemed to feel that he was about twice as large as he ought to be, and I felt that absence of body would be better than presence of mind on that occasion. But we had improved our works during the night, and though shells were bursting over and around us all day, still very few of the boys were killed or wounded. The Yankee infantry did not attempt our part of the line, and it would have been madness for them to have done so.[15]

But while we were lying idle, there was bloody work going on just down the line to our right. The Yankees came out in the old field near the Railroad, and attempted to break our lines there. Our boys who were lying behind a stone fence[16] let them approach to within thirty yards when they raised and poured such a deadly

---

more able leadership and more effective coordination of effort." E. J. Stackpole, *The Fredericksburg Campaign* (Harrisonburg: Military Service Publishing Co., 1957), pp. 137–38.

13. Lee's artillerymen could not see the river line, their view being blocked by the houses and further obscured by the fog. Also, as Patterson later observed: "Much damage could have been done had our batteries opened on them while they were crossing, but it would have completed the destruction of the city." (See below p. 90.)

14. Neither Lee nor Jackson mention any "unsuccessful charge" by the enemy on the Confederate right on December 12. The only references to even a minor action on that day along this portion of the front are to be found in the reports of Major General W. B. Franklin, commanding Burnside's Left Grand Division, and Major General J. B. Hood of Longstreet's corps. Hood was on Longstreet's extreme right. On December 12 he was "relieved" by General A. P. Hill of Jackson's corps. *O.R.*, XXXIII, Ser. I, 449, 622, 645.

15. General Wilcox reported his losses in the Battle of Fredericksburg as "but few men by the enemy's artillery, and none by the musket. . . ." *Ibid.*, p. 613.

16. The Telegraph Road, one of three main roads leading from the town to the battlefield, passed around the base of Marye's Hill. At the foot of the hill it became a sunken road, with a four-foot-high stone wall on the side facing Fredericksburg, continuing for over five hundred yards.

volley into them that there was not enough of them left standing to make a decent skirmish line. Line after line was brought forward, brigade after brigade swept over the same ground only to cover it with their dead bodies. They displayed daring bravery, but of what avail was it there? Already the ground was literally covered with their dead, while scarcely a dozen of our men were hurt. I cannot describe their repeated assaults. But it seemed almost cruel to shoot men down when they had so little chance of returning the compliment. There certainly was cruelty *somewhere* in sacrificing so many brave men. Farther down the line the battle raged fiercely but ended by the Yankees being repulsed at all points.

At night our regiment was detached and sent on picket, part of us on the canal and part on the hill near Mr. Stanbury's [17] and it was a miserably cold night. One of our guns fired occasional shots during the night, though it was too dark to fire with accuracy. In the morning where thousands had rushed to battle was the valley of the dead. Much damage could have been done had our batteries opened on them while they were crossing, but it would have completed the destruction of the city. And perhaps they have been sufficiently punished.

Last night I was put in command of fifty men to go down on the field and gather up arms. I have seen men lie thick on the battlefield, but never anything to compare with this one. It was a fearful sight to see so many hundreds lying there in the pale moonlight, looking as though whole regiments had fallen together. In some places their comrades had buried them in a line, by throwing dirt over them as they were, and so making a kind of breastwork. Most of those killed in front of the wall were Irishmen, members of Meagher's brigade.[18] It is a singular circumstance that during the

17. The Stansbury (not Stanbury) house was located between the Confederate line at its north end and the canal running from the river into Fredericksburg. It was approximately three quarters of a mile southeast of the Taylor home.

18. Brigadier General Thomas F. Meagher, a native of Ireland, organized the "Irish Brigade" in the winter of 1861–62 in New York City. This unit fought with the Army of the Potomac in all the battles from Second Manassas to Chancellorsville but none of its exploits exceeded the hopeless assault against Marye's Heights. Meagher resigned from the army in May, 1863, when he was refused permission to recruit his decimated ranks, and it was proposed to

great famine in Ireland,[19] the crop of corn raised on this very field was sent to Ireland by the citizens of Fredericksburg, and in all probability was the means of saving the lives of some of these men, who have thus repaid the kindness. Their bodies will soon become a part of that soil.

In Camp. December 25th. I had hoped that I would be able to spend my Christmas at Inglewood, but could not get even a three days leave of absence. Newson is there, and I would have had a delightful time; as it is I won't have any *turkey* or *chicken,* or pie or "sich," but still I will have a leetle drop of the crathur and have an egg-nog. Jones and Dick Hobbs have gone to Richmond. Wish I could have gone with them. Everything is very quiet now-a-days, and the Yankees seem satisfied with their attempt, and will not soon repeat it. We talk of moving our camp to a more favorable location. The weather is getting too cold to soldier with comfort.

Dec. 31st 1862. Well I have lived to see the close of another year and still a soldier. And now it seems that the war is just fairly begun.[20] During the year just drawing to a close many thousands have gone from the battlefield to the judgment bar. Poor deluded mortals, not content that the seeds of decay and death in our natures should produce their natural effect, we must kill each other. Only one way to come into the world and ten thousand ways to getting out of it. Instead of bearing each other's burdens, instead of shielding each other from danger, trying to prolong and make pleasant the few fleeting moments of time—all we have to fit us for eternity —we must tax our ingenuity to devise means of killing each other. If an inhabitant of some other planet could look down upon this

---

extinguish the brigade organization by distributing its units among other commands. The resignation, however, was not accepted.

19. In 1845 a potato blight reached Ireland and produced a famine that became devastating when the potato crop was again ruined in 1846 and 1847.

20. Whereas Patterson in December, 1862, could see the war as "just fairly begun," other Confederate soldiers took a more optimistic view after Fredericksburg. See J. G. Barrett, *The Civil War in North Carolina* (Chapel Hill: The University of North Carolina Press, 1963), p. 148; hereinafter cited as Barrett, *Civil War in N.C.*

little earth of ours, and have displayed to him all the wonders of creation, could see all that has been done to make this a happy home for man, and be told that among all these beings, all these wonders, man is the only being God has seen fit to endow with reason, he would undoubtedly think it had been given to the wrong class of beings, that the brutes of the field, the beasts of the forest, would make better use of it. And really they act more like reasonable beings than we do.

I suppose that we are but adding another to the list of the frolics that have risen in glory only to set in darkness and blood. It is the same attempt to solve the problem whether man is, or is not, capable of self government. I hope that I may live to see this war, and the questions arising out of it, settled. I think it will be a fine opportunity to study political economy.

During this year, some men have made themselves immortal. Some whose names will shine upon the pages of history until the pendulum of time shall cease to vibrate. Others have made records of infamy which will place their names side by side with those of Flagabulus, Caligula and Nero. In this latter class no name will be so prominent as that of "Butler the Beast." A disgrace to the American name, a fit representative of the state that produced him. His name will go down to posterity, as the very synonym of all that is vile, mean, low, contemptible. His career at New Orleans has "damned him to eternal fame." Strange that the Country that has produced a Washington, a Madison, a Lee, a Jackson, should produce a B. F. Butler.[21]

21. In May, 1862, Major General B. F. Butler occupied New Orleans after Admiral David C. Farragut had reduced its defenses. After being appointed military governor, Butler's subsequent conduct of office was controversial. He was vilified in the South and declared an outlaw by President Davis and was even accused of stealing the silverware from the house in which he had his headquarters. Thus he acquired the nickname "Silverspoon" as well as that of "Beast." The best known incidents in New Orleans were his hanging William Mumford who had pulled down the Union flag from the mint, his "Woman Order," and his confiscation of $800,000 that he claimed had been entrusted to the Dutch consul for the purchase of war supplies.

· VII ·

"We had the dirt road to travel on to reach Salem Church"

January 20, 1863, to June 14, 1863

January 20th 1863. I have almost given up writing in my journal for the fact that I have nothing in the world to record. There is too much sameness about this kind of soldier life. One day is the repetition of the duties of the day before, and I can always tell what (in all probability) I will be doing on the same day one month ahead. Capt. Crow is often on other duty, Cannon and Chandler on detached service, and I am generally in command of the Company. Every fifth day at three o'clock P.M. I go on picket and remain twenty four fours. We stand on our side of the river and look at the Yanks. They stand on their side and look at us. Sometimes we exchange papers, though in violation of orders, and sometimes the boys trade them tobacco for coffee. Just below the dam the water is not more than three feet deep, and the boys wade out to a little shoal of rocks in the middle of the stream and meet and take a drink together, make such trades as they wish, then each returns to his own side again. I have to visit some other post in the meantime, or make it convenient to have business in another direction, for it would not do for me to see these violations of orders. And yet I like to read a New York or Philadelphia news paper.[1]

The principal amusement of the troops now-a-days is snow-balling. A great many of them never saw any snow, or at least not enough to cover the ground, until last winter, and many of the Florida troops have never seen any at all. Sometimes whole brigades and even divisions, with their officers in command, get into a battle with snowballs. Then the sport becomes exciting, and the balls fly so thick that the opposing forces scarcely distinguish each other. I think this imitation battle is decidedly more pleasant than the real. The health of the company and regiment is much better than it was last winter. The men have become acclimated and accustomed to exposure, and it would be almost impossible to kill one of them now, by anything except a bullet. About this time last winter, quite a number of our company was sick, several of whom died. McKelvey, Fowler, Irion, Webb, and several others. Thus far our death from disease has been more than from battle. And I believe that the same thing is true with every command in the army, at least with those from the Gulf States.[2]

In Winter Quarters. Feb'y. 23rd 1863. Week after week passes without change. Still in the same camp and likely to be for some weeks and perhaps months to come. I am still the only officer with the company, the others being either on furlough in Alabama, or on detached service. Yesterday while on picket with my company

1. It was not unusual during the Civil War for Confederate and Federal pickets to fraternize.

2. The returns of the Confederate field and general hospitals for 1861–62 show:

Killed	19,897
Deaths in field hospitals from wounds	1,623
Deaths in general hospitals from wounds	2,618
Deaths in field hospitals from disease	14,597
Deaths in general hospitals from disease	16,741

Livermore, *Numbers and Losses,* p. 3.

down at the dam, I thought that another fight had begun, and was very much relieved when I learned that the Yanks were only firing a few shots in honor of the birthday of a great Virginia rebel, who figured years ago, or perhaps they were firing it in honor of the anniversary of our President's inauguration. I am sure that I don't care what their motive was, but I was glad that they used blank cartridges.[3]

We have made ourselves very comfortable here; most of the boys have built little huts of pine poles and roofed them over with pieces of tent cloth. They are chinked and daubed well, and have good fireplaces and chimneys. I am trying it in a tent. I have a good large wall tent and a chimney that draws well. And although the snow is over a foot deep outside, inside my tent it is as pleasant and comfortable as anyone could wish. I would not exchange it for a house. The 8th is camped over on the opposite hill just across the ravine and we have some wonderful snow battles.

March 20th 1863. On Picket at Scott's Dam. I have seen more pleasant places for spending one's birthday, but still in war times one ought to be thankful that he is not spending it with a few inches of soil over him. Twenty one years old, well I suppose that I am a man now, might vote if there was any voting to be done. I suppose that I can continue as a man what I began as a boy. I don't feel any older than I did three or four years ago. And I have been so little accustomed to receive advice from anyone for the last two or three years that I had almost forgotten that I was but a boy.

Co. "C." is on picket with my company, and Van Whitehead and I have been bewailing our condition. We have a fellow feeling for each other, as he is the only officer present for duty with his company and I with mine. The snow is something more than a foot deep but the air is mild and I think we will have a general thaw before many days. I like this weather much better than rainy weather for we are very comfortably fixed here now. Have snug little bivouacs built of brush and lined and floored with pine tops. I

3. On February 18, 1861 Davis was inaugurated provisional President of the Confederacy; on February 22, 1862, he was inaugurated President under the permanent regime.

don't want a better house to soldier in. The poor fellows across the river have a time of it, as their side has no timber to shelter them from the wind; but they are from a cold climate and ought to be able to stand it better than us. If they get too cold they can come over on this side and I think they will find a greater difference in the climate than they have any idea of. I think with our two companies properly stationed in the perfect works that we have built we could keep back a brigade of them attempting to cross the river. And the battery of the 24th Parrotts and the English breech loading guns could keep back another.[4]

I have at last received a letter from home, from Sister Sophia. When it was handed to me my hands trembled so that I could hardly open it. I feared that some of the loved ones were gone, that the home circle was broken. But no, all are well at home. Ah, there are few times in life that one can fully appreciate those words. Now, they are like angel whispers to me. It brings back the old home sickness on me again, and such a longing to see them all. It seems to me that I love them better now than ever I did in my life before the war, and oh, will I live through this miserable war and revisit the scenes of my boyhood home. I pray that I may.

"Hello! Ed, what makes you look so solemncholy? Must be writing to your sweetheart." "No, Van, my dear fellow, I'm just scribbling." "Well, just quit your writing and talk to me." "All right, Van."

In Camp. March 21st '63. My birthday was celebrated by at least one member of the Company. No, I won't call him a member of the company, for he has been here only a few days and a conscript[5] at that, and as he was the only one ever in my company and I intend that he shall be the last. Last night instead of watching the Yankees from a distance, he crossed over; I suppose he did not

4. The Parrott Gun was a rifled muzzle-loading cannon, varying in size from three to ten inches. It was named after its inventor R. P. Parrott. The Armstrong, Blakely, and Whitworth guns were English breech-loading cannons. Certain models of these pieces were muzzle-loaders.

5. In April, 1862, the Confederate Congress passed a conscription law that called into the service for three years all white males between eighteen and thirty-five who were not legally exempt.

like to stand on post. He must have had a sweet time getting across, for I could see this morning where he had pulled off his boots and gone barefooted along down the bank of the river in the deep snow and then waded across where the water was about three feet deep. It almost gives me a chill to think about it. I hope that he didn't catch cold. If I were on the opposite side of the river I might wade it to get to my company, but I can't imagine any other circumstances that would induce a cold water bath under so many disadvantages. No tears have been shed for his departure, and yet I can't blame him much. I can't see how any man in the South could feel justified in staying home at such a time. But still if I felt so, and was opposed to the war on principle, I would not fight. And if conscripted, I don't know but that I would do as he did, leave between two days without telling anybody goodbye. But he didn't have any such excuse, for he was a war man. He liked the war, but didn't like to do his share. Goodbye Green, I wish you no bad luck. But I would rather be lying out there in the old field wrapped in my blanket filling a soldier's grave, than to be in your condition.

April 10th. Instead of April showers with sunshine between them making the rain drops sparkle like diamonds, the rain falls ceaselessly and my tent gives back a hollow rumbling sound. The damp North wind comes sighing around my frail tenement, chasing the smoke down the chimney to seek room within, as if afraid to come in contact with the cold, cheerless air without. But the day's duties are done, the fire burns brightly and my tallow candle set in a genuine soldier candlestick, a bayonet, adds to the light and comfort-like appearance. Without darkness—within light.

It would not do for a soldier to look on the dark side, and the present would be hard to bear were it not for the faith in the future, though I must confess that mine is composed more largely of hope than of belief. Still it is a faith for that.

Occasional letters from the South tell me of burning houses and etc. The Union Heroes burned only fourteen in my section of the country, on their last visit, and did it without the loss of a man as they had only women and children to contend with. They were only private residences, so we say "ravages of war," and pass it by, as if there were not ten times more real suffering following the burning of one cottage home and leaving widowed mothers and her babes homeless than there would be in the destruction of the most magnificent public building.[6]

April 27th 1863. Still the same old "seven and six." Camping one place a few days and then change of location. In camp five days. Then on picket one day and night. More firing down the river and all kind of reports in circulation.[7] I, for one, wish we would commence fighting and stop only long enough to carry off the wounded and bury the dead, until the issues involved are fought out and settled, *once and forever.* I am tired of this long slow work, lying about in the mud and dirt and ashes, contracting all the bad habits that Satan can invent and fast becoming worthless for any other sphere in life than that of a soldier. It is all very funny and patriotic and glorious to walk over frozen ground, prickly pears and blackberry bushes, barefooted, and to wear your only shirt three or four weeks waiting for a sunshiny day to come so that you can stand

6. The people of north Alabama suffered fearfully during the war. Many of them had to leave the area in order to live. John E. Moore wrote to the Confederate Secretary of War from Florence, in December, 1862, that the people of north Alabama "have been ground into the dust by tyrants and thieves." Early in 1863 the citizens of Florence asked the authorities in Richmond for protection. "They said that they had been greatly oppressed by the Federal army in 1862. Property had been destroyed most wantonly and vindictively, the privacy of the homes invaded, citizens carried off and ill treated, and slaves carried off and refused the liberty of returning when they desired to do so. The harshness of the Federals had made many people submissive for fear of worse things. No men, except the aged and infirm, were left in the country; the population was composed chiefly of women and children." Fleming, *Civil War,* pp. 66–67; *O.R.,* XX, Ser. I, Pt. II, 442–43.

7. The firing Patterson heard marked the opening of the Chancellorsville Campaign (April 27 to May 6, 1863). Burnside, after his defeat at Fredericksburg, was replaced by Major General Joseph Hooker as commander of the Army of the Potomac. Since Lee had strengthened his defensive position overlooking Fredericksburg, Hooker evolved a plan for driving the Confederates back on Richmond by making a wide strategic envelopement by way of Kelly's Ford on the Rappahannock. Hooker was to lead approximately one third of his 134,000 man army in a turning movement while Major General John Sedgwick with another one-third was to hold Lee at Fredericksburg. The remaining troops were to be held in reserve. On April 27 three of Hooker's corps started for Kelly's Ford.

to go shirtless while you wash and dry it. It is very agreeable to get up at midnight and tramp through the snow four or five miles with the gentle breezes of heaven fanning your brow, and making an Eolian harp[8] out of the few remaining threads in the seat of your breeches, and then it is so nice after having been up all night to make one's breakfast off of "hard tack," manufactured in 1812, washed down with a cup-full or a gallon if you want it, of cold water. It is so warming and nourishing like. Yes, this is all very nice, but I don't like it, and I am getting madder every minute. Ten men hold me quick before I rush frantically down the bank—across the river with a gun under each arm, my sword in my teeth and a "Navy"[9] rammed down each boot leg and hurt somebody—Never mind, Here, Joe, give me a chew of that tobacco, and I'll consent to be pacified.

May 1st '63. Still big talk of a fight, rumors fly thick and fast. Have had us trotting around pretty well all day, and I can't see the beauty in being a reinforcing brigade. Most of the army is up in the vicinity of Chancellorsville, while here we are guarding the crossing at Bank's Ford and Scott's dam, and running back and forth from one position to another.[10]

May 5th. Almost all day on the 2nd we were moving about from Dr. Taylor's to Bank's ford thence to Chancellorsville, then back again.[11] At last we lay down at Scott's Dam on the morning of the 3rd, we marched out to the old field near the old "yellow house"

8. An Eolian harp is a stringed instrument played by the action of air currents.

9. The Model 1851 "Navy" (Colt revolver) was a 36-caliber pistol, weighing only two pounds.

10. When Stuart definitely established that Hooker was advancing in force through the Wilderness to strike the Confederate position in the rear, Lee decided to split his forces. Leaving ten thousand men behind to contain Sedgwick, he marched against Hooker. The Battle of Chancellorsville began on May 1.

11. On May 2 Jackson executed one of the most daring tactical maneuvers of the war by marching across the Federal front in broad daylight. His late afternoon attack drove in the Federal flank. However, later that night Jackson was mortally wounded by the accidental fire of his own men.

and lay down awaiting orders.[12] While there, the mail boy brought me a letter from the war department in answer to one I had written in regard to the promotion of Jim Crow. It was all satisfactory.

While we were all lying there we could hear fighting both above and below, and it was not long before a courier reached us from Gen'l. Barksdale, asking our immediate assistance. We double quicked as rapidly as possible down towards Fredericksburg and reached the top of the hill just above the Stanbury house, in time to see the Yankees come over the breastworks. By overwhelming numbers, they had succeeded, after several attempts, in running over his troops, and as we came down the slope of the hill we were met by a rapid fire from their sharp shooters. Old Wilcox immediately threw us into line, but we soon saw that we were not strong enough to check them for before we could get a battery in position the shells and shot were pouring into us in such a style as to become murderous. Quickly the order was passed to each regimental commander to make his way to the Brick Church.[13] Although we had been running until our tongues were hanging out still we saw no escape from capture or death unless we could reach that church before the Yankees did; and not only so—for if they arrived there first there would be nothing between them and the main army under Gen'l. Lee, who were fighting at Chancellorsville, with their backs to us.

The Yankees had secured the plank road and had us cut off between them and the river, and we had the dirt road to travel on to reach Salem Church. It gave them the shortest cut, but they were afraid to advance up rapidly. The fire of their sharp shooters was so severe that we were compelled to throw the brigade into column of companies, so as to bring the rear of the column far enough forward to be out of reach of the fire until we could throw out a line of

12. At dawn, May 3, Stuart in command of Jackson's corps launched a vigorous attack on the Federal lines at Chancellorsville. In the meantime Sedgwick had finally broken through Barksdale's Mississippians on Marye's Heights and started driving to the relief of Hooker.

13. The Brick Church was Salem Church west of Fredericksburg on the direct road to Chancellorsville.

sharp shooters to keep them back. In this way we double quicked back to the church.

I was almost dead when we got there from excessive heat, and no sooner had we stopped than I fainted. When I came to, some one was bathing my head and pouring some brandy down me. The command moved on, but Major Williams left a man with me, with orders for him to remain with me even if we were captured by the Yankees. But fortunately Dr. Minor heard of it and sent an ambulance for me. And I was snatched up and lifted into the ambulance and carried to the rear. About two miles from the church we stopped and I heard that the boys were fighting. Gladly would I have gone to them, but was not able to walk a hundred yards. In a little while they began coming in, mutilated and torn in every conceivable way. Poor fellows, how I pitied them, but they told me that they had gained a glorious victory.[14]

Yesterday I came down to the regiment feeling badly enough, but still able to go. I found that though the battle had been a severe one, not many had engaged in it on our side, and our brigade had borne the brunt of it. The loss in our regiment foots up twenty three killed and eighty nine wounded. In my company Charley Sharpe and Josiah Whitton were killed and quite a number of them wounded, among whom is Tom Harmon shot in the head, the ball entering his face just at the side of the nose, a little below the eye, and lodging in the back part of the head, Jim Edwards a bad gash across the top of his head, and quite a number of others.

The brigade had passed the church and then returned to it, forming line of battle on a line with it. Two regiments of the brigade on the right of the plank road and two on the left while ours was placed about thirty steps in rear of the 10th Alabama, with our left resting on the plank road. They had been there but a short time before Sedgwick got his command in order and charged them, the whole weight of his assaulting column was directed against the center of the line at the plank road. They came up to within about

14. When Lee learned of Sedgwick's advance, he rushed reinforcements to Salem Church. About five o'clock in the afternoon of May 3 the Federals launched a series of unsuccessful attacks on the Confederate position.

thirty yards before they fired, and the discharge was so terrific that it scattered the 10th and many of them came running back over our regiment. It was a critical time and Maj. Williams gave the command: "Forward, 9th Alabama!" Just as the boys arose to obey this order a fearful fire was poured into them by the 6th Maine and the 123rd N.Y. Regiment at a distance of not more than forty steps. This fire did most of the damage of the day. Nine men of Co. "K" fell dead in their tracks without firing a gun, and almost twice as many suffered severely. But the fire was well returned, and one hundred and fifty bodies were picked up off the ground where those two regiments were standing, (which) showed how destructive had been the fire. With a wild yell the brigade moved forward at the same time; the whole Yankee line was driven back in confusion, and the day was won.

The night was spent in gathering up the wounded and capturing prisoners, and this morning I have charge of about four hundred captured in the fight and in attempting to cross the river. The whole movement by the way of Fredericksburg has been a failure, and General Sedgwick was glad to get back upon his side of the river, with the loss of a thousand or fifteen hundred men.[15]

May 6th. The prisoners were placed in charge of the provost marshal yesterday to be taken to Richmond,[16] and we (were) ordered to move to Chancellorsville which we did in a hurry. The rain falling on us in torrents, the lightening struck a tree near the head of the column as we were marching and knocked down quite a number of men, and everyone in the regiment felt the shock to a greater or less extent. After arriving at Chancellorsville, and passing thru a portion of the wilderness where Howard's corps of Dutchmen[17] had left their overcoats, guns, cartridge boxes, rations

15. On May 4 Lee struck Sedgwick on three sides and slowly drove him back toward the river. Sedgwick, nevertheless, managed to keep his lines from being penetrated and by May 6 he had his entire command safely across the Rappahannock.

16. The estimated losses for the entire Federal army, May 1–4, are 11,116. Livermore, *Numbers and Losses,* p. 98.

17. Major General O. O. Howard took over command of the Federal XI Corps from Franz Sigel in March, 1863. This change of command was galling to the many German officers and men in the ranks.

and etc., we camped for about an hour, just got our fires built, and commenced drying our wet clothing when we were ordered to go back immediately to Scott's Dam. Back we went, grumbling and tired enough, but were glad to get into our old camps once more. The boys are nearly all footsore and weary.

We built our fires, spread our blankets, and as we heard the cold drizzling rain pattering against our tents, thanked our stars that we were under shelter. Poor, weak, short-sighted men, soldiers propose —but the Commanding General disposes. We had not been there more than an hour or two until Co. "D" was ordered to go on picket way down at Dr. Taylor's. Two miles thru the bushes over logs and stumps, through mud and water, through rain and darkness, the boys half sick, worn out with fatigue and exposure. What a task; the curses of some of them were not only deep but loud. And it was some time before I had them on the way. Just my luck, Jim Crow in Alabama on a furlough, Billie C.—acting adjutant, John Chandler in command of the ambulance corps. And I, the only officer with the company. Well, we arrived in due time and I stationed my pickets. Not allowed to have fire, so we shook and shivered and cussed and swore and charged around generally until daylight.

Now the sun is shining out bright and clear, and the boys and the yankees are abusing each other across the river. All in a friendly way however, as we have a tacit agreement that neither party is to fire at the other when on picket. I am anxious for the relief to come for I want to go back to camp and write a letter home, and get the surgeon who is over at the church to mail it, when he crosses to his own side of the river.

June 12th. Bank's Ford Virginia. For a month past we have been doing picket duty here and at Scott's dam alternately. Everything has been generally quiet, though some heavy firing in the direction of Culpepper C. H. and some rumors are now in circulation that we are about to move, though in what direction we do not know.

13th. We have been lying in the rifle pits here at the ford all day, though it rained on us all night last night. The Yankees have thrown up works all along the opposite bank of the river; they must think we are going to cross the river but there is hardly any danger of that.

Sunday 14th. Chancellorsville. After sleeping in a thicket last night we marched down to Bank's Ford, about 11 o'clock A.M. My company and companies A & F were thrown forward to the rifle pits. As we had been on such friendly terms with the yankees, Gen'l. Wilcox thought it would not be right to open fire on them without giving them proper warning, so he sent a man down to the edge of the river to tell them to get away. Some of them were busy and did not seem to think we were in earnest until the batteries commenced getting into position; then they slowly climbed the hill and got into their breastworks. We soon opened fire on them with our artillery and infantry, but I think without injuring anyone, then instead of crossing the river as I expected we would do, we were marched to this place where we have camped for the night, and are cooking rations.

· VIII ·

"When we reached the vicinity of Gettysburg the fight was still going on and the enemy falling back"

June 15, 1863, to July 16, 1863

Near Kelley's Ford, Monday June 15th. We left Chancellorsville early this morning and have been marching leisurely along all day. Crossed the Rapidann at Germania Ford, and have camped for the night.[1] We don't know where we are going, but "Marse Bob" knows, and that is sufficient.[2]

In camp near Culpepper C. H. Tuesday June 16th 1863. This morning we resumed our line of march and passing through Stevensburg and Culpepper C. H. and camped here some time before the shades of night had closed over us; that is, the Reg't. did,

1. Patterson in this entry misspelled Kelly's Ford, Rapidan (River), and Germanna Ford.
2. This is the beginning of the Gettysburg Campaign, June-July, 1863.

but Jim Crow, Dick Hobbs, J. R. Edwards, Willie Torrence and myself were out foraging. At dinner time we found ourselves seated in the shade of an old apple tree, up on the big hill on the other side of town with about two and a half gallons of butter milk before us, and of course we had a glorious dinner. As we were coming on to overtake the regiment we passed a house where we saw about half a dozen large cherry trees loaded with luscious fruit. Crow, with his most winning smile, approached the owner and asked permission for the party to destroy a few of them. The request was refused in a very harsh crabbed manner, and then Jim and I said to him, "My dear sir, will you please be so kind as to allow me to pluck a leaf from one of your trees, I wish to preserve it to remind me of you." The man seemed considerably plagued, but said nothing. We passed on, took supper at the hotel in town, and then came out here and are camping on our old camp ground of 1862.

"Hazel River."[3] ***Wednesday 17th.*** We have made but twelve miles today, and I like this kind of marching. Just as soon as we bivouac for the night, I pull off my shoes and socks and wash the latter and hang them up to dry, and take from my pocket a pair of clean ones washed the night before and put them on, thus carrying two pairs of them I manage to keep my feet from becoming sore.

"Flint Hill,"[4] ***Thurs. 18th.*** This has been by far the hottest day I ever experienced. A dozen or more of the men in the command have suffered from sunstroke, and I came very near it. Not a breath of air stirring, marching through long dusty lanes, beneath a burning sun, clouds of dust choking and smothering us. The suffering was fearful. I started out as the officer in command of the rear guard with the most positive orders to allow no one to "fall out," but the men could not stand it, and the surgeon finally told us to stop when we felt that it was necessary. I soon gave out and another officer was detailed to take my place. He was soon sun struck, and

3. The Hazel River flows into the Rappahannock approximately four miles northeast of Brandy Station.

4. "Flint Hill" was approximately twenty miles northwest of Culpepper.

by night the command had five different ones in command of the rear guard. I stopped at 11 o'clock A.M. and rested until three, then came on here in company with Van Whitehead and Todd, went out in the country, got a good supper and now feel "O.K."

Saturday 20th. Last night I felt more like "cussing" than I did like writing. Yesterday morning we marched to Front Royal, where we remained until 4 o'clock in the evening, waiting, they said until the pontoons were laid across both branches of the Shenandoah. In due time we moved forward, and the head of the column commenced crossing just at dark, and about the same time it commenced raining. We found the pontoons still upon the wagons packed near the river, and as regiment after regiment came up they made sport of them, and "waded in." It was no pleasant task crossing the river at that time. I pulled off my boots, socks, pants and etc., thinking I might keep them a little dry, but by the time I had cut my feet on the sharp rocks, and fallen down a time or two, I regretted it. The bank on this side of the river is steep and by the time we crossed it had become perfectly slippery and I had to go up it on "all fours." Some of the boys would nearly reach the top and then an unlucky slip would send them "sousing" into the river again. The rain poured down in torrents and the cussing of some of the boys was fearfully serious.

After reaching this side of the river, we went out into an old field, where I fell into a gulley; ran over a briar patch, scratched my face and nearly broke my neck, so dark that I could see it, feel it, taste it, and smell it, and such thick darkness that a streak of lightning could not have cut through it. After wandering about in the darkness a while I ran against a fence, and taking about half a dozen rails I made me a comfortable bed, so as to keep me out of the mud, laying them side by side, After getting into an easy position, I slept well, with my rail bed, and with the darkness and rain for a covering, and awoke this morning feeling a little stiff, but after shaking myself a time or two, felt all right. Came through White Port[5] today, and are camped on the road to Berryville. The

5. White Post (not White Port), Clarke County.

boys are all in fine spirits for *on dit* that Ewell is in Penn.[6] and that we are bound thitherward.

Berryville, Va. Sunday 21st. Here we are at the end of one week's marching at one of the prettiest spots in Virginia. On our march today we met our old war horse, Longstreet, and cheered him lustily.

Near Shepherdstown, Va.[7] Tuesday 23rd. Yesterday morning was so bright and beautiful that I determined to make the most of the day. Jim Crow, Dick Hobbs, and myself went by Gen'l. Wilcox's quarters and ascertained from Capt. Winn that it was the intention to remain during the day, so we set out on our day's ramble. Took breakfast at Mr. Wheat's; took dinner at Mr. Williams'. While there at 4 o'clock P.M., Mr. W. came in and while speaking of the army said that General Anderson's[8] division was the finest looking body of men that he had ever seen. Of course we felt complimented, and asked him where he had seen them, said that he saw them marching through Berryville about nine o'clock A.M. Here we were four miles in an opposite direction and the regiment had been marching all day. We thought it not worth while to grieve, so remained an hour or two longer, then took up our line of march. Went by the camps, found everything deserted, stopped in Berryville, had a serenade, laid in a supply of tobacco, then came out two miles this side and took supper at McCormick's, had a pleasant time, spent an hour or so, then set out for camps. Walked until about ten o'clock and then slept on the Pike without blankets for a couple of hours, then pushed forward and overtook

6. Lieutenant General Richard S. Ewell commanded Lee's Second Corp during the Gettysburg Campaign. On June 20 two of Ewell's divisions were in Maryland and one in northern Virginia along the Potomac. However, Brigadier General A. G. Jenkins' cavalry brigade, which was operating with Ewell, had by this date crossed into Pennsylvania. On June 19 he had been ordered forward to Chambersburg.

7. Shepherdstown is now in West Virginia.

8. After Jackson's death Lee reorganized the Army of Northern Virginia. He divided it into three corps. Longstreet commanded the First Corps, Ewell the Second, and A. P. Hill the Third. R. H. Anderson's division, to which Wilcox's brigade and the Ninth Alabama belonged, was part of Hill's command.

the regiment this morning as they were preparing to move forward to this place. I was awfully tired but it would not do to grumble, for we had been absent without leave. We passed through Charlestown, the scene of the last "tight rope performance" of John Brown, at an early hour.[9] The people were delighted to see us, and gave us a hearty welcome. We are to cross the Potomac in the morning into "Maryland, My Maryland." [10]

Near Boonesboro, Md.[11] ***Wednesday the 24th.*** This morning bright and early we crossed the Potomac at Mill Ford one mile below Shepherdtown. The water from three to four feet deep. It was a little cool but we were all in such fine spirits that we didn't mind it. We came up on the hill near Sharpesburg and halted for an hour or two; while there General Wright and staff rode into town and all came near being captured. All escaped but the General's son, who could not ride fast on account of the loss of a leg which he parted with at Manassas. The squad who made the charge escaped before our infantry could reach them.[12] Passed through Sharpesburg which is a hard looking dilapidated old town, and which still shows the marks of the battle fought there. The battle of Sharpsburg, or Antietam as the Yankees have it, will long be remembered. We have had an easy march today, and are now camping in a pretty meadow, in a valley three miles from Boonesboro.

Hagerstown, Md. Thurs. 25th. Passed through Boonesboro this morning just as the sun was rising bright and glorious over the South Mountain. Everything on the road looks strange to us coming

9. John Brown was hanged at Charlestown, Virginia (now West Virginia) on December 2, 1859.

10. In his poem "Maryland, My Maryland," James R. Randall was appealing to his native state to join the Confederacy. Clement Eaton, *A History of the Southern Confederacy* (New York: The Macmillian Company, 1954), p. 222.

11. Patterson usually misspelled Boonsboro and Sharpsburg. Neither was he consistent in his spelling of Shepherdstown.

12. Brigadier General Ambrose R. Wright of Georgia commanded a brigade in Hill's corps. In his official report of the Gettysburg Campaign he covers the operations of his command only for July 1–4. However, the *Official Records* do note a skirmish at Sharpsburg on June 24. Also, Patterson is correct in that General Wright's son had lost a leg at Manassas. *O.R.*, Ser. I, Pt. II, XXVII, 5, 622.

as we do from the desolate fields of Virginia. Here we see houses, barns filled with grain, fine stock etc. Today we met a fine large drove of beef cattle going to the rear. Some of the boys who have fully realized the effects of the war at their own houses are fairly itching to retaliate, but Gen'l. Lee's order issued the morning we crossed into Md. is too strict.[13] The majority of the people seem to be "loyal" tho we find quite a number who are with us heart and soul, though not bodily. Fungston [14] seems to contain quite a number of families who are Southern sympathizers. We reached this place at one o'clock this evening, and quite a number of the boys have been in the city. I preferred to remain in camp.

Two miles from Green Castle,[15] Penn. Friday the 26th of June. This morning Capt. Harry Lee, Jim Crow and I left camps about daylight and came into the city of Hagerstown. Had an old fashioned time. Patronized the barber shop, hotel, and saloon, and as it bade fair to rain all day we laid in a supply of the "needful." About 8 o'clock our command passed through Middlebury.[16] Crossed the Pennsylvania and Maryland [line] at 11 o'clock precisely. Jim Crow, Van Whitehead and I persuaded an old gentleman to show us exactly where the line ran and then standing with one foot in Maryland and the other in Pennsylvania, we finished the contents of a canteen, drinking some pretty heavy toasts. Green Castle seems to be a pretty little town but intensely "loyal." It would probably be more so, if it had passed through what many of the towns in the South have, tried with fire. Gen'l. A. P. Hill passed us on the march looking ready for a fight.

13. General Orders No. 73 reads: "The Commanding general considers that no greater disgrace could befall the army, and through it our whole people, than the perpetration of the barbarous outrages upon the unarmed and the defenseless, and the wanton destruction of private property that have marked the course of the enemy in our own country. . . . It must be remembered that we make war only upon armed men, and that we cannot take vengeance for the wrongs our people have suffered without . . . offending against Him to whom vengeance belongeth, without whose favor and support our efforts must all prove in vain." Clifford Dowdey, *Lee* (Boston: Little, Brown and Company, 1965), p. 363.

14. Funkstown, Maryland.

15. Greencastle, Pennsylvania.

16. Middleburg, Pennsylvania.

Saturday the 27th. On the march again. Passed through Marion [17] [and] Chambersburg. While passing through the latter place Gen'l. Lee rode up the column speaking kindly to acquaintances and passed on. The boys never cheer him, but pull off their hats and worship. The females of Chambersburg seem to be very spiteful, make faces, sing "Rally round the flag," wave their little banners etc. I think if they had a hole burned out in their town about the size and extent of that which the Yankees burned in Florence or Athens, Alabama, these patriotic females would not be quite so saucy.[18] A widow in the place discovered the knapsack of her deceased husband in the command, she wished it and the soldier gave it to her. He had picked it up on the battlefield of "Gaine's Mills," where we fought the "squirrel tail rifles." [19] I suppose that her husband has gone to that home from whence etc., such is war. We reached this place, Fayetteville, a little before sun down, and Jim and I went out and took supper with a good old Pennsylvania farmer; plenty of everything, especially apple butter, the first I have tasted since I left Ohio.

Fayetteville, Sunday Evening, 28th. I have been down town nearly all day sauntering about up and down the streets. No preaching either in camps or in town. Some of the boys have been "capturing" chickens. It is against positive orders, but I would not punish one of them, for as Joe McMurray says, it's not half as bad as they did, [to] his mother and sisters in Alabama, for they not only

17. Marion, Pennsylvania.

18. In May, 1862, Federal troops under John B. Turchin, Russian born colonel of the Nineteenth Illinois, thoroughly sacked the town of Athens. "Here for two hours, Turchin retired to his tent and gave over the town to the soldiers . . . after the old European custom." When he had to abandon the place, on the advance of Bragg across Tennessee into Kentucky, he set fire to and burned much of Athens. Fleming, *Civil War,* pp. 63, 65. For an account of Federal outrages in Florence see above p. 98 n. 6. Chambersburg, Pennsylvania was burned by Confederate troops July 30, 1864.

19. The Thirteenth Pennsylvania Reserves, known as the "Bucktails," were at Gaines's Mill. The regiment got its nickname from the custom of requiring a prospective recruit to bring with him the tail of a buck he had shot to show his skill with the rifle. Each man wore a buck tail on his hats as a unit identification. Possibly Patterson was referring to this unit when he used the term "squirrel tail rifles."

took such things, but took the rings from his sisters' fingers, and earrings from their ears, besides cursing and abusing them. It is well that Joe isn't General in Chief for he would try what virtue there is in fire, as well as the sword.

Tues. 30th. Still at Fayetteville, but there is something on the tapis, for yesterday Heath's and Pender's divisions [20] left, and have gone in the direction of Gettysburg. I took dinner yesterday at the hotel, and at night Jim Crow, Dick Hobbs and I went out about two miles into the country to get supper, and had a most magnificent time. The young lady was Union but called herself a "copperhead." [21] I would not mind being bitten by her a few times. On our way back as we were coming through the town we serenaded the citizens with "The Bonnie Blue Flag," "The Sunny South Forever," etc. Don't think it was appreciated though. Hood's and McLaws' divisions [22] passed through town late this evening. Met several of my old friends in the 4th Alabama. Also saw Cousin Frank. Had but little time to talk to him. Was on brigade guard today, and kept things *straight* around the hotel, took dinner there, and so won the heart of the old landlord that he filled my canteen with cherry brandy. I pronounce him a "gentleman and scholar and a judge of the article."

Near Gettysburg, Pa. Wednesday July 1, 1863. This morning we left Fayetteville at an early hour and reached this place while the sun was yet two hours high. On our way, we stopped on the mountain for some time in full view of the battle that has been raging in the valley, or rather in and around Gettysburg. While waiting on the mountain Gen'l. Lee passed us after a short conversation with out commander and we soon followed. When we reached the vicinity of Gettysburg the fight was still going on and

20. Major General Henry Heth's division (not Heath) was attached to A. P. Hill's Third Corps as was the command of Major General William D. Pender.

21. A "copperhead" was a northern Democrat who opposed Lincoln's war policy and favored a negotiated peace.

22. The divisions of John B. Hood and Lafayette McLaws were in Longstreet's First Corps.

the enemy falling back. We expected to be immediately ordered forward, but for some reason they have sent us away around on the right wing of the army, confronting the enemy's extreme left. We have bivouacked on a small stream and I suppose are placed here to prevent a flank movement by the enemy's cavalry during the night.[23] Our forces have captured several thousand prisoners today, and have driven the enemy through the town. But there will probably be more fighting tomorrow; and if so we are sure to get our share for Hearth's and Pender's divisions [24] have been engaged all today.

The boys seem serious tonight. No loud talking or card playing and it is natural that they should feel so.

"For well they know that on the Morrow,
Some must sleep beneath the sod."

[In the original manuscript, the following entry and those through October 6, 1964, are bound together with a cover page reading "Prison Life on Johnson's Island."]

The morning of the 2nd of July 1863 dawned on thousands of as brave hearts as were ever gathered together to battle for the right.[25]

23. Wilcox's brigade was engaged only in the fighting on July 2 and 3.

24. Patterson misspelled Heth. It was Heth's skirmishers who unexpectedly precipitated the Battle of Gettysburg on July 1, and soon after the fighting started Pender's division became involved.

25. On July 2 the Federal forces were disposed in the form of a fishhook, "with the tip at Culp's Hill, the hook curving around Cemetery Hill, the shank along Cemetery Ridge, and the 'eye' at the Round Tops." The Confederate forces were stretched around the outside of this hook, "with Ewell on the north, A. P. Hill in the center, and Longstreet on the south." Lee's plan of attack called for Longstreet to strike the Federal left flank with two division (Hood on the right and McLaws) then turn north and roll up the enemy line by an attack along the Emmitsburg pike. Ewell and Hill were to make the secondary effort; "that is they were to attack so as to prevent Meade from shifting troops from unthreatened parts of his line to reinforce against Longstreet's main effort."

A. P. Hill in his official report written several months after the battle had this to say about his command's part in the fighting on July: "The corps of General Longstreet [McLaws' and Hood's divisions] was on my right, and in a line very nearly at right angles to mine. General Longstreet was to attack the left flank of the enemy, and sweep down his line, and I was ordered to co-operate with him with such of my brigades from the right as could join in with his troops in the

And as the glorious sun rose in all his splendor shedding his rays on every hill top and flooding the Earth with light, the booming of artillery told us that all was not quiet along the lines, and that we had work before us. We had marched from Fayetteville the day before and had lain in line of battle all night protecting the extreme right flank of the army.

There had been hard fighting on the 1st and we well knew that one day's work could not decide the contest between two such powerful armies as now lay confronting each other near Gettysburg. Our noble army, flushed with a long series of brilliant victories and feeling unlimited confidence in the ability of General Lee and the justice of the cause for which we were fighting, were eager for the fray. We were soon in motion and with our gallant Wilcox at the head of the column were moving forward toward the center of the line of battle which was to be our position for the day. After marching some distance, we were ordered to halt, load our pieces and throw forward a skirmish line. We soon found our battle line, with the 10th and 11th Alabama Regiments a little in advance. These two regiments soon became hotly engaged with the enemy's sharpshooters, who were well posted behind a stone wall and in a strip of woods, but our boys soon succeeded in dislodging them, and our whole line moved forward and took position behind the stone fence from which we had just driven the enemy. During the little skirmish which lasted but a few moments, Maj. Fletcher and quite a

---

attack. On the extreme right, Hood commenced the attack about 2 o'clock; McLaws about 5:30 o'clock.

"Soon after McLaws moved forward, General Anderson moved forward the brigades of Wilcox, Perry, and Wright, *en echelon.* The charge of these three brigades was very gallantly made, and pressed on until Wilcox's right had become separated from McLaws' left. Wilcox and Wright drove the enemy from their intrenchments, inflicting a very heavy loss upon them. Wilcox's brigade succeeded in capturing eight pieces of artillery and Wright's brigade about twenty. The enemy threw forward heavy re-enforcements, and no supports coming to these brigades, the ground so hardly won had to be given up, and the brigades occupied their former positions in line of battle. The three brigades lost heavily in this attack."

Patterson's account of the fighting on his front must be basically accurate because it does not conflict with the reports either of his brigade commander (Wilcox) or his division commander (Anderson). *O.R.,* XXVII, Ser. I, Pt. II, 608, 614–15, 618; Boatner, *Dictionary,* pp. 335–36.

number of others from the 8th, 10th, and 11th were wounded and a few killed.

As soon as our regiment got into position, our company was ordered forward as skirmishers, Cannon commanding the 1st platoon, I the second and Crow in command of the whole. I immediately moved forward in obedience to the orders and formed line with the Fla. skirmishers on my left, and my right resting at a large barn which afforded considerable protection to my men and was also a good lookout. We immediately opened fire on the enemy's line of sharpshooters and succeeded in making them withdraw some distance and causing some of the more daring, or obstinate ones, to bite the dust, and this too without any loss on our side. We remained at the barn for some time and until the Yankees brought a battery to bear upon it, when I withdrew the men, placing them on line with the rest of the company.

We, however, still kept a lookout at the place, and about three o'clock in the evening I noticed battery after battery and brigade after brigade being moved up to our right and we knew that something of interest was soon to take place in that direction, and we were not long in suspense, for at a given signal our artillery opened fire throwing their missiles of death right down the enemy's line and making the very earth tremble with the thunderstones, and following in quick succession, a cheer such as Southern soldiers only can give and a terrible crash of musketry told us that Longstreet and his gallant braves had succeeded in getting on the enemy's flank and was dealing out death and destruction to them in their usual style.[26] But the enemy was too strong on that portion of the line to give way easily and fought for some time. But in half an hour from the commencement of the attack I saw the Yankees retreating, and our boys yelling like madmen in hot pursuit. The Yankees did not seem to be able to organize their shattered lines, and it was evident to all that if fresh troops were not on hand to check these flying fragments of regiments and brigades, the field would be ours.

26. After the war Longstreet was charged with losing the Battle of Gettysburg for Lee because of his delay in attacking on July 2. This unwarranted charge plagued him to the end of his life.

But about this time I saw immediately in our front solid masses of fresh troops, moving up between us and the victory, and now our time for action had come. The time to try our manhood, the long looked for hour when we should meet the enemy on his own soil. I prayed God in that hour to assist me to do my whole duty to my country. The spirits of the troops were never better, and as Gen'l. Wilcox rode along down the line giving orders to charge, cheer after cheer filled the air almost drowning the sound of shells that were bursting above and around us. The proud banner which waved amid the wild tempest of battle at Williamsburg, Gaines Mills, Frazier's Farm, Sharpesburg, and Chancellorsville never rose more proudly than today. And as we moved forward in a perfect storm of shot, shell and canister, we felt that the starry cross must triumph.

In less than five minutes from the time, the Yankees were seen advancing, and death had commenced his work in good earnest. The battle now rages furiously, but our lines move onward—straight onward. The roaring of artillery,—grape and canister that came plunging through our ranks,—bullets thick as hailstones in winter, men falling on every side as leaves fall when shaken by the rude blasts of Autumn, is terrible, yet our men falter not, and we succeed in breaking their first and second lines of battle, capturing many prisoners, artillery, and colors. At the third and last line we met stern resistance; here for the third time since the war began we met the famous Irish Brigade,[27] and they fought with a bravery worthy of a better cause. The troops on their immediate right and left gave way, leaving them exposed to an oblique fire from both flanks in addition to that from the front. Yet under the terrible fire they did not run, but retreated slowly and in good order, and returning our fire, but leaving the ground literally covered with their dead. They were, in fact, almost annihilated, and yet one regiment of them formed square around a piece of artillery and carried it some distance by hand, loading and firing it very rapidly,

27. The Irish Brigade under Colonel Patrick Kelly was attached to the First Division, Second Corps, Army of the Potomac. It had distinguished itself in attacks upon the Stone Wall at Marye's Heights.

the square opening to allow them to fire, but at last they had to abandon it.

We drove them to the foot of the hill on which was posted their reserve artillery, but there meeting reenforcements and seeing our terribly thinned ranks they made another stand. Wilcox seeing the valor of his troops, moved among them and before them, as if courting death by his own daring intrepidity. The fight goes on, and the blood flows like water. But few are left unhurt, and with ranks now torn and bleeding, capture or annihilation inevitable if we remain longer, we all feel that something must be done, and that speedily. Some one gives the order to fall back, no one knows from where the order emanated. Some obey it, some do not. There were no longer companies or regiments, scarcely brigades, for Barksdale's had completely overlapped ours and we were mingled in glorious confusion. It was a line where every man seemed satisfied with any place and cared little for others, or what command he was fighting in. "Whiz" went a ball and burned the side of my head, just above the ear, cutting the hair nicely. The air was hot, and filled with sticks, rocks, dust and black smoke, almost suffocating, when I, with a few Mississippians, tried to make our way out back to where the line was trying to form.

After getting back about a hundred yards, we found that we had run into a gang of Yankees. For some unaccountable reason the troops on our left had not advanced and thereby had allowed the enemy to get into the rear. The first thing I knew there was a line of guns leveled on us, and one of the Yankees yelled out, "Surrender, you d—d gray backs." I saw at a glance that we were "gone up" and no help for it. In company with a large number of officers and men who had been captured in the same trap, I was hurried to the rear, feeling badly enough, and could have been bought for five cents. When I arrived in the rear of the lines, I found about fifty men and about a dozen officers from the old 9th. I was glad to see them, for misery loves company.

July 3rd 1863. (Friday) In company with forty or fifty officers, including from my regiment Capt. Smith and Chisholm, and Lieuts.

Cartwright, Chisholm, Sharp, Gamble, and Nicholson and about five or six hundred men, we set out for Westminster.[28] We had been engaged with the enemy during the day before and had not eaten anything since our breakfast of that morning, and if anybody thinks it is an easy thing to march thirty miles over a dusty road, the sun shining in a cloudless sky, and the hottest that ever shone, without having eaten anything for twenty four hours, just let them try it. We were fortunate in having a very gentlemanly sort of a fellow in command, who endeavored to make us as comfortable as the circumstances would admit, often walking and letting some one else ride his horse.

Weary and worn we reached Westminister at sun down, and created quite a sensation. With a single exception the people treated us respectfully. The exception was an officer, with the rank of captain, and wearing the badge of the Eleventh,[29] which corps, by and by, has the reputation of being the most cowardly in the army, and has never failed to run at the first volley. "You d—d sons of bitches," said he, "If I had *my* way with you, I'd have you shot down in the street where you are." And then followed a string of abuse that cannot be repeated. Cowardly Dog! thought I, there is no probability of you ever seeing any of us shot down unless it is in the street of some quiet town at least thirty miles from the front. For I am sure that his cowardly legs will never carry his worthless carcass nearer. The officer begged us to pay no attention to what the man said, saying by the way of mitigation that he was drunk.

Passing down through the principal street in town, we were taken to the outskirts of the place and huddled together in a little enclosure that had been used as a stock pen, with barely room enough to lie down. About nine o'clock they gave us a day's rations of hard tack and salt pork which was very acceptable, as we had eaten nothing at all since the morning of the day before. We were

28. Westminister, Maryland.

29. The Eleventh Corps was known both as "The German Corps," because of its high percentage of German-speaking units, and a "hard luck outfit." At Chancellorsville it bore the brunt of Jackson's brilliant surprise envelopment, and at Gettysburg two of its divisions were routed on the first day.

so completely exhausted that we were not choice in position and were soon sleeping the sweet, yet heavy sleep of a weary soldier.

July 4th 1863. Eighty Seven years ago today, our forefathers declared that henceforth and forever they were and of right ought to be free. 'Twas a noble sentiment and nobly did they conquer. Today the South contends for the same principles which fired the hearts of our ancestors in the revolutionary struggle, and as sure as right and justice prevail, so surely will we finally triumph. Men of the North tell us that our cause is a doomed one, that the populous North by sacrificing man for man will eventually exterminate the Southern people. Cool calculating murder. I might believe this if I did not know that the race is not always to the swift, nor the battle to the strong. There is a God above us that holds the destinies of Nations in his hands, and who in his own good time will bring us safely out of the fiery ordeal through which we are now passing.

This is a day that will be long remembered by all who were in our party. Early in the morning we were marched down to the depot and hurried on board a train of box cars where we could not even sit or lie down, we were so crowded. And even had we been so situated that we could have lain down, the cars were too filthy, and then they were so close that we could scarcely get a breath of air. How different this from the treatment of the Yankee officers captured at Chancellorsville. They were sent to Richmond in elegant passenger cars.[30] In these cars we were kept all day, expecting every moment to start for Baltimore. But it was no go, and we had to pass the night on the train. They were afraid to start for fear that Stewart [Stuart] was waiting somewhere along the line to capture the train.

On the following morning however, we went to Baltimore,

30. Federal prisoners traveling on Confederate railroads were not always placed in "elegant passenger cars." In early 1864 when the first Federal prisoners from Virginia were sent to the new but soon to be notorious camp at Andersonville, Georgia, they were crammed into half-ruined boxcars that offered little protection from the weather. Robert C. Black, *Railroads of the Confederacy* (Chapel Hill: The University of North Carolina Press, 1952), p. 234.

arriving at 11 o'clock, and marched down through the city of Fort McHenry. Although from nearly every building in the city the Stars and stripes were flying, I learned that many of them were not put there willingly, but had been put there by order of the provost marshall of the city. A kind of forced loyalty or patriotism.[31] In passing through we recognized many friends, but the guard watched us so closely that we could not converse with them. About midnight we received quite an addition to our number, including Jones, Patton and Seward of the 9th.

July 6th. About sundown we went aboard the steamship Susquehanna and started for Fort Delaware,[32] where we arrived forty eight hours afterwards, having undergone some sea sickness and rough weather, and suffered some inconveniences in consequence of having nothing to eat. The captain commanding the vessel assured us that it was unintentional, that the rations intended for us had by mistake been put on board the wrong boat. Quite a serious mistake, we poor hungry souls thought before we reached our destination.

Immediately on our arrival, we were conducted to the barracks situated in a vast mud hole. It is useless to attempt a description of the place. A respectable hog would have turned up his nose in disgust at it. But this was not all, the fare was worse, if possible, than the lodging. Twice each day we marched or waded through the black mud nearly knee deep to a low dark and filthy hall to eat what little their generosity allowed us. Here without knife or fork (having stolen our pocket knive previously) or plate, we found each man's rations lying on the table (single planks running the entire length of the hall). Each man's ration consisted of three small musty crackers, and a piece of salt pork half cooked, about the size of my three fingers, and occasionally by way of variety, a cup of

31. One of the earliest manifestations of southern sympathy in Baltimore occurred on April 19, 1861, when secessionist sympathizers in the city attacked Federal military units en route to Washington. This was known as the Baltimore Riot.

32. Federal authorities used various forts as prisons. One of these was Fort Delaware in the Delaware River. Among Confederate soldiers it was probably the most dreaded of all Federal prisons.

some kind of liquid called soup. It seemed to be the odds and ends of a week's cooking boiled in water used in washing the pots, kettles and c., in the kitchen, and as no one was allowed to commence eating until all were served it was generally cold. I think on the whole, with Schenk in command, it would answer very well for a second class hell.

Around the Fort was a moat which was always filled with water, as the ground on which the Fort stands is lower than the river. Within this enclosure were about seven thousand prisoners, and all of them wash not only themselves, but also all their clothing in the moat. I have often seen two or three hundred men washing in there while the cooks were dipping up water out of it, with which to make our coffee and "soup." On the surface of the water may always be seen a coating of soapsuds mixed with a green scum. The outhouses are built extending over the river, and here all these men had to come from all parts of this Hell on earth, through mud and filth in many places over knee deep. Of course deaths under such circumstances were frightfully frequent. The men died by hundreds and I might say by thousands, and no effort was made by the authorities to better this state of things. Even in going from our barracks to the dining hall, we had to wade through black slimy muck to our knees. By the blessing of God I remained well, but I was pained by seeing those whom I had known strong, stalwart, noble men and heroes of many a hard fought field, grow weaker day by day, with sunken eye and pallid cheek, staggering along through the mud to get their little morsel of bread and meat, just enough to keep them from starving. In a few days I would lose sight of them. Death had claimed his victim, another martyr to liberty, another soul gone to eternity to accuse his persecutors at the judgment.

Here men seemed to lose their own self-respect, with no change of clothing, nothing but cold water, without soap to wash with, covered with vermin, no hope of getting away, with almost certain death staring them in the face, if they remained long. Is it any wonder that some of them took the oath of allegiance? No, I think not. It is said that the U.S. Authorities have condemned this as a prison, and it is to be hoped that no more prisoners may ever be incarcerated herein. God pity them if some are so unfortunate.

July 16th 1863. Today we were informed that all officers here confined would in a day or two be sent to Johnson's Island, Lake Erie.[33] This is glorious news to us, for we are anxious to go anywhere (except to Hell and some even said they would prefer the aforementioned place for the same length of time) in preference to remaining here.

33. Johnson's Island was near Sandusky, Ohio.

· IX ·

"Now, I am a prisoner of war on the little island of Lake Erie"

July 18, 1863, to December 31, 1863

July 18th. Farewell old Fort Delaware, with all your pleasant associations, and you abject cringing puppies who hold sway there. Fit tools ye are for your master Abraham Lincoln, ye have done your work well and will be welcomed to a seat side by side with your illustrious master in the dominion of his Satanic majesty.[1] We reached Philadelphia about noon, and after remaining an hour left for Harrisburg, where we arrived during the night. Along the road between the two places is some magnificent scenery. But I was not in a condition to appreciate its beauty.

1. A Texan who was a prisoner of the Federals had this to say about Fort Delaware: "It happened to be my good fortune not to go to Fort Delaware during my involuntary stay in the North. But this place is spoken of by all who have been confined there as a perfect hell on earth." R. H. Shuffer, ed., *The Adventures of a Prisoner of War 1863–1864* (Austin: University of Texas Press, 1964), p. 88; hereinafter cited as Shaffer, ed., *Adventures of a Prisoner.*

Johnson's Island, Ohio. July 20th 1863. At the end of our journey at last, just about as far North as we can go, unless Uncle Jonathan rents land enough from John Bull to build him a soldier pen on. For some reason the cars did not leave Harrisburg until the morning of the 19th. Probably our considerate guardians wanted to give us an opportunity to see the country through which we had to pass; or perhaps they did not wish to disturb our slumbers. We reached Pittsburg about sundown, and found the city fortified as if anticipating an attack from the East. Here we managed to elude the vigilance of the guard and get hold of a newspaper.

On today we came through Alliance and Orville, changed cars at Mansfield, and arrived at Sandusky about sundown, and at the island about an hour later. The whole population of Sandusky were ready to swear, when they saw so many of us, that now indeed the "rebellion is crushed." As the train neared the depot they commenced running pell mell, men, women, children, of all ages, sexes, conditions, and colors. Dogs, cats, cows and mules joined in the drove and helped make up the show, almost running over each other to get a good look at the "Rebs" (as the smart little boys in the North have been taught to call us). The word "*we*" has become a common one in this part of the country. Little ones suspendered, ruffle shirted, quartermaster and clerks, fancy dry goods merchants with their pens behind their ears and yardsticks in hand, divinity students with their unapproachable neckties and immaculate shirt fronts, smelling like a drugstore, all saying that "*We* have got you this time." "You might have known that we could whip you. We will teach you how to rebel against the best government under the sun." Yes, and *we* have played H—l, and not one in a thousand of them was ever near enough to a battle to hear the thunder.

21st. We all like Johnson's Island much better than any other we have found since leaving Dixie. Here we have no guard standing at our doors, and in fact are not brought in contact with the Yanks at all.[2] This is the anniversary of the first battle of Manassas,

2. Young Henry Kyd Douglas, while a prisoner at Johnson's Island, wrote that the "officers and guards with rare exceptions, were civil and considerate." Four hundred men, called the "Hoffman Battalion," served as guard from the

—then the Yanks were going to put down the rebellion in thirty days, and after McDowell and his forces were sent flying back to Washington, they gave us ninety days and from that day to this they have been giving us a little more time. I do not know exactly the date now predicted for us to lay down our arms but it cannot be far in the future, as Vicksburg and Port Hudson have fallen and Lee's army "utterly demoralized," and its capture or annihilation a "moral certainty," and in addition to this "Charleston just about to fall."[3] *Will it not be a wonder* if we hold out three months longer?

22nd. Met my old friend Billy Casey from Lauderdale, Ala.

July 27th. After a week's sickness I am just beginning to feel all right again. Nothing of much importance has transpired during the week until today, when a large number of Gen. Morgan's officers came in; among them were Col. Basil Duke and several others of note.

28th. Officers from Port Hudson arrived.

30th. Father, Sister Sophia, and Uncle Edmund[4] came to the Island to visit me, but they were not allowed the privilege. I managed however, by going up on the platform at the steps of Block one, to get a peep at them and exchange a few words with Uncle Ed, though I had to speak loud enough to be heard all over the barracks in order to make him hear me.

---

spring of 1862 until January 1864 at which time six more companies were added. Having reached full regimental strength, the ten companies became the One Hundred Twenty-eighth Ohio Volunteer Infantry, and Lieutenant Colonel W. S. Pierson was replaced by Brigadier General H. D. Terry as commander of the unit. He in turn was replaced by Colonel C. H. Hill in May, 1864. Henry K. Douglas, *I Rode With Stonewall* (Chapel Hill: The University of North Carolina Press, 1940), p. 263; hereafter cited as Douglas, *I Rode with Stonewall.* E. T. Downer, "Johnson's Island," *Civil War History, VIII* (June, 1962), 210; hereinafter cited as Downer, "Johnson's Island." *O.R.* VII, Ser. II, 140–41.

3. Vicksburg fell on July 4 and Port Hudson on July 8 but Charleston was to remain in Confederate hands until near the end of the war. Federal authorities mistakenly thought that Fort Sumter could be destroyed by naval bombardment after which the fleet could land an army corps to occupy the city. All efforts to carry out this plan (April-December, 1864) were unsuccessful.

4. Uncle Edmund was Uncle Edmund Brooks.

31st. This day closes a very eventful month. On the 1st, 2nd, and 3rd the terrible battle of Gettysburg was fought. On the 4th Gen. Pemberton[5] surrendered Vicksburg, with all the forces in command, to Gen. Grant. On the 8th or 9th Port Hudson also surrendered. During the month there have been minor battles fought. Dick Taylor captured Brashear City with the forces stationed there.[6] Gen. Morgan and his command have also been captured during the month,[7] and the siege of Charleston has commenced.[8] The month has been a very fortunate one for the federals, and an unfortunate one for us.

After quite an extensive trip through the North I am more fully convinced that this war will last during Lincoln's administration. No one who knows anything about the vast resources of the North can hope for a speedy termination of the war. The feeling of the North is so bitter against us that as long as they can get men, and means, the war will continue. As for myself, I see before us as citizens of the confederate states, *war* for years to come. And although we have suffered much, I believe it has been nothing compared to what is yet in store for us. It is not for us to pretend to say when peace shall be made, but it is our duty to fight on and on, until our enemies shall find that they are making a losing business of it and conclude to terminate it.

August 2nd. Well here we are still at Johnson's Island, and nothing that I can see to indicate a speedy release. We ramble about through the pen, which comprises sixteen acres,[9] during the day and

5. Lieutenent General John C. Pemberton.

6. Major General Richard Taylor, in command of the District of Western Louisiana, captured Brashear City on June 23, 1863. It was reoccupied by Federal forces on July 22, 1863.

7. In early June, Brigadier General John H. Morgan received permission to make a raid with his cavalry division into Kentucky, but he was forbidden to cross the Ohio River as he had proposed. Notwithstanding the prohibition he decided to invade the North and on July 8 crossed the Ohio below Louisville. He was captured near New Lisbon, Ohio, on July 26. He and others of his command were placed in the State Penitentiary at Columbus.

8. The first assault on the city's defenses had taken place on April 7 when a Federal fleet attempted to force the entrance to the harbor. In July the operations centered around Fort Wagner on Morris Island, and major Federal assault on the fort was turned back on July 18.

9. The following is a prisoner's description of Johnson's Island: "The prison was an oblong, bare piece of ground enclosed by a high fence, and perched up

at night retire to our quarters, some to read, some to write, and others to play chess, whist, Old sledge, Euchre, Cribbage, and a dozen other games unnecessary to mention. We spend our time in this manner until half past nine o'clock, when at the tap of the drum, all of the lights must go out. And we retire to our "bunks," some to sleep—"aye, perchance to dream," and others to study of home and loved ones there. Last night I was vainly trying to sleep, and thinking first of the friends of my childhood, of home, father, brothers and sisters, then of warm hearted friends in the South, and wondering if I would ever see them again, and if so, under what circumstances, when I was surprised to hear the hoarse cry of the sentinel, "Half past two and all's well." And it instantly diverted my thoughts and sent them in another channel, and after considerable study and reflection, I came to the conclusion that, "All is not well," but as I could not see how I could better the matter, I let the subject pass for future consideration.

August 4th. The officers of Morgan's command who were captured in the recent raid through Indiana and Ohio, were today sent to the penitentiary at Columbus, and will probably be held there until Straight and his band of thieves are released at Richmond.[10] The officers are a noble set of fellows, high minded and honorable men, and they will show that they can suffer as well as fight for their country.

---

on this fence, or barricade, at intervals, in sentry boxes, were armed sentinels. The barracks or prison houses were long buildings, hastily erected of wood and weatherboard, called wards. The weatherboarding was a single layer nailed to upright beams, and there was no plastering of any kind. The weatherboarding would sometimes warp, and in all rooms there were many knotholes, through which one lying in bed could look out upon the moon or the water; but when the weather got below zero, the scenery was scarcely compensation for the suffering. Bunks were ranged along the walls—if they can be called walls—in three tiers. In my room or ward, there were sixty of these. There was one stove in the middle of the room, which kept the room fairly comfortable within a certain range, except in very cold weather. It was about like living in a canvas tent. Of course out on that lake, the weather became excessively cold, below zero, and not infrequently drove the sentinels from their posts, knowing well enough that no prisoner could escape and live." Douglas, *I Rode with Stonewall,* pp. 260–61.

10. In late April, 1863, Colonel A. V. Streight (not Straight) left Tuscumbia, Alabama, with fifteen hundred men, mostly mounted, to cut the railroad in Georgia below Rome. Nathan Bedford Forrest, sent in pursuit, caught up with Streight as he was about to enter Rome and compelled him to surrender.

We still hear nothing definite in regard to an exchange. Some Northern journals state that there will not be any more exchanges until our government consents to treat captured negroes as prisoners of war. If this be the case, then I hope that there may never be another exchange. If the Yankee government will persist in arming the negroes of the South and sending them against us, I believe it will amount to the "Black Flag." One thing I think is very certain and that is that the army in Virginia will not take negro prisoners. Much as we would deplore such a state of affairs I say let it come rather than take the alternative. If we lose everything else, let us preserve our honor.[11]

I have just received a letter from my old friend, Sam Bassett, which is decidedly interesting, abounding in such wise predictions as the following: "The confederacy is completely played out," "the war will end this fall," and advising me to take the 'oath.' But I would prefer taking almost anything else that I could lay my hands on than that.

11th. My mess now consists of the following named officers. Capts. Ballantine, Mosely, and Brown. Lieuts. Adams, Burtcheall, Breare, Dewees, Thigpen, Mosely, Clark and myself. A jolly set of fellows, and most of the boys have a supply of greenbacks.[12]

"Despondency of the Rebels." "North Carolina anxious to return to her allegiance." "The rebellion crushed."[13] Day after day, and week after week, can these meaningless expressions be seen in glowing capitals at the head of leading articles in all the abolition

11. In July, 1862, a general plan for the exchange of prisoners was worked out by General John S. Dix for the Union and D. H. Hill for the Confederacy. This system soon broke down and from 1863 forward the number of prisoners on each side increased enormously. There were a number of reasons for this failure, among them were Butler's conduct in New Orleans (see above p. 92 n. 21) and Davis' hot retaliation in declaring the Union general an outlaw. Also on December 28, 1862, Secretary of War Stanton ordered the exchange of commissioned officers to cease. Further difficulties arose over the use of Negro troops by the Union, refusal of Confederate authorities to exchange these Negro soldiers and their white officers as prisoners of war, and misunderstandings as to southern prisoners released on parole at Vicksburg and Port Hudson. In 1864 Grant put a stop to all exchange of prisoners. This order remained in effect until January, 1865.

12. Greenbacks were United States fiat money.

13. For a description of North Carolina's "despondency" see Barrett, *Civil War in N.C.*, pp. 171–201.

papers of the North, and then in the very next column will be a pitiful howl about the defenses of Washington. The New York Herald, after assuring its readers that the rebellion was crushed, and that all the hard work had been done, turns around and tells them that Gen'l. Lee has an army of one hundred and fifty thousand of the best troops in the world, twenty five thousand cavalry and three hundred pieces of artillery, and that he is about to make another advance on Washington, that Meade's army will be unable to check him and calls loudly for a Peninsular campaign as the only means of saving the capitol. This is all very ridiculous, but the fact of the business is, they have undertaken a task that they begin to see they will not be able to finish.

16th. Received a letter from Uncle Samuel Brooks, filled with the same trash about taking the "Oath,"[14] "Downfall of the Confederacy," etc. This would be quite amusing if it were not so stale. I have heard so much of that kind of talk since I arrived at this place that it is beginning to annoy me, but I generally write such answers that I am not troubled with a repetition of the dose from the same person.

18th. Pa has been here all day. I went outside and remained with him during his stay, took dinner at Capt. Linnel's. Pa still thinks me wrong, and gives me advice which I cannot accept. He urges me to give up the cause of the South which he pronounces a doomed one and one which he is willing and anxious to see put down even though it should take years to accomplish and all the treasure and blood both North and South have. I can scarcely consider myself a member of the family—we have nothing in common. They pray Almighty God to visit the Confederate States with swift destruction while I am risking my life in defence of the South and am willing if necessary to lay down my life in defense of her principles. Those who have fond mothers and fathers, loving sisters in the South to bid them "God Speed" when they go forth to

14. Prisoners taking either the "Oath of Allegiance" or the "Oath of Obligation not to Bear Arms" could be released. *O.R.*, III, Series II, 52.

battle, telling them that their prayers shall go with them, cannot appreciate my feelings. With how much better spirit would I go into battle if I had a father or mother, sister in the South to pray for me and encourage me by their counsel. Now as I go forth to battle, although I have the proud consciousness of right within my own bosom, I cannot help thinking of those far away in the North who are praying for the success of our foes. I cannot help calling to mind the language of one who used to be very dear to me. "If you fall in battle, we shall be compelled to admit that you met your just deserts."

Years must pass before this war will be settled and thousands upon thousands of noble forms must lie cold in death, and I may be among the number. I pray however, that my life may be spared. I wish to live to see the Confederate States an independent Nation, loved at home and respected abroad, and at peace with all the world. I believe that this war will be the downfall of slavery, or that it will not exist in all the Southern States as it once did exist. What effect this will have on the future wealth and greatness of our country, I am unable to say. Present appearances indicate that a large portion of our country will be overrun by the invaders and will become a desert waste. Wherever the foot of the Yankee hireling presses the sacred soil of the South, it carries with it the torch as well as the sword. Not confining themselves to making war on armed men, as our noble army does, they satisfy their insatiable thirst for plunder and revenge by burning dwellings, by turning defenseless and helpless women and children out of their homes, and burning their only shelter before their eyes. Many have thus been left penniless and homeless, dependent on the charities of the world, but it will be remembered to the honor and glory of the Southern people that they, during this terrible struggle, have always been ready to open their heart and their homes to these poor homeless wanderers.

21st. This day has been generally observed by the prisoners here as a day of fasting and prayer, and the entire day devoted to religious exercises. And I believe all felt benefited by it, felt more hopeful, and more like putting our entire trust in the God of battles. We are told that the draft is going on very peaceably in N.Y. City; strange, "passing strange," what a pacifying influence twenty thousand bayonets together with artillery and cavalry in proportion will have in executing the laws of a *"free government."* It is not strange that this number should be required in New York City, when two and a half millions of men cannot enforce the laws of Abraham in the South.[15]

August 25th. Have just received two letters, one from sister, and one from Miss Mattie B., the latter announcing the death of the mother of a young man in my company. It seems that I am destined to carry news of sadness to the boys from Kentucky in my company, to one the death of a mother, to another the death of a sister. Really the devil seems to be gaining ascendancy over the hearts of a large number confined here. Only a few nights since, while some of the more religiously inclined were holding prayer meeting, another party set up a Faro Bank and carried on the game all through the services in the same room, and not more than twenty feet from the meeting, and mingled their horrid oaths with the prayers as some unlucky turn would make them lose heavily.[16]

August 26th. Have been on detail today, and perhaps some one will wish to know what kind of duty I have been doing. Well then, each day we have three men detailed whose duty it is to set the table, clear them off, sweep the rooms, scour the knives and forks, receive and divide the rations, and etc., and all this to do three times during the day, and this is what I have been doing today, and those who have had experience in the matter will agree

15. The bloody "Draft Riot" in New York City occured July 13–16, 1863. Order was restored only with the arrival of Federal troops from the Army of the Potomac.

16. Gambling "was a popular pasttime. It was very common to see a colonel sitting at a table dealing 'faro'; whilst officers of all grades bet at it or played 'poker.'" Shuffer, ed., *Adventures of a Prisoner,* p. 98.

that it is no small job, where there are between eighty and one hundred men to feed.[17]

The other day I came across the following lines, and though written and applied to the North it is far more applicable to the South.

"Abroad in the breeze waves our 'glorious flag.'
Beneath its folds toil we,
While other nations their harvests reap,
And some are at play and some asleep
We are writing our history.

We write—not one to labor alone,
But thousands hold the pen
Delicate Youth and hoary age,
Fair women and stalwart men.

Oh, scornful world watching without,
Stricken of God ye say,
Nay through the cloud as our fathers trod,
We are marching to meet our God,
His promise our only stay.

There is hardly a home whose every chair
Is filled as it might have been,
Were there no blank sheets in our history
To be filled ere another year we see,
And faster travels the pen.

It matters not, O, doubting world,
That our labor be hard or long,

17. Nine of the buildings or "blocks" were partitioned into two large rooms below and three above, with a small room attached to each for cooking purposes. Arranged along the walls were three tiers of bunks and at the end of the room were a number of plank mess tables. Thus a single room served as living quarters, mess hall, storeroom for rations and clothes, and a sleeping apartment. Finally, in 1864, as a result of the unsanitary conditions resulting from this arrangement, two mess halls and a wash house were constructed. The prisoners attributed the unsanitary conditions to a scarcity of water; prison officers explained them on the grounds that "the prisoners being nearly all officers makes it difficult to obtain the necessary amount of dirty work from them. *O.R.*, VII, Ser. II, 468; Downer, "Johnson's Island," pp. 204–7.

For never by man was a good work wrought
But Angels first with the devils fought,
Yet right will conquer wrong.

Float on in the breeze then flag of hope,
Bravely beneath toil we,
While other nations their harvests reap—
With glorious deeds for memorys keep,
We are writing our history."

We are indeed writing a history that will interest the world not only now, but as long as time shall last. I am glad to think of the glorious record my Alabama, my sunny home, will have. Even now, when the enemy have possession of all her northern border, and are threatening Mobile, our legislature has passed a series of resolutions pledging the last man and the last dollar in the state toward the carrying on the war until every invader is driven from our soil.[18]

28th. I continue my journal,—It has become a sort of task of duty to me without the discharge of which I do not consider the labors of the day performed. I feel disposed to write though I should have to destroy my journal as soon as I leave this place, simply for the love of writing. I feel better satisfied when writing than at any other time, whether writing a letter to a friend or penning my thoughts here for my own perusal. Today I was elected

18. The port of Mobile was under blockade in 1861 but no attacks were made on the defenses until August, 1864. The legislature, however, stated in August, 1863: ". . . the war was unprovoked and unjust on the part of the United States government, which was conducting it in utter disregard of the principles which should control and regulate civilized warfare." The legislators "renewed the pledge never to submit to abolitionist rule. The people were urged not to be discouraged by the late reverses, nor to attribute their defeats to any want of courage or heroic self-sacrifice on the part of the armies. All the resources of the state were pledged to the cause of independence and perpetual separation from the United States. It was the paramount duty, the assembly declared, of every citizen to sustain and make effective the armies by encouraging enlistments, by furnishing supplies at low prices to the families of soldiers, and by upholding the credit of the Confederate government." Fleming, *Civil War,* 131–32.

postmaster of this mess. The supply of greenbacks at our table has just about played out, and each one looks out for himself.

31st. Another month draws to its close. And it is well sometimes to take a retrospective view of the past and see how our condition has been bettered by time. During the month we have inaugurated some measures calculated to improve us all. In the first place, we have a flourishing debating society, where we have readings, essays, declamations and debates. This is both interesting and instructive. Then we have several Bible classes. This is also instructive as well as interesting. And for amusements we have concerts, vocal and instrumental, on Fridays and Mondays of each week. Yesterday we had preaching by Col. Lewis of Missouri. It was one of the ablest sermons I ever heard. And besides this, he is a very eloquent speaker, and everybody likes him. I hope that I may hear him often while we remain here. Sumpter[19] they say, has been battered down, but still our flag floats over the grim ruins.

September 2nd. Capt. Bob Brown received a box containing eatables, clothing, and reading matter, all of which I suppose was acceptable, at least the reading matter was very acceptable to me, and as I am one of the mess, I come in for my share of the good things.[20]

4th. Received a letter from Cousin Frank today. He thinks he will have to remain in this God forsaken country as long as any of us, and that I am afraid will be a long time. If I credit newspaper reports, the day of exchange is past.

9th. Well here we are, Capt. Ballantine and myself, sitting up with our sick friends in the hospital.[21] Since I watched with the sick one week ago, death has been among them and two from this room

19. Fort Sumter.

20. Prisoners were permitted to receive clothes from friends and relatives provided the cloth was gray and the design was not in the nature of a uniform. To supplement the monotonous prison diet, they were allowed both to receive boxes of food through the mail and to purchase supplies from the prison sutler and from outside sources. Prisoner's were also given permission to receive books, with the exception of geographies, military histories, and military treatises. Downer, "Johnson's Island," pp. 205–8.

21. The hospital contained beds for sixty-eight patients. *Ibid.,* p. 209.

have been taken. I too, must die sooner or later, and so must all. Some of us who are longing to return home will never again see the bright faces and hear the sweet words of welcome of those loved ones at home, but 'tis a pleasing thought, that although in this world we meet but to part, and love only to have the object of our affection snatched from us when it seems most dear,—that there is a world above, a heavenly home, where friends never part and where sorrows never come. 'Tis this that supports the christian in his darkest hour—Oh, that I were a good humble devoted christian.

I went to the debate today, but heard only two speeches, as we were interrupted by the gruff insolent order of the sentinel to "disperse." This is not the first time even in my recollection that "Rebels" have been commanded to disperse. Abraham the 1st once ordered them to disperse and lay down their arms but was not obeyed, though the sentinel was, for none of us cared about being shot at. A few prisoners have just now come in. Well it is some satisfaction to know that while Southern officers are coming in here, that our armies are taking some of *them* in "out of the wet."

Really it is almost impossible for me to write tonight, I am thinking so much about my friends in Virginia and Alabama, thinking of the many bright mornings and happy evenings I spent last Autumn. Would that I could live over again those happy fleeting days I spent at Inglewood, Belle Monte and Richmond, and in old Lauderdale too last Autumn. I fancy that the time is coming when I will again visit those places, but will it all be the same? Will I find them all there, not one missing? I hope so. How different is the prospect before me. Time will now drag heavily instead of flying swiftly, but perhaps it is best that some bad should be mixed with the good. What would I not give for a good long letter from some of my lady friends in the South tonight. But as I am likely to have a carpet sack full of journal, I must be more brief, not write so much, and yet, as the lonely hours of the night pass wearily along, I feel that in no other manner can I pass them so pleasantly as in writing.

11th. This has been one of the pleasantest days I have passed in a long time; probably the letters I received this morning have had much to do with it. Five letters and two of them from Dixie. I had been thinking for some time of the chances I had whether I would ever receive a letter from my friends in Virginia, and I had given up hope almost, and concluded that I would never hear from the dear creatures during the period of my prison life. How gladly did I welcome a letter bearing the post mark "Old Point Comfort," (it was New Comfort to me), and in the well known hand writing of one "Thomps," and how eagerly did I devour its contents. Ah, I knew that I was not forgotten, I knew they would sometimes think of me and speak of me, but I feared I would never have the pleasure of reading a letter from one of them during my stay. How refreshing were these two letters from Miss Sallie and "Thomps," coming as they did, from the spot connected with so many pleasant associations of the past. I also received a letter from Miss Kate D. and one from Miss Mattie B.

15th. Still another letter from "Dixie." I did not believe that so good and kind a friend as Miss Jennie had so soon forgotten me, and I was right in my belief.

19th. Rumors afloat of a victory in the west over Rosencranz by Bragg, but we have been so often disappointed that we do not consider it safe to brag on Bragg, until something more definite is known.[22]

About five years ago, I remember writing out a kind of history of my future life. And according to that history I would now be in the far west, but I went South. I intended to spend about one year there. I liked the South, I found nothing existing as I had heard it represented, and I concluded to make my home there. Soon the dark clouds of war arose and grew blacker and blacker until the muttering of the storm could be heard in the distance, and then it was that I saw that there was no alternative but war or disgrace and everlasting dishonor for the South, and embraced the first opportunity of becoming a soldier in the confederate army, and can truly say that I

22. Bragg won a resounding victory over W. S. Rosecrans (not Rosencranz) in the Battle of Chickamauga, September 19–20, 1863.

have never for a moment regretted the course I have pursued, although had I returned North at the commencement of the hostilities, I would have had the benefit of a thorough education, which I fear that I now never will have. The time that has been devoted to my country might have been spent in acquiring knowledge which would have been more advantageous to me individually than anything I have learned or will learn in the army, but then, I have the consciousness within my bosom of having done right which amply repays me for all I have lost.

Sunday Night, 20th. Young, healthy and active, of a lively disposition, gay and careless, light hearted (and for all I know, light headed also), still I am subject to fits of despondency and gloom when I hate the light and trivial things by which I am surrounded, when I care little for life and sometimes impiously wish that I had never been born. Perhaps the peculiar circumstances by which I am surrounded may account for these feelings. Here I am near the spot where I passed the sunny hours of childhood and the golden dreaming days of youth and under what circumstances—a prisoner of war. I am devoted to a cause that I esteem a just and holy one, and here is a kind father who I believe loves me as he loves his own life,—two sisters whose love for me is as pure as an Angel's love, and my brothers too,—yet all regard me as forever disgraced and dishonored. They consider my course a stain on the family name and with their every prayer for my safety is mingled a prayer for the speedy overthrow of the Southern cause. Their letters, too, give me much more pain than pleasure, telling me that I am worse than wasting the early years of my manhood. I do not mind these letters which speak reproachfully; I can answer them in the spirit they deserve. But when I read the letters of my sisters such as only a sister can write, not written in a spirit of reproach but speaking so sadly of the present and recalling to my mind the beautiful long ago, begging me with such simple, honest earnestness to come home, it is no wonder that I am sometimes sad. Should any other eye peruse these pages, they will doubtless pronounce these sentiments unworthy of a man; but do not judge harshly of these thoughts, nor smile that I put them on paper, unless you too have been placed in similar circumstances. I neither can nor will confide to any human being my joys and sorrows, so when my heart overflows with felicity or misfortune I take great pleasure in making these mute confidences on paper. But I hope and pray that ere long this prison life will cease, and I return to the land I love best, and then where the fire flashes hottest and the wounded lie thickest, I wish my friends to hear of me.

25th. Debating societies continue to be held, but are not so interesting as formerly, as the brave commander of the Post[23] will not allow any question to be debated which has any bearing on the present war or upon the Confederate States as an independent Government hereafter. (Bah!)

Cumberland Gap prisoners came in today. They seem to have been captured with all their dry goods about them.[24]

—Night—

This is indeed a lovely night. The moon, "Pale mistress of the Night" robed in fleecy clouds, rides the heavens in all her glorious majesty, and the rippling waters of the lake shine and sparkle as burnished silver, as they reflect the silvery light of the moon. On such a night as this my thoughts wander back to the happy days of last autumn. The moonlight promenades—the lovers' seat on the hill, where we used to sit and talk of friends near and dear to us who had fallen in battle.

27th. I am very prone to lament over miss-spent time, but thus it ever is. When the golden opportunities are passed, then and not until then do we realize the value of what we have lost. Our youth is gone almost before we know it. It is generally filled with ardent longings for manhood, and all its cares and responsibilities. We are then ambitious without any definite object in view, anxious to

23. Colonel W. S. Pierson, a Yale graduate, and former mayor of Sandusky.

24. Cumberland Gap, Tennessee, was captured by the Federals under General Burnside, September 8–10, 1863. The Confederate garrison of 2,500 men under J. W. Frazer surrendered unconditionally.

throw off the restraint of parental authority, and launch out for ourselves on life's tempestuous ocean. Soon, Ah, soon we find that the future is not what we pictured it to be. The flowers of youth become withered and dead, fond hopes and bright anticipations blasted. We can then see the golden opportunities that have passed unheeded by. If we wish the memory of the past to be pleasant we must improve the moments as they pass. We have every encouragement to work, for here in this fleeting world of change we may exert an influence for good that can never die.

"Press on—press on, nor doubt nor fear,
From age to age, this thought shall cheer
Whate'er may die and be forgot,
Work done for God, it dieth not."

Sunday October 4th. We are receiving additions to our number almost daily, some from the prison hospitals in and around Baltimore and some from the army of the West. We have several Generals here now: Major Gen. Trimble, Brig. Gen. Archer, Frazer, Beall, Jeff Thompson, and Jones. Gen'l. Trimble is really a noble specimen of manhood.[25] He has a real martial look about him. I am sorry to see him here, and especially to see him hobbling about on crutches, minus a leg, but he still looks hale and hearty, and I hope will long be spared to the Confederate cause. Good men are needed and we could ill afford to lose him. "Old Jeff" too, as the boys call him, though tall and slender is wiry and active, and looks able to brave a score of battles yet.

Oct. 10th. About seventy five officers came in today from Camp Chase,[26] met with an accident on the way resulting in the death of a Col. and the wounding of several other officers. Received a letter from Belle Monte. About a dozen officers came in who were

25. I. R. Tremble lost a leg at Gettysburg; J. J. Archer was captured in the same battle; J. W. Frazer surrendered Cumberland Gap to the enemy without a fight; W. N. R. Beall was captured at Port Hudson; M. J. Thompson of Missouri was captured in Arkansas; and J. R. Jones fell into enemy hands at Smithburg, Tennessee. Johnson's Island was primarily a prison for Confederate officers.
26. Camp Chase was a Federal prison at Columbus, Ohio.

captured around Charleston: [27] Last Friday about thirty of the privates who were confined here took the oath of allegiance to the Yankee government, and went out amid the taunts and jeers of their loyal companions in arms. We are glad to get rid of such men; they are worth nothing to either side and are despised by both Yankee and Southern men.[28]

13th. Election day in Ohio.[29] We had quite a lively time in the morning, holding a sham election and having several very spicy little speeches from McKnight, Houston, Fellows, and Col. Province.

14th. The following named chaplains left this morning for Dixie: Bouchelle, Granden, McGill and Perry. This evening Col. Davis of Virginia delivered a very interesting address on the subject of "The qualities of a general."

16th. A few prisoners came in from New Orleans; all belong to the trans-Miss. department.[30] The Herald today contains an account of recent movements of importance of the armies in Virginia in which they acknowledged being compelled to fall back some thirty or forty miles, losing some prisoners, stores and etc., and still with their usual inconsistency claim to have gained a decided advantage over us by the move.[31]

27. See above p. 125 n. 3.

28. John Dooley, a prisoner at Johnson's Island, recorded in his journal that one prisoner who took the "great oath" was "kicked downstairs by his room mates. . . ." J. T. Durkin, ed., *John Dooley Confederate Soldier* (Washington: Georgetown University Press, 1945), p. 158; hereinafter cited as Durkin, ed. *John Dooley.*

29. The candidates were John Brough and Clement L. Vallandigham.

30. The Confederate Trans-Mississippi Department was created in May, 1862, to include Texas, Indian Territory, Arkansas, Missouri, and West Louisiana. On February 9, 1863, Kirly Smith's command in West Louisiana and Texas was expanded to include the entire Trans-Mississippi Department. On March 7 Smith took command of all Confederate troops west of the Mississippi.

31. This a reference to the Bristoe Campaign, October 9 to November 9, 1863. Although this campaign had no significant results, it illustrates the principle of the offensive that made Lee such a great commander: "Although Meade had a numerical superiority of eight to five, he retreated about forty miles and permitted his adversary to destroy the railroad which it took a month to repair." G. J. Fiebeger, *Campaigns of the American Civil War* (West Point: United States Military Academy, 1914), p. 179.

17th. Had quite an interesting discussion in our bible class today, on the subject, Soul and Intellect. Intellect was defined as follows: "Wherever we find combination and conclusion, there is Intellect."

Friday 23rd. The day is cold, and dark and cheerless, fit day for the scene I have just witnessed, the execution of a deserter. It is said that he first deserted our army and joined the federals. Soon after that he deserted them and killed the Provost marshal who was attempting to arrest him. At half past two o'clock P.M. the Batallion was marched down and formed on three sides of a square on the beach in front of our quarters. The convict was led out, heavily ironed, and placed within the square just at the lake shore. The execution was delayed some time while the chaplain prayed and talked with him. He was then seated on his coffin, facing his executioners. At this time the suspense became painful in the extreme. His crime was for a time forgotten, and we saw only a fellow being, trembling on the verge of another world, with but a very few swiftly fleeting moments between him and eternity. A deathlike stillness prevailed, unbroken by a single sound. The command was given to fire and the roar of the volley echoed over the still waters of the bay, the convict fell back upon his coffin, a corpse. The Batallion then marched back to their quarters with the band playing that mournful dirge, "The dead march."

Sunday the 25th. This is a very dark and gloomy day, but I suppose that a person should not allow the day to have any controlling influences over his or her mind, but somehow I can't help it. I cannot see anything bright or cheering in the future on such days as this, but generally manage to call up some shadow of a half forgotten hope or fear and call it presentiment and thus manage to borrow what I can never hope to repay, trouble from the future, for to us the future never comes.

27th. Received a letter from Miss Sallie, all well at Inglewood, Belle Monte, and Clenmore.[32]

32. Since Patterson refers to Clenmore along with Inglewood and Belle Monte it must have been a plantation.

30th. The enlisted men all sent away this morning, destination Point Lookout,[33] this may be a preparatory step to an early exchange. One year ago this very hour, I was enjoying the society of Cousin Ella Edwards and Miss Mattie Fowler, and we were talking of happy days in the future, indulging in dreams, and at that time it little troubled me that there was a prison in the world.

31st. If a stranger were to look in on us this morning he would hardly think we were prisoners. While I am scribbling down a few thoughts, just to pass off the time, Mosely is sitting at my side, studying away at his French as though life depended on it. Just opposite sits my worthy friend, Ballentine, engaged in a novel, while at my left sit Dennis and Clark trying their skill at chess, Burtchell watching the game, and Captain Brown looking over the papers of the day. Farther down the room I see a table surrounded by parties playing whist, euchre, solitaire, and etc., and still beyond them Apperson and Adams writing letters. Thus we employ the time. Received a letter today from Miss K. containing the photograph for T.

[Page torn out containing the description of the second attempt to escape from the prison.][34]

. . . in the mud and water rather than attract the attention of the guard by calling for assistance. Unfortunately those outside the walls did not succeed in reaching the mainland and were discovered about daylight and sent again within the walls. This is the second attempt that has been made to escape.

8th. [*Nov., 1863*] Have been out this morning assisting to dig a grave for Lieut. Barnett, who died yesterday evening after an illness of only a few days.[35] While digging the grave a party of

33. Point Lookout was a Federal prison in Maryland.

34. Most attempts to escape were made during the winter months when the lake was frozen solid and cold guards either huddled in their sentry boxes or left their posts.

35. The cemetery was located near the northeast point of the island. Today it contains the graves of 206 Confederate soldiers who died on the island while prisoners of war.

ladies and gentlemen (I suppose I must call them so, it is customary) visited the burying ground. Besides this we had a visit from two gentlemen from the town of Monroe, Michigan, and a person (I cannot call him a gentleman) from Sandusky. When this person come up to where we were at work his first remark was "You would not be so lively, would you boys, if you were digging a grave for a white man?" One of our party replied that we were digging it for a white man. "Why," said he, "you don't call a rebel a white man do you?" "Yes, sir," said Capt. Ballantine, "as white as you and much more of a gentleman." The old fellow said that he did not notice that we were prisoners, as we had no guard with us, or he would have made no such remark. We told him that it made the matter no better by placing it in that light. Soon after this conversation, he commenced telling us of a cousin he had in the army in Mississippi, and asking if any of us had ever met him, when up stepped Billie Avant and putting on the real Yankee whine said, "Look-a-here, stranger, is this here cousin of *yourn* a white man?" This used the old fellow up completely and he had nothing more to say. A gentleman was baptised this evening in the Lake by Rev. Littlebury Allen.

9th. Received a letter today from Miss Mattie B.; says she will send me some books in a day or two. These will be very acceptable, especially if I have to remain here during the winter. There is a great deal of sickness here now. Pneumonia seems to be the prevailing disease, and nearly every case proves fatal. No one from the 9th Alabama delegation has died yet, and I hope that we may all live to return to our regiment.

Tuesday the 10th. First snow of the season, snow fell to the depth of an inch but did not remain on the ground twenty four hours. Several died at the hospital last night.

12th. The Yankees have had a section of a battery in a position to command the channel all day. They refuse to deliver express packages. It is reported that they anticipate an attack from Canada.[36] Sutler was ordered today to close his business within twenty four hours.

14th. About a hundred officers came in last night; they are from the army in Virginia and were captured on the Rappahannock. They are all from Ewell's corps and are North Carolinians and Louisianians.[37] The Yankees are at work fortifying on the peninsula opposite the island, constructing works close to the light house. They now have several pieces of artillery in position along the beach besides a large force of infantry on the island. They refuse to allow any newspapers to come in, and are nearly frightened to death.[38] Yesterday the "Rebel Thespians" played the battle of Get-

36. The small steamer, the U.S.S. "Michigan" stationed on Lake Erie, was the only Federal warship on the Great Lakes and Confederate authorities were quick to see her value. As early as February, 1863, a plan was proposed for the capture of the "Michigan" but this undertaking had to be abandoned. Then in August of the same year Secretary of War J. A. Seddon and Secretary of Navy S. R. Mallory suggested to Lieutenant R. D. Minor of the Confederate navy a plan for seizing the "Michigan" and using her guns to force the release of the prisoners on Johnson's Island. Twenty-two men supplied with $110,000 in gold were sent to Canada in October. After establishing contact with the prisoners through the columns of the *New York Herald,* the party (its numbers increased by escaped confederate prisoners found in Canada) planned to "embark on one of the lake passenger steamers, overpower her officers, and use the captured ship to take the Michigan." But the Canadian government got wind of this plot and informed Washington. Immediately troops were rushed to the Great Lakes region and the area defenses strengthened. The plot to free the prisoners on Johnson's Island thus had to be abandoned just as it was about to be put into effect. Shuffer, ed., *Adventures of a Prisoner,* pp. 79–80; Philip Van Doren Stern, *Secret Missions of the Civil War* (New York: Bonanza Books, 1959), pp. 201–2; hereinafter cited as Stern, *Secret Missions.* See also R. W. Winks, *Canada and the United States: The Civil War Years* (Baltimore: Johns Hopkins Press, 1960); F. J. Shepherd, "The Johnson's Island Plot, An Historical Narrative of the Conspiracy of the Confederates, in 1864, to capture the U.S. Steamship Michigan on Lake Erie, and Release the Prisoners of War in Sandusky Bay," *Publications of the Buffalo Historical Society,* IX (1906), 1–51.

37. These officers were captured in the fighting at Rappahannock Bridge and Kelly's Ford (Bristoe Campaign) November 7, 1863. Ewell, in these two minor engagements involving two of his divisions, lost in killed, wounded, and captured 2,023 men, a "figure that outraged the Second Corps and shocked the entire army." Freeman, *Lee's Lieutenants,* III, 267.

38. See above pp. 143–44, n. 36.

tysburg. The piece was well written and reflects credit on Lieut. Peeler, the author.[39]

17th. All is still bustle and excitement around our island home. There are now about two thousand infantry besides several batteries guarding us, and I do not know but we are furnishing employment for about as many of Abe's soldiers as we could manage in the field, and with this advantage, that Abe is feeding both sides. We receive re-enforcements occasionally, sent us no doubt by "Uncle Jeff" for strategic purposes. The Vallandigham fleet, that great "bug bear" which has so terrified the Yankee nation for the past few days, has not yet made its appearance, but they seem to be expecting it as they have been practicing with solid shot and shell lately for the purpose of getting the exact range of the channel through which the boats must pass in approaching the island.

21st. The Yankees have got over their big fright, and the regiment of militia which had been stationed here for some time was sent away last night.[40]

24th. Weather quite mild and pleasant. Have been writing some "dime letters," or in other words, letters of four pages. The examining clerks will read a letter of any length provided they find money enclosed in the letter to pay for it, at the rate of two and a half cents per page, and although this seems to be a very small matter, they make several dollars a day at it. Letters of over one

39. "The Battle of Gettysburg" enjoyed a successful run of three weeks. A minstrel band known as the "Rebellonians" also provided entertainment from time to time, always playing to crowded houses. But, said one prisoner, "we never succeeded in putting on a first class ballet," H. Carpenter, "Plain Living at Johnson's Island," *Century Magazine,* XLI (November, 1890 to April, 1891), 712; hereinafter cited as Carpenter, "Plain Living."

40. See above p. 144 n. 36. The "Vallandigham fleet" mentioned in the entry of November 17 is a reference to the Confederate plan to use captured vessels to free the prisoners on Johnson's Island. Clement L. Vallandigham was a controversial Ohio politician. He was a member of the Knights of the Golden Circle (a secret order of southern sympathizers in the North) and a bitter critic of Lincoln who once banished him to the Confederacy.

page in length from our friends come through the same channel and are paid for at the same rate.[41]

29th. I have seated myself in the middle of this large room to try to write a few lines but am afraid I will have to give it up, for the ink freezes as fast as I write, and I have such a "buck ager" that I cannot hit the lines half the time. The ground is covered with snow, and the air is bitter cold and here we are without a stick of wood, unable to build a fire, and will have to go without our dinner, not because we haven't the rations but because we haven't the wherewith to cook them with. Some of the boys are in their bunks trying to keep warm by putting on all of their clothing and wrapping up in a blanket, others by double quicking up and down the room and as might be expected, none of them in a very good humor. My friend Brown is in bed with his overcoat on, and rolled up in three or four blankets,[42] trying to read "what will he do with it?" He holds the book in one hand, while he has the fingers of the other hand in his mouth trying to coax the blood into circulation once more. After all, if those who howl so about the treatment of Yankee prisoners in Richmond could see us today it would afford them great satisfaction. A writer in the National Intelligence says, "Let the howls of rebel officers on Johnson's Island mingle with the cries of the half starved union heroes in Richmond." What a christian spirit.[43]

41. All letters to and from Johnson's Island were limited to one page in length and were censored. If the letters were found in order, they were stamped with "Examined" and initialed by the censor. But, as Patterson points out, the letters could be longer if the prisoner had the money to bribe the examining clerks. On the other hand if the money were not available and the letters were too long, the prisoner was placed on the "black-list," which meant the stoppage of his mail. In many ways this was the most severe punishment a prisoner could receive. Carpenter, "Plain Living," pp. 712–13.

42. Not until 1865 were blankets a scarce item at Johnson's Island. Downer, "Johnson's Island," p. 205.

43. During the winter of 1863–64 some one thousand Federal officers were crowded into Libby Prison in Richmond. This three-story warehouse on the bank of the James River was originally intended to serve only as a place of temporary confinement. Belle Isle, on an island in the James River, also served as a prison. Richmond was always congested with prisoners, but the situation became so critical by 1863 that it was decided to set up a prison compound in Georgia (Andersonville).

December 1st. Good news. Gen'l. Morgan has made his escape from the penitentiary, and the "Yanks" will have to be pretty sharp if they get him again. Woe to the Yanks that fall into his hands; they will pay dearly for his treatment while a prisoner. Received three letters today, two from the South and one from Maryland. Chandler says that he is about to send me some money. I have a faint recollection of having seen something of this kind years ago, when I was a small boy. No such thing is known here now. The word money is marked "obsolete" in all the late dictionaries calculated for this meridian, a word formerly used to denote coin, used as currency; still I would like to have some, more out of curiosity than anything else.

5th. After a day or two of pleasant weather, it has again become extremely cold, and we are again threatened with a "wood famine," and tables and benches are in imminent danger of being sacrificed to meet the increasing demand for wood, to say nothing of our bunks, or as they may more properly be termed, "shelves," on which we lay ourselves away at night, after the labors of the day are over, which labor consists in having nothing to do all day and nothing to do it with. Yesterday brought me a nice letter from one of my lady friends in Kentucky, and also another white winged messenger from the South, both of which I intend answering very soon as by a system of financiering which would have done credit to a secretary of the treasury, I have managed to get hold of a ten cent "shin plaster" [44] which if judiciously expended in purchasing stamps and paper will enable me to write two letters and still have one cent left, which I will deposit as a sinking fund to be drawn upon in case of absolute necessity.

6th. Postage stamps are above par, and the dime I had intended to dispose of so advantageously has purchased only two stamps and nothing remains. I once thought that the tales told me on the Yankees about making wooden nutmegs and basswood hams were

44. Shinplasters were small paper notes, usually in denominations from five to fifty cents.

fabulous, but when I see the Yankee retailing postage stamps @ five cent piece each, as they do here, I am ready to believe anything.[45]

8th. Last night about one hundred and thirty officers came in. A large number of them belong to the Florida Brigade, and were captured at Lookout Mountain and Mission[ary] Ridge, during the late battles in the West.[46]

10th. I can see no reason why there should be so much sickness here at this season of the year. Some attribute it all to the climate, but I am compelled to lay the blame at the door of these Yankees. I am told by the surgeons at the hospital that it is often impossible to get such medicine as is absolutely necessary to check a disease and save a patient's life, and thus many valuable lives are lost that might be saved. Something is wrong somewhere or men would not be dying at the rate of four and five a day.[47]

I have noticed since I have been in the army, and more especially perhaps since I have been a prisoner, that where a large number of men are thrown together, entirely cut off from the society of ladies, that they seem to forget themselves and make use of language that they would not think of using at home, or in the presence of ladies. I have also been pained to see men, professing to be gentlemen, speak lightly and thoughtlessly a lady's name in a mixed crowd. Every one has seen or known of instances during their life time, of where a few words lightly spoken, and in jest perhaps, has blasted the reputation of a woman forever. Although I am far from being what I should be, no one can justly accuse me of this fault. I make it a rule never to say anything of any woman which I do not know to

45. Wooden nutmegs and basswood hams refer to anything false or fraudulent.

46. Lookout Mountain (November 24, 1863) and Missionary Ridge (November 25, 1863) were Federal victories in the Chattanooga Campaign of October–November, 1863.

47. Only in the fall of 1863 was the hospital crowded. During this period the health conditions were at their worst. The total number of deaths during the whole of Johnson's Island, however, was only 221 from approximately 12,000 men. At Elmira, New York 2,963 out of 12,123 succumbed to sickness, exposure, and associated causes. Downer, "Johnson's Island," p. 209; James I. Robertson, "The Scourge of Elmira," *Civil War History* (June, 1962), VIII, 200

be the truth, and never make any allusion to any of my lady friends which I think they themselves would blush to hear. There is nothing more disgusting than to hear a lady's name bandied about from lip to lip by gentlemen who pride themselves on being very intimate with their lady acquaintances and for fear that everybody will not know it, persist in using their names on every occasion, without taking the precaution of prefixing the Mrs. or Miss. Woman's friendship is too priceless a treasure to be lightly thought of, or hastily thrown aside. And I pity the man who cannot say with truth, that he has at least one good, kind, warm hearted lady friend.

December 11th. One year ago today, I was sitting on the hill near Dr. Taylor's house, watching the bombardment of Fredericksburg. It was one of the grandest sights that I have ever witnessed, but I hope that I may never witness another like it. All day from forty minutes past five o'clock A.M. more than a hundred pieces of artillery thundered forth their missiles of death into the doomed city, balls went crashing through church steeples, through dwelling houses and in fact, everywhere, driving the citizens into the cellars for protection, "while ever and anon" a fiendish yell of hellish delight from the Yankees told when another building was in flames. And amid all that storm of shot and shell, stood Barksdale [48] and his men who have so often proved themselves worthy sons of glorious Mississippi, disputing inch by inch the ground with these Yankees.

Tonight I am sitting up in the hospital with a sick friend, and not likely to hear the thunder of artillery soon. At least I am afraid I will not.

13th. Last night one of the Yankee sentinels shot an adventurous yank who was prowling about during the night, probably trying to steal something; unfortunately however, he was only wounded, and it is feared that it will not prove fatal.

15th. Received a box of clothing from Miss Tena Crum, for which I am thankful enough; also a few books from Miss Mollie

48. General Barksdale was killed at Gettysburg.

King. Yesterday during the heavy gale a new building on which the Yanks were at work came down with a crash, annihilating one and wounding several. "Small favors thankfully received, large ones in proportion."

17th. 3 o'clock A.M. at the hospital. All this long winter night have I been sitting here by the fire, reading, writing and thinking, the wind howls and whistles around the house mournfully enough and the waves of Erie beat and break against the rocky shore with never ceasing roar, while the snow and sleet pattering against the window and forcing their way through every crevice makes one thankful for fire and shelter even in a prison. My thoughts have wandered far tonight, to Alabama and to Virginia and sometimes to old La Porte in this my native state. I have been thinking of the old homestead, and of the friends who nightly gather around the old hearth stone. In days gone by I formed one of the group, but times have changed, and I will change my thoughts and think of the happy days spent in Alabama and Virginia. What good old times I used to enjoy in old Lauderdale. How I would enjoy a visit with my good friend Mr. Whitsett, what tales I would have to unfold, tales of battles won and battles lost, of midnight marches, of hardships endured and occasionally of pleasures enjoyed. What tales of prison life, of scenes at Fort Delaware and Johnson's Island. Yes, I would like to be once again in my little room at Mr. Whitsett's and feel myself at home.[49] At home, did I say?—I am at home anywhere. (Northern prisons excepted). Richmond has become one of my homes, and so has Inglewood and Belle Monte. If ever again sick or wounded, let my lot be cast in no pleasanter places than Alabama or Virginia.

18th. This is real winter weather; the snow is falling thick and fast and "out of doors" looks cheerless enough. Lieut. Cherry better today. Capt. Smith taken sick very suddenly, erysipelas in his face. One eye entirely closed, and the other nearly so. Dewees received a nice box of eatables, a portion of which "I fell heir to."

49. See above pp. v–ix, xiii–xix.

19th. Last night for the first time this winter, the bay was frozen from the Island to Sandusky. Paid a visit for the first time to the erysipelas ward in the hospital; there are about thirty patients there, and they present a sad appearance. Capt. Smith worse today.

20th. My friends, Capt. Mosely, Capt. Smith and Lieut. Cherry all improving. Several cases of the scarlet fever in the hospital now, and some are afraid to go there on that account, but I have never seen or heard of a disease that I would flinch from, if one of my friends had it and needed my assistance.

23rd. Midnight. Last night Gen'l. Archer and several others got outside the prison walls by bribing a sentinel, but the sentinel played them a real yankee trick, having men stationed near the lake to pounce upon them as soon as they should leave the wall; thus the sentinel and his party received a fine gold watch and a hundred dollars in green back.[50]

25th. This is the first Christmas that found me in limbo and I sincerely hope that it will be the last. "Nary drop" of "eggnog." But thanks to some of my Mississippi friends I have had a nice dinner, as any one could wish for anywhere. I had anticipated eating my Christmas dinner in Virginia, and of course was disappointed; still I have much to be thankful for. About two hundred boxes came in by express today filled with eatables and Christmas gifts. It makes me a little mad to think I cannot get anything, not even a letter of condolence while others are getting so much.

26th. Brown, Butchell and Adams received boxes today and we have had quite a day of feasting.

Sunday 27th. Rev. L. W. Allen preached in this Block to quite a large congregation. After the sermon, quite a large number of mourners went forward and three of them professed to have found

50. Another account has it that Archer had to return to the island when the ice on the lake began to crack. Durkin, ed., *John Dooley,* p. 153.

faith in believing. There seems to be much interest manifested by nearly all the prisoners here on the subject of religion. Why is it that I am not interested, why is it that I can sit perfectly unmoved and listen to sermons of the ministers here day after day? I know that every word they say is true, my mind assents to every truth they utter, I acknowledge everything and try to examine my own heart to see what I shall do. If I had felt the least inclination to go forward as a mourner I would have gone, but I did not. I feel sometimes that I am a christian, and then I can realize the feelings of a christian as they tell of their happiness and their hopes of heaven. At other times I doubt my being a christian, as one of our ministers said the other day that a man was not a true christian who could not point to the very day when he became converted, and everyone feels a great change within their own heart at the moment his sins are forgiven, as would be experienced by a man coming from total darkness to the broad light of the noon-day sun. I have never experienced this feeling and still down in the very deepest depths of my heart I wish to be a christian.

29th. Night. A very interesting prayer meeting was held in our room last night. About a dozen mourners went forward, among whom was myself. If I am not a christian I am determined to become one. I feel like consecrating myself entirely to the service of God. I cannot understand my feelings entirely. After a conversation with some of the preachers, I have determined to unite myself with the Church. Among the mourners last night were Lieuts. Sharp and Gamble, for whom I have often prayed.

31st. Night. It is proper and right that as time hurries on toward that bourne from whence no traveller has ever yet returned, to let our minds wander back over our past life. I am startled to see how swiftly time has been passing. One year ago tonight I was sitting in my tent writing, thinking then as now of

"Forms and scenes of long ago."

Then I was with my command, and although our duties were anything but pleasant, still I had nothing to complain of. Then, as now, I was writing in my journal, recording the scenes of my every day life while doing picket duty on the banks of the classic Rappahannock. Now, I am a prisoner of war on the little island of Lake Erie, and with a prospect before me anything but cheering; entirely separated and cut off from the outside world, unable to take any active part in the struggle which is still going on between justice and injustice, right and wrong, freedom and oppression, unable to strike a blow in the glorious cause of Southern independence.

Now, the end of the war seems more distant than ever. Time only shows on the part of the abolition government a firmer determination than ever to subjugate; while on the other hand time only shows on the part of the South a stronger determination to fight to the bitter end, trusting alone to the god of battles for success at last. And we *will* succeed. Who will say that a country such as ours, rich in everything that makes a nation great and prosperous, a country with broad valleys unequalled in fertility by any others upon which the sun shines, a country abounding in natural fortresses and inhabited by eight millions of brave people determined to be free and willing to sacrifice everything even life itself upon the altar of their country, united as no people ever were before, I ask, who will say, in view of all this, that the South will not be free. I engaged in this war firmly believing that the South would be successful and now after nearly three years of war, I find that time has only served to strengthen that opinion. I believe that winter will pass and spring come again with its verdure and flowers—I believe it as I believe anything that I see around me,—the fair fields of the South may be transformed to deserts, and the places where now may be seen stately edifices, tokens of wealth and refinement, may be made as howling wildernesses, Yankee hirelings may occupy every state, every County in the South, they may occupy our state capitols and our seaport towns,—but our hill tops and hollows,—never. We will carry on the war even there.

During the year that is just closing, many battles have been fought and many, many thousands of the young men of the South have fallen. Their bones lie bleaching in the sun on the fields of Chancellorsville, Fredericksburg, Gettysburg, Vicksburg, Chickamauga, and in fact all over our land from the Potomac to the Rio Grande may be seen the soldiers' graves. No sculptured slab of marble marks their last resting place, but they are not forgotten, and the memory of their deeds will ever be cherished by a grateful people, and the story of their deeds will be handed down from sire to son as long as noble deeds are admired and respected by mankind. When I think of the many thousands who have fallen in battle and the still greater number who have sickened and died from disease during the year my heart is filled with love and gratitude to that God who has so mercifully spared my life until this time. Surely he has covered my head in the day of battle, —why is it? All that I have and am belongs to God, and even now, as I think, I thank God for the capacity of thinking and writing.

In a few short hours the year 1863 will be numbered with the years that are past. Its great events, its battles won and its battles lost, its fields of carnage and bloodshed, its mighty hopes and expectations, its fond anticipations, its sin and sorrow, its suffering and toil are almost ended. They have passed before us, shifting scenes in the great drama of life, and as the year 1864 opens up before us, we will miss many actors who have figured conspicuously before the country, during the year. The one most missed will be Jackson. He is fallen. The places that once knew him will know him no more forever. Never has the army before or since been half so much affected as it was by his death. They could look defeat cheerfully in the face knowing that finally they would triumph, but when Stonewall Jackson died, a sad and solemn gloom seemed to hang over our entire army, and this feeling pervaded the hearts of all. We will always have to acknowledge the battle of Chancellorsville, though such a brilliant victory, dearly won by the death of this God-like man. Many have been swept from the stage of action and the cry goes up from many bleeding hearts, "Oh, Lord, how long?" Our brothers go halting by on crutches; our husbands, our fathers languish and die in the hundreds and thousands of hospitals scattered all over the South. And again the cry, "Oh, God, stay thy hand!" And still the war goes on.

We have met with many reverses during the year, but the spirit of our people remains unbroken, and always rises equal to the occasion. We are learning to bear misfortune, and we must expect to bear still more. I expect to see during the coming year a larger portion of our country subjected to Yankee rule than has been at any previous time. Our armies are growing smaller day by day, and we have not the men to supply the places of those who fall in battle. It seems to me that we should fight only when some decided and important result is to be obtained, and save men as much as possible. Meanwhile our people at home where the foe has possession should remain quiet, take no step toward forming a state government in accordance with Lincoln's directions,[51] treat all citizens of the U.S. as invaders and enemies, let them have nothing except what is taken by force, show no desire to have anything to do with the U.S. Government, and the Yankees will soon find that it will require a standing army in every Southern state to enforce their laws. A great party will be raised up in the North who will demand that the war shall cease, and it will cease. Such a party is growing now, and is becoming stronger every day. But enough, 'tis almost midnight and as soon as the New year comes, I must lay myself away on my shelf.

51. In December, 1863, Lincoln issued his amnesty proclamation outlining the steps southern states could follow to get back in the Union. This became known as his 10 per cent plan.

· X ·

"I am worn out with this prison life"

January 1, 1864, to October 6, 1864

Jan. 1st 1864. As I turn over a new leaf in my journal, so may I in my life. This year is like the page before me, pure and spotless, all as yet. A blank. Who can tell what may be written on it before the year closes. This year opens up before us dark and gloomy. We can not, nor should not, wish to lift the curtain that hides from us the future. A kind Providence has mercifully hidden from us the blood and the tears and suffering which the future will disclose. Battles are to be fought and fields are to be deluged with blood; we know it, we realize it in its full force, but the darkest hour is just before day, and out of this universal gloom and thick darkness I believe that we as a nation will soon emerge into the glorious light of peace and prosperity. The New Year asserts its rule with vigor; last night it was warm and misty, but about midnight the weather became colder and by morning was terribly cold, and has been growing colder every hour, and now, at sun down, mercury indicates twenty two degrees below zero.

10th. Col. Lewis preached to a very large and attentive audience: text, "At evening time it shall be light." Made an application of the text to our present difficulties.

11th. Anniversary of the secession of Alabama, and gloriously has she sustained herself during the last three years of trial. The fires of patriotism still glow unquenchably in the bosom of every true son and daughter of that lovely, noble state.

21st. Today the great snow battle came off. Lower forces commanded by Col. G. Troup Maxwell and the upper forces by Gen. Jeff Thompson, resulting in a drawn battle after half a day's hard fighting and a large number of sore heads and black eyes.

February 1st, 1864. L. B. Johnson [the sutler] brought in a lot of pictures of the Island and its surroundings and enforced their sale in the following manner: A man would go there to trade with him, perhaps to buy some tobacco or some papers, or no matter what, he would hand one of these pictures and tell you if you would buy one for three dollars he would sell you other articles, but unless you did buy one he would not open an account with you, and as those who had money outside could only make it available through the sutler, he succeeded in selling quite a number of his pictures. All this was done by Col. Pierson, but as soon as the facts were made known to Col. Bassett,[1] commanding the post, he compelled the sutler to take them back and pay money for them.

9th. First installment of officers left this place, destination probably Point Lookout.

22nd. This day was celebrated by both yankees and rebels, the former by firing big guns and listening to the reading of Washington's farewell address—the latter by listening to speeches appropri-

1. Colonel I. C. Bassett, Eighty-second Pennsylvania Volunteers, evidently was in charge of Federal forces on Johnson's Island at the time and Lieutenant Colonel W. S. Pierson of "Hoffman's Battalion had control of the administrative powers of the prison." *O.R.*, VI, Ser. II, 902–3.

ate to the occasion delivered by Capt. Fellows, Col. Lewis and Lieut. Houston. It seems to me right and proper that Southern men should celebrate this day as the birthday of the first original "Rebel," a man who fought for the same principles for which we are fighting. But for the Yankees to celebrate it is very mockery. I cannot conceive of anything more out of place. They celebrate the birthday of a Southern gentleman and a slaveholder, and this while they are straining every nerve to tear down what he built up, while they are laboring to destroy every vestige of constitutional and to establish a military despotism over a part of the lands for which he fought. And these yankees, who are so loud in their hurrahs, have planted their impious footsteps on the soil of his own native state and have even robbed his last resting place. *We* have *two* reasons for celebrating this day. We hail it as the anniversary of the birth of our young republic, the day on which Jefferson Davis was first elected President of the provisional government of the Confederate States.[2] In honoring the name of Washington we cannot forget the name of Davis; these two names will be handed down side by side to posterity as long as history shall endure and will be honored and admired as long as noble deeds and undying love of country shall meet the admiration of mankind.

March 2nd. Received the first news of the victory in Florida.[3] It is reported that there will be preaching in the prison by a Yankee divine next Sabbath. I do sincerely hope that no confederate officer will attend. After dragging our own ministers from the pulpit and thrusting them in prison, simply because they would not pray God's blessing on old Abe, I think they could offer us no more gross or greater insult than to offer to preach their Yankee religion to us. The idea of a man getting up before a congregation composed entirely of confederate officers and praying for the overthrow of the cause for which they have sacrificed everything. (And if they do

2. On February 9, 1861, Davis was elected provisional President of the Confederacy. His inauguration took place in Montgomery, Alabama, two days later. Then in October of the same year he was elected permanent President. His second inauguration occurred in Richmond on February 22, 1862.

3. Olustee (Ocean Pond), Florida, February 20, 1864.

not pray thus they act the hypocrite.) It is simply out of the question. As for myself, I want no advice on religious matters from any one who at the same time is urging yankees to join in the attempt to subjugate us, and who upholds the damning deeds of Abe Lincoln and his army. Besides we have plenty of preachers here of our own, Southern men, and the long and short of the matter (as a negro said the other day, when looking at one of their tracts with a big yankee flag on the cover) "It ain't our religion no how."

3rd. Big Dixie Mail. Received a letter from Miss Sallie Q. Good news from the South—all the troops re-enlisting for the war.

8th. Well, the yankee preached sure enough and I understand had about fifty listeners. No comment necessary. Joined the B.S.C.[4]

10th. This morning the Yankees ordered a detail to be made from the several Blocks to build a road from the lower gate up through the prison yard, but all refused to have anything to do with it and they gave it up.

12th. Today closes another week of the "living death." Time drags heavily. I can't tell how I would have managed to get along even with the assistance of my friends in Kentucky, had it not been for my friend Capt. Moseley, from the 2nd Florida. Others in the prison have done considerable for me, but none so much as "Mose." He it is that furnishes me in tobacco, in postage stamps, in paper and envelopes and in fact whenever I want anything I go to him for it. I wish all who profess to be friends of mine to regard him with special favor. "Long may he wave, etc."

4. The editor was unable to identify specifically the "B.S.C." but in all probability it stood for something like Block Security Committee or Court (see diary entry for June 8, 1864). At least two other prisoners on Johnson's Island at this time make references in their journals to the organization of a "Court" by the prisoners themselves for the trial of offenses committed in the barracks. Shuffer, ed., *Adventures of a Prisoner,* p. 82; Durkin, ed., *John Dooley,* p. 151.

17th. Last night the negro Fred Douglass [5] spoke in Sandusky; his theme, "The mission of the war." The Sandusky Register says that he had a very appreciative audience, and I don't doubt it. I learn that Sergt. Joe McMurray, who lost a leg at Gettysburg, was among the number exchanged the other day. I am very glad to hear this, for he has already suffered enough. He is a good, noble, brave soldier, and shall never want for anything while I have it in my power to assist him.

March 20th. My 22nd birthday.

" 'Tis greatly wise to talk with our past hours,
And ask them what report they bore to heaven,
And how they might have borne more welcome news."

'Tis twenty two years today since I made my advent into this breathing world and became one among the millions of actors on the world's great stage, upon which is being played the great drama of life which shall have its grand finale in eternity. Twenty two years gone, and how little I have accomplished! It is with a feeling of sadness that I view the scene which memory too faithfully spreads before me. When I realize what I am and contrast it with what I *might have been,* I pronounce my life a failure. I see so many priceless moments wasted, and these in the morning of life when they are most precious. How true it is that,

"We take no note of time, but from its loss."

But I love to compare one year with another and one birthday with another, to see what changes have taken place in and around me. Until my seventeenth birthday each had been spent at home. My eighteenth in Alabama at Mr. Whitsett's. My nineteenth in the dry goods store at C. & J. Higgins,[6] and behind the counter all day. My twentieth with a party of friends, visiting the tomb of Madison in Virginia. My twenty first at Scott's dam on the Rappahannock, in

5. Frederick Douglass was a free Negro who was very active in the anti-slavery crusade. He edited an abolitionist newspaper. At one time he was employed by the Massachusetts Anti-Slavery Society as a lecturer.

6. See above p. xvii.

command of my company, and this my twenty second finds me where I hope never another will find me, on Johnson's Island in a federal prison.

26th. For the first time in several days, we have had communication by boat with Sandusky.

30th. United with the Church.

April 3rd. During the week just passed, I have received letters from Miss Kate, Miss Tena, Miss Mattie, and from Cousin Josie and Lizzie, one from home and one from my "sweet heart"——, also one from my old "Chum" H. M. Bassett,[7] now signing himself Asst. Surgeon in one of Lincoln's regiments. These letters have served to make the week pass quite pleasantly. The sutler came in and sold goods on only one day in the week. His sales for the day amounted to over Three Thousand Dollars.

8th. Prayer meeting at each Block at nine o'clock A.M. Preaching in our Block at 10 o'clock; day very generally regarded by all as a day of fasting and prayer.

10th. Received a letter from Miss Kate, and through her heard from friends in the South. We have had no flag of truce for a long time, and that is enough to give us the blues.

14th. It is now four days since we have had a mouthful of meat of any kind, and no prospect that we will have any soon. I am getting as lean as "jobe's Turkey."

15th. I must hasten to record that the Yankees have just issued a day's rations of beef to us. Our Young Men's Christian Association met this morning, had a very interesting meeting.[8]

7. A cousin.

8. The "Young Men's Christian Association of Johnson's Island, Ohio" was an interdenominational group whose principal aim was to look after the sick and needy among the prisoners. The society also cultivated religious, social, and literary interests among its members. Its constitution required an original address or essay to be read at each weekly meeting by a member or invited friend. Shuffer, ed., *Adventures of a Prisoner,* pp. 82–83.

23rd. About one hundred and fifty officers left here this morning (sick and disabled). I understand that it is for exchange. Among the number were Lieut. McBride and Capt. Chisholm from the old 9th.

30th. Received a box from Miss Tena C., containing clothes, eatables, and etc., all of which were very acceptable.

May 2nd. Strange weather. Only yesterday the weather was so warm that we were all out in our shirt sleeves, in fact a coat was uncomfortable. Today an overcoat is comfortable, and there is a snow storm going on, and in fact one can hardly realize that it is not mid winter.

3rd. Prayer meetings are being held almost every day, for the special purpose of invoking God's blessing on our arms during the coming campaign and to thank him for the successes already gained; more especially however, the object is to pray for the success in Virginia, that our army there may go forth conquering and to conquer, and that we may there gain a victory which will give us peace. After attending these meetings I feel better satisfied. Today as one brother prayed that God would spare to us Gen'l. Lee, that he would cover his head in the day of battle and give him wisdom to direct his army aright, I felt that even then that God had answered the prayer. I feel almost certain that our noble Lee will live to see his work accomplished, to see the South free and independent.

May 5th. I have today listened to one of the most eloquent and instructive lectures which it has been my good fortune to hear. It was delivered by Col. L. M. Lewis, before the Y.M.C.A. He pictured a glorious future for the young men of the South, if they only prove true to themselves.

6th. Last night Captain Fellows, in compliance with a request from the officers of this block, delivered an address on the state of our country, and our duties to it. It was a very stirring address and the Block was crowded and all listened with marked attention. I have seen but very few men in my life who were his equal in debate, and then he is a natural orator and uses the most elegant and chaste language. I would be in all my glory if I could speak as he can.

We begin to hear all kind of rumors in regard to movements of the armies in Virginia. Some say the two armies are fighting,[9] other rumors have it that Meade[10] has succeeded in crossing the Rapid Ann[11] and has the force drawn up in line of battle near the old Chancellorsville battle ground;[12] nothing reliable is known. We are all in great suspense knowing that on this battle depends almost everything, among other things our deliverance from this prison.

8th. No news received yesterday that we can consider at all reliable, and as we receive no mail today we are of course left entirely to conjecture; all sorts of reports are being spread through the prison; no one can trace them. We feel pretty confident that our army will be victorious, but still cannot help but feel uneasy.

9th. All the news we get today is from the Sandusky register and a more muddy list of dispatches I never saw. It is perfectly impossible to form any correct idea of what has been done. All I can gather from the paper is that on last Thursday and Friday a severe battle was fought and I think from their account we must have got the best of it, as they say that Gen'l. Hill's corps[13] attacked them driving them back with great slaughter, but that afterwards they gained the ground.

9. After his selection as general in chief of the Armies of the United States in March, 1864, U. S. Grant devised a grand strategy to end the war. One phase of his plan called for a major drive in the East against Lee's Army of Northern Virginia. The first major engagement in the campaign to follow was the Battle of the Wilderness, May 5–7, 1864.

10. General George G. Meade commanded the Army of the Potomac but Grant directed its operations in the field.

11. Rapidan River.

12. The Battle of the Wilderness was fought in a region already scored by the Battle of Chancellorsville.

13. A. P. Hill.

10th. I really hoped and believed that today would bring us full accounts from the battles of last week, but if possible the dispatches were more unintelligible than yesterday. One thing is certain,—there has been hard fighting and heavy losses, but the paper says that no official accounts have been received, but says that it is believed that General Lee's army is falling back in the direction of Richmond.[14] Another dispatch states that Beast Butler has captured Petersburg, Virginia;[15] another dispatch, that the Yankees have advanced as far as Spottsylvania Courthouse; another that both armies are holding their same positions, confronting each other in line of battle. Still another that Longstreet is mortally wounded, being shot in the neck with a musket ball. They also state that Gen'l. Lee is wounded,[16] also that all their troops have been engaged, and that they have lost heavily but hope to be able to resist Lee's army. Of all this I think that there is nothing that can be relied upon. It is very *probable* that Gen'l. Lee will be the victor, but it is *possible* that he may not, and that is just as the case stands in my mind at present. I do not believe that the engagement is decided yet.

11th, 12th, 13th. Continued news of the battle raging in Virginia, the Yankees admitting that they are getting worsted, but still claim to be driving Lee towards Richmond.

14th. Morning papers contain an account of the terrible battle of Tuesday at Spottsylvania Courthouse, Yankees claim to have

14. In this spring campaign of 1864 Grant was able to drive Lee back to Petersburg-Richmond.

15. As part of Grant's over-all strategy for the final phase of the war, B. F. Butler was ordered to operate against Richmond from the south side of the James River. In operations around Drewry's Bluff, May 4–16, 1864, he was turned back by Confederate forces under General P. G. T. Beauregard. Butler then withdrew to Bermuda Hundred (northeast of Petersburg on the James).

16. Longstreet was seriously wounded on May 6, 1864, by his own men, almost precisely a year after Jackson had been mortally wounded under similar circumstances but a few miles away. The rumor that Lee had been wounded was false.

taken the place. Really this state of suspense and nervous excitement is wearing me down.[17]

2 o'clock P.M. The Sandusky Register has an extra out in which are reports dispatches purporting to come from Gen'l. Hancock[18] stating that he has captured Gen'l. Ed. Johnson's division[19] entire together with the officers commanding and thirty three pieces of artillery. Of course none of us believe this very improbable statement but we are fearful that they have had some little success on which to found this news. But though we all feel perfectly confident that Gen'l. Lee will win out, and that it is merely a question of time, still such reports have an unpleasant effect, and I do not like to hear them being circulated. Today while out at work improving the appearances of our prison cemetery, I met one of my old school mates, Ed. Thompason, a private in the 122th——.

Sunday night. *[May 15, 1864]* This is the third night I have watched with the sick in the hospital. Lieut. Jones is no better, and I am afraid he will have a very severe time of it, if indeed he recovers at all. Ruffin is nearly well, Bowen and McRae are still quite unwell.

Wild rumors are in circulation in regard to the movements of the armies in Virginia. All bad and no good; the latest is that Gen'l. Lee is retreating toward Danville, leaving Richmond, and Grant in hot pursuit. Of course none of us believe any of these reports but our fears are always ready to picture something dark and gloomy. There is however one good sign for our country. Prayer meetings, —largely attended,—are held daily and nightly in the prison for the special purpose of praying for the success of the armies defending the capitol. Many strong earnest prayers are offered up daily and I believe that almost every man in the prison, whether saint or sinner, has been praying sincerely and earnestly for the blessings of God on our noble army ever since the fighting commenced in Virginia.

17. Following the Battle of the Wilderness the armies of Lee and Grant engaged in bitter fighting around Spotsylvania Court House May 7–20, 1864.
18. Winfield S. Hancock.
19. Edward "Allegheny" Johnson was captured at Spotsylvania.

Never since the sound of the first shot echoed along the lovely valleys and wooded hills of Virginia has there been so bloody a sacrifice offered upon the altar of the God of war,—so fierce a struggle as is now raging.[20] Would to God that the people of the North would pause and think, but I have no hope that they will. Madness rules the hour. Why this terrible sacrifice of human life? —Why will they rebaptise Virginia in blood?—think of the last ten days. The sacred soil of Virginia has echoed to the tread of nearly half a million of men, armed and set in battle array to destroy each other. What a sight for the world, what a scene for God and the angels to look upon. And what a sight for devils in hell. 'Tis a bright May morning in Virginia, the glorious sun arises in beauty, Nature has put on her most beautiful garments, and the birds pour forth their songs of sweetest melody. The hills and the valleys are covered with a carpet of green, the dew drops sparkle like gems of silver in the sunshine—Soon, ah, too soon, this carpet of green, these hill sides and valleys will be stained with blood and hell with laughter loud shall ring long ere the setting of the sun. At an early hour the storm bursts forth, and all through the long day the lines sway to and fro like a monster serpent writhing in agony, and where all this beauty was before, now can be seen nothing but scenes of destruction and death. The sun goes down in blood, sets on a field red with carnage and hoarse with the groans of the dying. This is the record day after day.

During last week I received letters from home, from Miss Duval, and from the South; Miss D. tells me to call on her for anything I may need while a prisoner.

18th. It is quite amusing to read the editorials of the administration journals. They have had Lee retreating from Spottsylvania C.H. on several different occasions. Or at least they claim to have commenced fighting there and to have driven him all day, but

20. Grant's losses at the Wilderness and Spotsylvania numbered approximately 29,000 and by June 3 (Battle of Cold Harbor) the figure would reach at least 50,000. Lee, as a result of this incessant campaigning, lost around 32,000 men.

always wind up by reporting him in the vicinity of the Courthouse, and the only explanation that I can give is that Lee must have the place on wheels, and moves it about with him as he falls back.[21] It seems to be to him and to our army what the ark of the Covenant was to the children of Israel, and by and by—the Lee-vites [Levites] still have charge of it.

Two weeks ago the Cincinnati Times said that Grant had an army of over two hundred thousand men, and that he would make quick work of finishing Gen'l. Lee with his sixty thousand half starved troops. On the 14th inst., the same paper thanks God that Grant with an army of eighty thousand has been able to withstand the onslaught of Gen'l. Lee's army of one hundred and fifty thousand veterans. Ah, "Consistency thou art a jewel."

20th. About ten days since the Yankees came in and made up clubs to the following named papers: "New York News," "Cincinnati Enquirer," "Chicago Times," "Columbus Crises."[22] The subscription price to each, one dollar per month for the daily, and including the four papers there were about one hundred and thirty copies taken. The paper had just been coming five days when "Lo!", an order from the outside informed us that henceforth all papers of this class would be considered contraband, and the subscribers can now get neither money nor paper. The Yanks very graciously tell us that we can take the "Herald" or the "Tribune" or in fact any other administration paper, but none of us feel willing to subscribe not knowing how soon they might declare these contraband. A day or two since I received a package from Miss D. of Baltimore, containing paper, pens, stamps, envelopes, and other articles. These were very acceptable.

Sabbath, 22nd. Have listened with great interest today to a sermon by Col. L——. Text—"And having done all to stand." He divided his subject and spoke of the injunction, first from a social

21. The fighting around Spotsylvania raged from May 7–20 before Lee retired toward Richmond.
22. *Columbus Crisis* (not *Crises*).

point of view, then religiously. Have received during the past two days letters from Cousin Annie, Miss Tena C., and from some of my old friends at Point Lookout, all of which have been answered. Lieut. Jones who has been very sick but was (I thought yesterday) nearly well was taken much worse this morning and I am afraid he has much suffering still before him even if he succeeds in living through it.

27th. Three years ago today we (our company) received "marching orders," an order from Pope Walker [23] directing us to proceed immediately to Richmond, Va., and to report to Gen'l. R. E. Lee, who was at that time commanding in Western Va.[24] The order was afterwards changed; we reported to Gen'l. Johnson [25] at Winchester. I wish that some one whose order would be as effective would order us today to proceed immediately to Richmond and report to the same great man.

28th. Very little news from the army—learned a few days ago of the death of my Brigadier General; he was killed at the battle of Spottsylvania Court House.[26] Col. Forney of the 10th was also killed, and Col. Herbert of the 8th wounded. The Yankees have countermanded the order in regard to newspapers and the old order of things is restored.

29th. Sunday. The "patriotic" contemptible whelps who are guarding us seem to take a great delight in harrassing and annoying us in every conceivable manner. This morning, under the pretense of searching for ladders, they made a strict and thorough search of all our goods and chattels. After getting us all outside to roll call, they stationed a guard at each door to prevent any one from coming in the house and then a "shoulder strapped" gent for each block commenced their work going into carpet sacks, trunks and boxes in a manner that would have done credit to old Butler himself. I stood

23. Leroy Pope Walker, first Confederate Secretary of War.

24. Dispatched on July 28, 1861, to Monterey, Virginia, Lee succeeded in halting a threatened invasion from western Virginia.

25. General Joseph E. Johnston.

26. Brigadier General Abner M. Perrin was killed at Spotsylvania on May 12.

at the window and watched our "Bandy legged, slab sided, whining, white livered, hypocritical scoundrel" while he rummaged my carpet sack looking into my private letters and papers and examining my scanty stock of clothing as though he thought some day he might need some of them. My equanimity of temper was not in the least disturbed but he was, if possible, cooler and more composed than myself. He seemed to handle property belonging to another like an adept and I haven't the slightest doubt that he has followed the business of going into trunks and valises previous to his coming here, and probably under more unfavorable circumstances. I could not help thinking that in a carpet sack or letter box was a rather strange place to look for a ladder. This agent rejoices in the suggestive cognomen of Star (or Starr). I expect some day to see it occupying a prominent place in the "Police Gazette,"[27] a paper published for the benefit of men of his stripe. After a thorough search lasting several hours, they succeeded in bringing to sight one or two small confederate flags, over which they rejoiced considerably but were compelled to return them to their owners by Col. Hill of the 128th, who is commanding at this post.

June 1st. Grant seems to be making for the old McClellan line around Richmond, after being whipped at Spottsylvania C.H. He concluded to change his position and accordingly moved down the Rappahannock and now gets his supplies from Port Royal, and from the White House.[28] I have no fears that he will do any damage down there. I am a little fearful that Gen'l. Johnson will have to go back too far.[29]

27. *National Police Gazette* was first published in New York City in 1845.

28. As Grant marched southward, he moved out of the supply area of Belle Plain on the Potomac. The next river supply base was at Port Royal on the Rappahannock. Later he was to use White House landing on the Pamunkey, the same base McClellan used in 1862.

29. Patterson evidently is referring to General Joseph E. Johnston who at this time was in the West commanding the Army of Tennessee. In May, 1864, he was skillfully falling back before the forces of the W. T. Sherman in north Georgia (a phase of the Atlanta Campaign). The Federal offensive was a part of Grant's grand strategy of 1864. Sherman's orders from the commanding general were "to move against Johnston's army, to break it up, and to get into the interior of the enemy's country as far as you can, inflicting all the damage you can, against their war resources." Boatner, *Dictionary,* p. 30.

Jones getting along finely.—Took supper with May, Saunders, and Caldwell.

Jun. 3rd. Grant still occupies about the same position that he did on the 1st.[30] Have received letters during the week from Cousin Lizzie, Brother Joe, and from Avont from Pt. Lookout. Last night the Yankees discovered a hole commencing under the "dead house"[31] and running under the wall. It was completed and the boys were only waiting for the night to get a little darker when the Yankees found it. They came straight to the spot without waiting to look around at all. Some spy had told them all about it.

7th. Either Col. Hill thinks us all fools, or is one himself. Today I noticed an order on the Bulletin board, as follows: "Chiefs of messes will be held strictly responsible for any damage that may be done to the Blocks or other U.S. Property, with[in] this prison.—Tunneling for the purpose of escape will come under this head. It will be the duty of any prisoner who may discover any tunnel to report the same immediately to these Hd. quarters. A failure to comply with this order will be deemed sufficient cause for retaining the rations of the whole mess or inflicting such other punishment as may be deemed necessary." I give it just as it is. No comment is necessary. It would give any of us much more pleasure to cut his throat than to make any kind of a report to him, though so base a coward as he has proven himself to be (in Virginia) does not deserve an honorable death.

8th. Still another order from the "Powers that be": "Information having reached these head quarters that the safety of one of the

30. Having failed at Spotsylvania, Grant planned another turning movement to the south but Lee anticipated this move. He managed to intrench at Hanover Junction before Grant could mass his forces against that point. The fighting in this area (generally referred to as North Anna River) lasted from May 23 to 27. During the night of 26–27 Grant moved south again. After some skirmishing along Totopotomoy Creek the two armies took up positions at Cold Harbor where on June 3 one of the bloodiest battles of the entire war was fought.

31. The bodies of those who died in prison were kept in the "dead house" before burial.

inmates of mess No. 2 Block 7 has been threatened, I hereby notify the mess that each and every member of this said mess will be held strictly responsible for the safety of its members." None will be "screaned."

By command and c., and c.

It will be noticed that the education of our venerable commandant was sadly neglected in his youthful days.

It has been made plain that we have traitors within these walls. But the eyes of the B.S.C.'s are upon them, and when once the proof is plain, they will have no hope. They must get out of this place or take the consequences of their guilt.

10th. Since the 7th inst., quite a change has been made in the way of rations. We now get meat, bread, salt, and soap. Previous to this we received in addition to this coffee, sugar, candles, and occasionally a few potatoes. I believe I am getting along just as well without these latter articles as I did with them. And I know we will be healthier without them, especially the villianous compound called coffee.

I have just read a pamphlet called "Miscegenation,"[32] the contents of which are endorsed by Wendell Phillips,[33] and Mrs. Harriet Beecher Stowe, and others of the same stripe. I have no words to express my opinion of the book or its author. The doctrines it advocates are damnable, they are hellish. Never before has any man or woman been found so degraded, so lost to all sense of shame, so devoid of every enobling principle which makes a man, as to breathe such foul slander against the noble women of the South.

Sunday 12th. Perhaps one of the worst features of prison life at this place at present is that it is so public, that is, it is impossible for one to get away from the crowd, the bustle, and confusion. From morning until night it is the same, talking, reading, walking, play-

32. It is, of course, impossible to know which particular pamphlet Patterson read but in 1864 one entitled "Miscegenation: The Theory of the Blending of the Races, Applied to the American White Man and the Negro" was published in New York by H. Dexter Hamilton and Company.

33. Wendell Phillips was a Massachusetts abolitionist.

ing all kind of games, in doors and out, and there is not a spot within the walls of this prison to which one can go for quiet reflection and meditation. I like company most all the time, but there are times when I love to be alone, yes, alone. At such times I cannot express the deep emotions that throb in my bosom, as I look around and think of the goodness of God in providing so much innocent pleasure, so much that is grand and sublime, so much that is wonderfully beautiful and lovely even in this world. Oh, that I were where I could enjoy it, appreciate it more fully. For one long, long year shut up in this prison, and still no prospect of a speedy release. It is a harrowing, soul sickening thought. Thank God the sunlight finds its way even into this place, but it is the only thing we enjoy pure and uncontaminated.

17th. A special order from the post commander now permits us to go out in the lake bathing, two or three times a week. This adds much to our comfort and relieves in some degree the tedium of prison life.

18th. Reports by the morning papers are to the effect that Petersburg has been captured. I am almost sure that this is a Yankee lie, for I believe it is the intention of Gen'l. Lee to hold both Petersburg and Richmond, and if he wishes it he can do it.

20th. The papers came out this morning and "owned up" that Petersburg is still in the hands of the "Rebels."

21st. About a score of officers belonging to Morgan's command came in this evening; they were captured recently in Kentucky.[34] Vallandigham, who arrived on the 17th, seems to have settled down to private life, after defying the Yankee government and

34. After escaping from the Ohio State Penitentiary, Morgan made his way back to the Confederacy. In April, 1864, he was put in command of the Department of Southwest Virginia. Two months later he led his cavalry into Kentucky on a raiding mission. At Cynthiana, Kentucky, on June 11 he captured almost three hundred officers and men of an Ohio regiment. The following day, however, he was defeated by a Federal force under General S. G. Burbridge, suffering heavy losses.

telling them in so many words that he will not remain longer in exile in obedience to a decision of a military tribunal. If Lincoln does not take the matter in hand he confesses his own weaknesses, and if he does re-arrest him, it is likely to work against him in the coming election. Either side of the dilemma is bad enough.[35]

22nd. News today of the grand assault on the works of Petersburg, which was repulsed with "terrible slaughter" according to their own accounts. Yankees place their loss at twelve thousand.[36] Further reports from the west confirm the reported defeat and utter rout of the command of Sturgis. A dispatch from Forest states that he has killed and wounded and captured more of the enemy than he himself had in the engagement.[37] Lincoln has left Washington on a visit to Grant. If he will only let Grant alone for only one month more, I think we will no longer be troubled with an army advancing on Richmond; in fact, Gen'l. Grant is just the man to make a finishing job of the Yankee army in the East.[38]

23rd. Something rotten in Denmark. Gold advanced from $1.96 to $2.10 in Wall Street yesterday. Last July it was selling at $1.23.[39]

35. In 1863 Vallandigham was arrested by military authorities for speeches he had made against the war. He was sentenced to imprisonment but Lincoln commuted his sentence to banishment to the Confederacy. After a short and unwelcomed stay in the South he made his way to Canada. In 1864, in spite of the order for his banishment, he returned to Ohio and took an active part in the campaign of that year.

36. Having repeatedly failed in his attempts to turn Lee's flank and capture Richmond, Grant shifted his line of operations to the south side of the James. His object was to capture Petersburg and then move on the Confederate capital from south of the river. By June 16 he had his entire army on the south bank. In the meantime (June 9) Butler had bungled an attempt to capture Petersburg while it was held by a very small Confederate force. Major assaults on the Petersburg defenses during May 15–18 by the Federal Eighteenth Corps, General W. F. Smith commanding, also failed.

37. At Brice's Cross Roads, Mississippi, June 10, 1864, a Federal force of 7,800 under General S. D. Sturgis was defeated by N. B. Forrest (not Forest) who had a force only one half as large.

38. The staggering losses suffered by Grant in his struggle with Lee caused northern morale to sag.

39. The Gold Exchange and its adjunct a Gold Exchange Bank were located in New York City.

Pork is now selling for $40.00 per barrel in New York. If I mistake not, it will soon equal Richmond prices.

24th. Great day with the "Free Masons." Col. Lewis is president of the Masonic Association of this place, delivered a very eloquent and interesting address this evening which was listened to with marked attention by the largest audience ever assembled within the prison. Although not a mason myself, I believe I enjoyed the address as well as any of them. I shall certainly join the Masons if ever an opportunity occurs, and I am so fortunate [as] to escape Black Balling. In the course of his remarks he was led to speak of the acts of the Yankee army in terms of bitterness, speaking of their destroying the property of the lodge at Fredericksburg and other places, and also of their refusal to recognize Southern men as entitled to the privileges of brother masons.

25th. The news is still good. Correspondent of the "New York Times" states that in the last four days they have made several assaults on the works of Petersburg but have been unsuccessful, and that up to the present time they have fought none of Gen'l. Lee's troops. Beauregard is holding them in check, I suppose, while the main army is resting from the terrible ordeal through which they have passed during the last six weeks.[40] "Madam Rumor" states that Gen'l. Hunter has been soundly thrashed losing two thousand men, all his artillery and wagon trains; good if true.[41] Received a letter today from Sister Belle, learned that Grandma Brooks is dead.

26th. This has been a dark day with me. I have just learned that my dearest friend was killed in one of the recent battles in Virginia, and among all the noble ones who have fallen during this struggle, not one more brave and noble man, or more devoted to

40. Lee arrived at Petersburg the morning of June 18 and A. P. Hill's Corps started arriving that afternoon (see above p. 173 n. 36).

41. On June 18 General David Hunter attacked the defenses of Lynchburg which were manned by John C. Breckinridge's troops and a part of Early's corps. Hunter was repulsed and that night began a retreat to West Virginia. The fighting at Lynchburg was not heavy.

the cause of his country has fallen than Maj. James M. Crow. Having been his intimate friend and companion for nearly three years, having been with him on the march—around the campfire, —and in the dread hours of battle I had learned to love him as a brother. As an officer, he was kind, but firm and conscientious in the discharge of his duty. As a man he was generous to a fault. None spoke of him but to praise him and none knew him but to love him. He has left a large circle of friends and relatives to mourn his untimely death. His country has lost one of its most gallant defenders, and I have lost my bosom friend.

I cannot call thee back, but we can all swear that thy death has not been in vain. Thou hast fought well and nobly, and hast found a grave in Virginia where lie buried so many of those dear boys whom you have in days gone by led to battle. Thy warfare is accomplished, but ever in my heart's deepest depths will I cherish thy memory, and if again permitted to join the strife may I be inspired by thy example and strive to imitate thy noble deeds of daring, and if fall I must, Oh, let it be as thou didst fall in the front of battle, struggling manfully for the sacred principles of right and justice.

"Another hand thy sword shall wield,
Another hand the standard wave,
Till from the trumpet's mouth is pealed,
The blast of triumph, o'er thy grave."

"But never shall the land forget
How gushed the life blood of her brave,
Gushed warm with hope and courage yet
Upon the soil they fought to save."

27th. Anniversary of the battle of Gaines Mill where six brigades of us carried the whole line of the enemy's works driving the demoralized troops of Fitz John Porter before us and shooting them down at every step and with very little loss on our side, after the works were carried. Several more of Morgan's raiders came in last night in a very demoralized state. They seem to imagine that when

Morgan with his little squad of a few hundred men are whipped, that the confederacy has received a blow from which it cannot recover.

Received a letter today from Miss Duval. Played chess nearly all day and played chess nearly all night in my dreams to pay for it.

[Entry undated, but should be June 30, 1864] This is a kind of "landmark" in my life's history. Just two years ago this evening, I was lying wounded and helpless on one of the famous battlefields near the good old city of Richmond. It was the battle of "Frazier's Farm," or as the Yankees style it, "Glendale."[42] Our brigade had just made the famous charge resulting in the capture of a splendid battery, which is described in the report of the General commanding as a reckless and desperate charge of a brigade in the shape of a wedge and which he acknowledges was perfectly overwhelming. We were about a half mile distant from the battery when the order was received directing our brigade to take it. The command was immediately given "By the right of Companies to the front." "March." We advanced in this manner until within about three hundred yards of the battery when the command was given, "By company into line,—March." And in quick succession, Forward guide, double quick march, and forward we went sweeping everything before us, but with a loss in killed and wounded of about two thirds of our number. My company was losing twenty one out of twenty seven engaged. I was not one of the lucky ones, and fell just at the muzzle of one of the pieces. A glorious place to die, but a much better place to live, at least so I thought after they had shot me through the shoulder and both legs and I had begun to be accustomed to it. So much for my personal history. That I did not then and there die is sufficiently proven by the fact of my being here today, but I did feel rather squeamish as a ball would strike me, go through me "seeking what he might devour," and out on the other side and "on its way rejoicing."

42. The spelling should be Frayser's Farm. This engagement was also known as Charles City or New Market Crossroads, Nelson's Farm, and Turkey Bend.

July 2nd, 1864. I am almost ready to say let this day be stricken from the calendar and let it be remembered no more forever. Dark and gloomy day, which one year ago witnessed the bloody scenes of Gettysburg. Oh, how well I remember the lurid glare, the stifling smoke, the almost deafening roar of musketry and artillery and cheers and the groans of that day. But not for these do I hate the day. I had witnessed all these things before but I hate it for the fact that when that eventful day closed, it found me in a condition that God grant I may never again experience, (If ever again free), a prisoner. Little did I think at that time that long weary months would elapse ere I would again join my company of brave boys.

But to come to scenes of today. While busily engaged playing the innocent but very unintellectual game of "marbles" one of the boys informed me that there was a package at the "express office" for me. It is not necessary to record the many speculations of surprise and wonder that found expression on the receipt of this intelligence. Strange visions of good things to eat floated before me, (as I was *very hungry*). Something as a thirsty man in his sleep, dreaming of cooling springs and sparkling fountains. I thought of butter, ham and eggs, nice vegetables such as I had seen in the good old times before I found myself a prisoner, and I wondered if those dear people of Laporte[43] and vicinity had relented, and knowing that I was dragging out a miserable existence on scanty bits of salt pork, a little bread and plenty of water, while they, like the rich man of the parable, were faring sumptuously every day, had concluded to send me a few crumbs from the table. I could not find out by guessing, and I soon came to the conclusion that the quickest way was to go and see, and go I did and very soon the reality dispelled the illusions or fancies in which I had been indulging. I found two packages, neither of which I was expecting. One from Baltimore, containing a lot of books, some canned meats, a little coffee and sugar, and a letter; the other bearing the express mark Mansfield Indiana, containing a large lot of books, magazines, Reviews, pap-

43. Laporte, Ohio.

ers, etc., but no letter accompanying it to show from where it came, but after a while I found on the fly leaf of one of the books the name Mollie L. K.——. Ah, I have heard of her, she is the cousin of one of my friends. Well, I can feed the mind if I cannot feed the body.

3rd. Here I am in a terrible fix; just now a letter—no, not a letter—but an empty envelope, was handed me directed in the same delicate hand as the name in the book, and mailed in Madison,—but across the letter was penned these ominous words—"Letter contraband and destroyed." God bless her Southern heart; she could not write without offending the Union ears of these "Simon pure" Yankee letter examiners. But how shall I answer this empty envelope. "Aye there is the rub." I must do it somehow, but I will wait for tomorrow and trust to the memories connected with the day to inspire me.

8th. Very busy today acting as Secretary for the Committee appointed to draft Constitution and By Laws for the Grand Assembly of Social friends of the Confederate states of America. My friend, McRae, growing worse day by day; it is impossible to tell how long he may last. If he could only go to his own home in Southern Georgia, I believe the change would give him a new hold on life, and he might live for years, but as it is he cannot live more than a few weeks or months at farthest. Each succeeding day finds him weaker than the last and very soon we will in all probability follow his body to its long resting place on this lonely island.

Sunday 10th. It seems that I am to be pretty busy for a while. Most of my friends are getting sick and need attention in the hospital. McRae, Ruffin, Reed, and Hoy, besides several acquaintances are in hospitals now, and if I half way do my duty, I will be there a considerable portion of the time each day. Received on yesterday a letter from my friend, Miss Kate, which I answered this morning.

12th. Bully for the "Rebs." We learn by the papers today that our forces are on this side of the Potomac, have captured Boonesboro, Harpers Ferry, Hagerstown and Frederick and are threatening Baltimore and Washington.[44] They are taking the proper course this time, sending back into Virginia large droves of horses, sheep and cattle besides immense trains of wagons loaded with supplies. They are destroying large quantities of stores. Have burned Gov. Bradford's residence only four miles from Baltimore.[45] The Sandusky predicts, however, that the "raid" will soon play out, and that our forces will soon be back in Virginia again.

13th. Still better news. Our boys have cut off communication between Baltimore and Philadelphia, have burned the bridges on the Northern Central R.R., captured five trains of cars at "Magnolia" with quite a number of prisoners, among them Maj. Gen'l. Franklin.[46] No communication whatever with Baltimore or Wash-

44. In this entry, as well as the ones for July 13, 14, and 15, Patterson makes reference to Jubal Early's raid on Washington, June 27 to July 12, 1864. "Early's raid occurred because General Lee needed somehow to relieve pressure on Richmond after Grant had hammered his way from the Wilderness through the gore of Cold Harbor. When Lee sent Early westward toward the Shenandoah, first to deal with a Federal raid against Confederate communications, then to move upon the enemy capital if possible and perhaps force Grant to reduce strength in front of Richmond, a whole new phase of military operations began."

On July 2 Early was at Winchester. The next three days were spent raiding in the vicinity of Harper's Ferry. The Federal forces at Harper's Ferry, however, were strongly entrenched on Maryland Heights, opposite the town. Early considered the position too strong to assault, so he crossed the Potomac at Sheperdstown and reached Frederick, Maryland, on July 9. Here he levied a requisition of $200,000 on the town. Three days earlier General John McCausland had entered Hagerstown and levied a requisition of $20,000. (Boonsborough was between Hagerstown and Frederick.)

Following his victory in the Battle of Monocacy on July 9 (southeast of Frederick), Early threatened Baltimore with a cavalry brigade and marched on Washington. He reached the outskirts of the city on July 11. An assault was ordered for the following day, but the arrival of Federal reinforcements caused Early to abandon the idea. He withdrew his forces on the night of July 12 and two days later crossed the Potomac at Leesburg. Frank E. Vandiver, *Jubal's Raid* (New York: McGraw-Hill, 1960), p. viii.

45. Not only was the home of Governor A. W. Bradford destroyed but also that of U.S. Postmaster General Montgomery Blair. Although Early did not order this destruction of property, he thought the acts entirely justifiable in view of earlier Federal depredations in the Shenandoah Valley. *Ibid.*, p. 172.

46. General W. B. Franklin was captured on July 11 while on sick leave from duty in the West. He escaped the next night.

ington from Philadelphia. The "Rebs" go through the pockets of the prisoners, and take in gold watches etc.

14th. The banks have placed their funds, and the city of Balto. its papers and records, in board of a boat in the harbor, not knowing at what moment our forces might be upon them. Communication has been re-established between Baltimore and Philadelphia, but nothing from Washington. Wild rumors prevail at Baltimore that Washington has been attacked. One corps from Grant's army has arrived at Baltimore, and another from New Orleans. The Yanky army is now South of our capitol and we North of theirs, and both places in a state almost amounting to a siege. It is impossible to divine the result of these movements.

14th. Nothing of importance from the front. Our forces still continue their labors in "My Maryland," driving across the Potomac large droves of cattle, sheep, hogs, etc.

15th. Our forces falling back across the Potomac carrying their spoils with them. Last night a squad of Yankees came into the yard and fired four shots into different blocks, then retired in good order, giving the order that no man should step outside the door during the night on penalty of being shot.[47] They seem to apprehend an attempt to take the island, or something of that kind. Last night the battery stationed here was sent to Coveington Ky.,[48] and today the old Gun Boat, Michigan, came steaming in and anchored close by to take its place. Was elected to the General Assembly of S. F.[49] to meet on Monday the 18th.

17th. No preaching this morning. This evening at five o'clock Col. Lewis preached to an audience of nearly two thousand. He

47. Much of the shooting seems to have been prompted by two rules: no visiting between wards after 9 P.M. and all lights out after 10 P.M. (see also below pp. 182–83.).

48. Covington (not Coveington), Kentucky.

49. General Assembly of Social Friends of the Confederate States of America. (See also Patterson's entry for July 8, 1864.)

always finds it necessary to preach in the open air, as none of the "Blocks" will contain all who wish to hear. His text was "But the name of the wicked shall rot."

18th. Very little news today. Part of Sherman's army reported to be across the Chattahoochie River.[50] Our forces have evacuated Maryland.[51] Grand Assembly met; did not finish our business, adjourned until tomorrow.

20th. One year ago this evening in company with nearly four hundred other unfortunates, I arrived on Johnson's Island. Little did I think at that time that the Summer of 1864 would find me still a prisoner. It is so hard to be shut up here when our country needs us so much. It would be better, it seems to me, to be killed at once on the battlefield. We can do nothing but pray, but thank God, we can always pray for the right, and for the last three months we have had prayer meetings daily, and it does the soul good to hear the warm, earnest petitions that go up day after day and night after night, from the very depths of the hearts of the noble ones who linger here, to God, our Father, that he will have mercy on our bleeding country, and save her and our people.

My heart sickens as I read the records in the papers of the damning deeds done by Sherman and Sturgis, and others of the same stripe. It is a wonder that the very stones do not cry out against them. Surely swift judgment must overtake them. If it is not wicked, I *thank* God that there is a *terrible hell* where the Shermans, Butlers and Sturgis and all those who uphold them will finally receive their just deserts.[52] The blackest, foulest, and most

50. Johnston made a stand at the Chattahoochee (not Chattahoochie) River, July 4–9, but Sherman turned his position forcing him to withdraw to Peach Tree Creek (see above p. 169, n. 29).

51. This is a reference to Early's Washington Raid.

52. W. T. Sherman, B. F. Butler, S. D. Sturgis. Patterson did not have to concern himself with Sturgis because this Federal officer's Civil War career had been terminated by N. B. Forrest at Brice's Cross Roads the previous month. After his defeat in this battle Sturgis saw no more service in the field. (See also above p. 173, n. 37.)

damnable deed that has ever been done, even in this war, is one recorded in the papers today. A deed so black, so diabolical that the fiends of Hell or even "Butler the Beast" would never have been able to originate unaided. It was left for Gen'l. Sherman, high in rank in the U.S.A. to perform it. A body of cavalry sent out by him to burn houses, steal negroes, and ravish women, came upon a factory some distance South of Marietta where were at work four hundred girls and women making tents; they burned the factory, which of course was to be expected, but after that instead of going on and making war on armed men they actually took these young girls as prisoners, and marched them into their lines. They were aiding the "Rebels," making an honest living, that was a sufficient cause to justify Sherman in his own sight in doing as he did. He put them in wagons, sent them back to the depot at Marietta with orders that they be sent immediately North of the Ohio River and "turned loose."[53] (To use his expression—let it never be forgotten). And to think today, thousands of hypocritical, blasphemous Yankees are praying God to give Sherman success, to enable him to make our land a wilderness and our people worse than slaves. To what brutal insults these unprotected females may be subjected. How many of them may be forced to sell their honor—their hope of heaven, their all, for bread, he cares not. I would as soon pray for the success of the Devil as for the success of Sherman.

26th. Tuesday. On last Saturday night, while all was quiet and all who had no tobacco to smoke or chew had retired to their bunks, and were sleeping soundly, and others more fortunate ones were sitting around in groups in various parts of the room, one of the

53. A young officer in Sherman's army wrote from Marietta: "We have some 400 young women in the old Seminary Building near town. They have been working in a factory at Rossvill [Roswell?] making cloth for the Confederate government. The factories were destroyed and the girls are to be sent South or North whichever way they want to go. Some of them are tough and its a hard job to keep them straight and to keep the men away from them. General Sherman says he would rather try to guard the whole Confederate Army, and I guess he is right about it." O. O. Winther, ed., *With Sherman to the Sea* (Baton Rouge: Louisiana State University Press, 1934), p. 119.

Yankee Sentinals on the wall below our block cried out, "Lights out in Block 5." As there was no light in the Block and had been none for a week, we, of course, replied to him that there was no light here, but that it was the light from the hospital windows shining through our windows. He replied that he knew there was a light in block 5 and thereupon fired into the Block. The ball passed through the wall, then through one of the upright pieces that supports the plates, four inches thick, then striking one of the bunks, glanced and passed through Lt. Dillard's arm, shattering the bone below the elbow and finally lodging in the shoulder of Lt. Inman, making a very dangerous wound. This is the fifth time they shot into the blocks, but fortunately heretofore their shots have been harmless. In fifteen or twenty minutes, the officer of the day came in and pretended to regret the occurence, and stated that he would have the sentinel punished (As if that was any satisfaction). This thing has been going on a long time, and every soldier on the Island knows that there has been no violation of orders at any time when the various shots have been fired. It is simply a cowardly base way the sentinels have of getting promotion, which always follows when one of them makes a lucky shot and wounds one of our officers.

A Dixie mail arrived day before yesterday by which I received letters from Inglewood and Petersburg. I received also at the same time two from Baltimore and one from Kentucky. Clark received a large box the other day, and as a matter of course we, Dewees, Clark and I, live very well, especially as on the same day I received a supply of sugar and coffee. Assisted in burying the body of Lt. Jackquess who died night before last. Disease eryesipelas.

28th. Yesterday went to Gen'l. Trimble's room to give in evidence in regard to the "shooting affair." Col. Hill, (U.S.A.) shows a disposition to do justice in this case; whether it is all make believe we cannot tell. Received a letter from Joe yesterday, enclosing a note from Sophia. Received a paper from Thead (I suppose). Am very unwell today, hardly able to be up. My general health is very bad, and has been for some time.

July 29th. Received several very interesting volumes from Miss King, also a letter insisting on my sending a list immediately of all my wants and let her supply them. I am sure that I shall accept this offer. This is very kind to offer to do so much for an entire stranger.

30th. Extracts from "our papers" speak of another brilliant affair in which Mahone's Division alone was engaged.[54] It, the division, consists of three small brigades, Wright's, Mahone's old Brigade, and the Alabama Brigade, to which I belong, commanded first by Gen'l. Kirby Smith, then by Forney, Wilcox, and Perrin, and since the death of Perrin by Col. Saunders of the 11th.[55] The "last affair" took place on the 19th inst. They captured sixteen hundred and fifty prisoners, the same number of small arms, four pieces of artillery and ten stands of colors, with a loss on our side of fifty five killed, two hundred and sixty three wounded, and fifty six missing. This makes over five thousand prisoners, eight pieces of artillery, and more than a dozen stands of colors during this campaign, captured by this little division. "Bully for them." I wish I could be with them. Received a letter from Dixie.

Sunday 31st. Terribly hot, and scarce a breath of air stiring. The weather is very unpleasant for those who are sick. My friend, McRae seems to be getting lower every day. I fear that he cannot live long. Major Moore is also quite sick, and if I am not much mistaken, has the consumption. The cold and exposure of last winter is beginning to have its effect and many will doubtless die (with that fatal disease, consumption) before another winter

54. The *Official Records* do not mention any engagements as having taken place on either June 19 or July 19 in which General William Mahone played a prominent role. However, on June 22, 1864, General Lee wrote James A. Seddon, Secretary of War: "The enemy's infantry was attacked this afternoon on the west side of the Jerusalem plank road and driven from his first line of works to his second on that road by General Mahone with a part of his division. About 1,600 prisoners, 4 pieces of artillery, 8 stand of colors, and a large number of small arms were captured." *O.R.*, XL, Ser. I, Pt. I, 750.

55. A. R. Wright, William Mahone, E. Kirby Smith, W. H. Forney, A. M. Perrin, J. C. C. Sanders (Patterson misspelled Sanders). By the date of this entry Sanders had been promoted to brigadier general.

passes. I was so delighted to hear a few days since that my dear friend, Jim Crow, is still alive and well, notwithstanding the reports to the contrary. He writes me as follows on the 16th inst. "Dr. Pat, I am here and well, boys in the command well and c." That is truly good news. Only one death reported among my friends there, and that is the death of Sergt. Dolph Owens, as good and noble a soldier as ever went forth to battle.

August 3rd. Mess 3 had quite an engagement this morning among themselves. Lieut. Black was so unfortunate as to be knocked down with a chair, which struck him on the right side of his face, fracturing his jaw and endangering his eye. The doctor pronounces it quite a serious wound. Lot of officers came in from Johnson's army today,[56] they represent matters in the West to be "all right." I wish I could think so.

4th. Sat up last night with McRae, he seems to be sinking very rapidly. He may live a week, not longer though. Yankees are building some large dining halls and when they are completed we will have no more cooking done in the "blocks." I am very much afraid that they will stop the sutler establishment also, and then goodbye to everything in the shape of vegetables. We now get exactly three ounces of beef per man for a day's rations, and five ounces of salt pork, about a peck of hominy each week to be divided among a hundred men, and about half enough bread and for the last few days, hardly that.

As for the sick, they get along the best they can. The doctors at the hospital have been without medicine for five days, and no hope of getting any soon, though I understand that money is to be appropriated for the purchase of morphine and other necessary medicines out of the treasury of the Young Men's Christian Association. We have collected quite a large sum and perhaps we cannot do better than to dispose of a portion of it in this manner.

56. On July 14 President Davis had ordered John B. Hood to replace Johnston as commander of the Army of Tennessee.

Sunday August 7th. My friend, Lt. McRae, died. I hope he is better off now. He suffered much during the last few days of his life, but without a murmur. One by one they are passing away. God, grant that I may live to return South! I do not wish to die on this lonely island. Yesterday evening my friend, Lt. J. B. Murphey, made his escape and has not since been heard from. I hope that he is on his way to Canada. He had managed to get hold of a pair of blue pants and a blue blouse and yesterday, when the Yankees who had been at work inside went out, he picked up a shovel and stepped in among them, and deliberately walked out without creating any suspicion. Prayer meetings were held at various places in the prison this morning immediately after roll call. Our association meets at 4 o'clock P.M. and Col. Lewis preaches at five o'clock in the open air. Wrote to Miss Sallie Q—today. No further news of Grant's army since the terrible slaughter of his troops on the 28th of July.[57] His army and ours must be about equal in numbers now, and I shall be much surprised if Gen'l. Lee does not persuade Grant to leave his present position in a very short time.[58]

6th. The Sermon preached by Col. L—on yesterday could not have been more direct and pointed to my particular case if it had been preached exclusively for my benefit. Text, "If ye suffer, ye shall also reign with him." His sermon was based on the principle that *suffering is the law of human elevation,* and that when there is no suffering, there cannot be elevation. During his remarks, he paid a tribute to Gen'l. Lee in the following beautiful language. "For thousands of years men have lived and moved upon the earth, men of profound wisdom and learning, men who have made their mark upon the age in which they lived, and men whose names will live as long as history shall endure; but during all this time, the front-piece in the great book of fame has been left blank until the present

57. In the fighting at Deep Run Bottom (July 27–29) Federal losses were reported as 334 killed and wounded. Confederate losses are not known. However, on July 28 Kershaw's division (Confederate) alone had 300 men captured.

58. Grant had suffered staggering losses in his struggle with Lee (May–July) but he was able to replace his losses whereas Lee was not. So the armies were not equal in number as Patterson thought.

time, and today the Angel of Destiny stands ready with pen dipped in immortal remembrance to write upon that page the name of Robert E. Lee."

But leaving all these thoughts,—the boys have, some of them, been having a very lively time today. The Yankees were hauling sand into the prison, and some of the boys formed the notion of getting in the wagon and riding out. Lt. Elkins was the first who tried it, and succeeded admirably; immediately afterwards half a dozen or more walked out dressed in full Yankee blue, and as wagon after wagon went out, they hardly ever failed to carry at least six or seven until some twenty odd had found themselves outside the walls; but unluckily they tried it once too often, and one was caught in the attempt. Of course they immediately started out a strong line of skirmishers and went over the island, looking behind every bush and behind every stump and finally succeeded in finding sixteen of them. The boys were having a fine time of it, but those who were captured say that they will not patronize that line of omnibusses again, as it failed to make the connection with the ferry. If they had been a little more careful, I suppose that we could have all left as fast as transportation could be furnished.

9th. Late last night they brought in a few more of the raiders. I think none are missing now but Lt. Williamson and Lt. Murphey.

12th. Received a letter from Miss Mollie this morning. Says that she will send my box and money this week. My friend Maj. Moore returned this morning from the hospital looking much better than I expected to see him, so soon too.

13th. A well filled box from Miss King this morning, containing pair pants, jacket, two shirts, pair of shoes, two pairs of socks, hat, paper—two quires, stamped envelopes, 1 package plain ditto, needles, case, thread, buttons, etc., besides a fine large bacon, ham, two huge pound cakes, biscuits etc. Received a letter stating that the money was sent on the same day that the box started. It will probably reach me in a day or two. Received also a letter from Mrs. L. Virginia Brown from Columbia, Tenn.

14th. Received a letter from Miss Martha Baeuchamp giving me more bad news to communicate to her brother when I write South, namely—the death of a sister. Prayer meeting this morning at sunrise in the open air.

20th. Cold driving rain, more like December than August. Went down to the sutler's shop this morning and tried to make some purchases but failed, as an order was received while I was there making a complete change in the selling arrangement. An order from the war department now limits the list of articles which the sutler is allowed to sell to stationery and tobacco, and the same order cuts off all express boxes. I am afraid that there will be much suffering this winter if this order is enforced, for the rations we receive from the Yankees are not sufficient to keep body and soul together. And we are dependent entirely upon our friends for clothing. Yesterday our association met and after transacting some business, Capt. Strickler addressed the society upon the subject of "faith." He was listened to with much interest.

Sunday 21st. Wrote to my friend at Inglewood. Dixie mail received but no letter for me. The papers today contain extracts from Southern papers, among which is an account of the "affair" at Petersburg.[59] It is now proven that only two brigades on our side were engaged—viz.—Mahone and Saunders (mine). Mahone says that they captured one thousand one hundred and one prisoners, including seventy eight commissioned officers, thirteen hundred small arms, seventeen stands of colors, and all with a loss on our side of five hundred men killed and wounded. The two brigades numbered three thousand effective men; [60] these trophies added to

59. The Battle of the Crater (Petersburg Mine Assault) occurred on July 30.

60. Mahone was the hero of the battle. His command cleared the crater of Federal troops. For this action Lee gave him an on-the-spot promotion to major general. Approximately 11,466 Confederate troops from various commands were engaged in the battle. Livermore, *Numbers and Losses,* pp. 116–17.

the former ones of this splendid little division during this campaign foot up over six thousand prisoners, and about three thousand stands of arms, eight pieces of artillery and thirty one stands of colors. The paper states that the immortal Beauregard complimented them on the field, and that furthermore they had been complimented by every Lt. Gen. in the army, and that it has been ordered that these two brigades have inscribed upon their banners, "Carter" "Petersburg."

After this war what a time I will have in talking about what *we* have done. When the question is asked, where were you when the battle of the wilderness, the battle at Spottsylvania, Cold Harbor, and Petersburg were fought, I can only answer at Johnson's Island, but if there is a man in all the Confederacy who wishes to change places with me, be he sick or wounded, in jail or out of it, no matter what his condition, he can "get a trade." I am worn out with this prison life. I feel that I am growing old before my time. My disposition has become soured against the world generally, and I am afraid that if a change does not come over the spirit of my dream, that I will soon get to be a very unlovable object. I will be so old and so cross that my sweetheart won't own me, when I go back (if I should be so highly blessed as to go back). The chances are that a man will not make a [illegible] of it. Half starved, poorly clothed and not allowed to buy food or clothing, and not even allowed to receive them from friends. Our case is quite desperate, or will be when cold weather comes on.

25th. After three months silence Cousin Angie[61] again writes me; she says that she has nothing more to say, that our separation is final, that we can never meet as once we met. She cannot find a place in her heart for a rebel cousin. She also regards the separation between herself and brother as final, but still takes an interest in him, and writes me for the purpose of ascertaining his address. She seems to think there is but little chance for Frank (God bless him) and myself. I am sorry that any political difference between us and our friends in Ohio should be the means of forever separating us,

61. Sister of Frank Patterson.

but if they will have it so, we cannot help it. If they could answer for me and my conduct in the great day of accounts, I might pay some heed to their counsel, but as I know that I alone am to be held responsible in that day for my actions I dare not swerve from the path of duty. I wrote Cousin A—a cousinly letter giving her the desired information. I cannot but believe that they will all acknowledge that they were wrong and I right before many years pass by.

Received a letter from my friend, Miss D—of Baltimore. She continues to send me the daily papers which of course are very acceptable, as they always contain extracts from Southern papers. Subscribed today for the Sandusky Register. Received a letter also from Brother Joseph, tells me that one of my former acquaintances, ("Oscar Bush") is dead. He was one of the "one hundred day's men," and died of the fever in Baltimore.

This evening we had quite a storm, hard enough to make these old buildings totter. It laid a portion of the prison wall (on the West side) flat, but by the time any of the prisoners found it out, they had a sufficient force in the gap to repel an attack if any of us had been so disposed, which we were not, seeing that there was a regiment of them in battle array besides a piece of artillery.

Saturday 27th. The match game between the "Confederate Base Ball Club" and the "Southern Base Ball Club" took place this evening, resulting in a brilliant victory on the part of the "Southern Club." The first innings were won by the Confederate club, and they made a run of three; the first innings of the Southern Club amounted to nothing. The Confederates led until the fifth innings when the Southern took it from them and maintained it throughout. The sympathies and good wishes of the crowd were decidedly with the Southern Club from the commencement. At the close of the game the scorers reported as follows:

Confederate Club............Eleven
Southern Club..............Nineteen

Another game is expected next Saturday. Among sporting characters a considerable amount of money changed hands.

30th. I was somewhat surprised as well as pleased when a Yankee handed me a note from Pa—saying that himself and brother "Thead" were on the island and hoped to see me soon, but about an hour afterwards I received another note from him informing me that he had made the attempt and could not get permission to have an interview with me. I went to Block 1 where I could see them (over the wall) and bowed to them. Thead looks much younger than I expected to see him, and in fact one would think to see us together that I was the elder of the two. He has not "roughed it" as I have and by the time he goes over the same road that I have travelled, he will not look as boyish as he does now.

Chicago Convention in full blast. Chances seem to be in favor of McClellan's nomination.[62]

Sept. 1st. An order issued from Hill's Headquarters limits us to two mails per week. No man allowed to write excepting on Mondays and Thursdays, and no man allowed to send out two letters at once. Of course we have the privilege of evading the order as all others, if we are able to do so.

2nd. John K. Nickell, a member of the second Batallion Ky. Cav. was hung today on the island. He was charged with having killed two men in Kentucky. I know nothing of the circumstances, but men who do know them seem to justify him and they also state that his brother, a "Bushwhacker," has ten Federal Officers in prison, and that he notified the U.S. Authorities that he would hang them all if any harm was done his brother. He was hung this evening between the hours of one and two. I noticed quite a large number of women among the crowd who went to witness the execution.

Sept. 7th. Sent the picture to Miss K— received a letter from my lady friend in Paducah. Says she will send me something soon. She writes me that her brother John is a prisoner, but does not tell me where is. Wrote to Miss D. of Balto.

62. General George B. McClellan was the Democratic candidate for the presidency in 1864.

8th. Moved to the dining halls all of our cooking utensils, provisions etc. A prospect of pretty general starvation seems to be staring us in the face; no rations today but bread and rotten fish, which we would none of us eat only as a matter of necessity to keep soul and body together; not a particle of meat or grease of any kind to cook them with, and so salt that we have to boil them in three waters, and when they are finally cooked there is about as much nutriment in them as there would be in the same quantity of boiled shavings.[63] I feel confident that if our government officials knew the facts in the case they would give Andersonville and Macon[64] prisoners something to whine about; then perhaps retaliation in kind would bring about an exchange. The news of the fall of Atlanta is now fully confirmed and though it is a heavy blow to us, we may yet make it a terrible success for the foe. I do not believe that Sherman will be able to remain there, and he may yet be driven back to Chattanooga.

9th. Officiated for the first time today as Sec'ty. of our Y.M.C. Association. The meeting was a very interesting one, several resolutions being offered which elicited quite an animated discussion.

10th. Received a letter from my friend, Major Jim Crow; it contains sad news. My friend, Lieut. John D. Chandler was killed at the fight of Petersburg on the 30th of July. Received a letter also

63. During the period from 1862 to early 1864 the quantity and quality of food seems to have been, on most occasions, satisfactory both to the prisoners and to Federal inspectors. However, a radical change took place in the spring of 1864. Rations were sharply reduced and heavy restrictions were placed on purchases. "This more rigorous treatment of the Johnson Island prisoners cannot be explained on the grounds of any shortage in the available food supply, inadequate transportation facilities, or lack of funds. The changes coincide in time, however, with the widely-circulated atrocity stories about the ill treatment of Union soldiers in Southern prison camps. Therefore, one finds it easy to believe that these harsh measures were in response to the public clamor for retaliation, or at least as insurance against the coddling of Rebel prisoners. Writing in July, the Commissary General of Prisoners asserted: 'It is not expected that anything more will be done to provide for the welfare of Rebel prisoners than absolutely necessary.'" Downer, "Johnson's Island," p. 207.

64. Andersonville Prison (open stockade) was located near Americus, Georgia. The first prisoners arrived there in February, 1864. The Confederates also maintained a prison at Macon, Georgia.

from Miss Mollie King asking if she will be allowed to send money and stamps and regretting that the present orders from Washington will not allow her to send me a box of eatables.

11th. Received a letter, no, an envelope from Dixie. By the handwriting I judge that it must be from my good friend at Inglewood, Va. I cannot see what right Col. Hill has to stop letters from the South. An arrangement has been entered into by the two governments to allow persons in this country to write to their friends in the *Confederate States,* and for *our* friends to write letters to the *United States.* Examiners are appointed by each government and after a letter passes their hands I cannot see the use of another examination after it reaches this place, and even if they do examine it they have no right to stop it.

Sept. 14th. The wolf, which has been of late barking around us, seems to be growing more fierce and I have nothing to defend myself with against him but an empty coffee pot and a crust of dry bread. I hope to keep him at bay for a while at least. The authorities have declared that hereafter candles are contraband, and we now have to remain from dark until daylight in total darkness. As the nights become longer this is becoming very unpleasant; no one wishes to spend twelve or fourteen hours of each twenty four in sleep, and no one wishes to sit for four or five hours (from dark until bedtime) without being able to read, write, or play any game for amusement. This presents quite a contrast with the Yankee officers who are confined at various places in the South, who have gas light furnished them and are allowed to buy such things as they need which our government does not furnish them.

The Difference. About two weeks ago, Father and brother "Thead" came to the island to visit me; this was right enough and I was very glad to see them, though I could not talk with them. All the friends at home sent messages of love etc. A day or two since Caldwell's father (who is also an Ohian) came to see him; he also was unable to talk with his son, but with the messages of love from his brothers and sisters came something substantial. Each had something nice to send; one a lot of fine grapes, another a half bushel of nice sweet potatoes, and other articles of this kind; not one of those at home but had his or her little gift to send thinking how good they would be, and how highly their brother in this loathsome prison would appreciate them. Now what makes this difference? I am confident that his relatives love him no more than mine do me. It is from no want of affection that my relatives (and as they say friends) never have once sent me anything of the kind. It is simply a blind indifference and a fixed faith in the various articles in the abolition journals of the country to the effect that we are well fed, clothed etc., not that I care particularly, for if the authorities would permit I can get anything I need from friends farther South. It helps to answer the question that I have seen somewhere propounded— "Is not the kindred of common fate a closer tie than that of birth?"

Friday 16th. Twenty five sick left today for exchange, and Col. L. M. Lewis on special exchange. He will be missed more than any one else who has ever left this prison. He has wielded a powerful influence for good during his stay and those who have enjoyed the benefit of his society will never forget him. Always foremost in every good work he had endeared himself to all who knew him. I am sure that he will give an accurate account of our treatment to our government, and exchange business is a paying one on our side if we can get such a man as Col. Lewis for any officer of the U.S.A. that we hold. Association met in Block 7.

Saturday 17th. For several days some of the boys have been killing and eating rats, of which there are thousands in the prison. I have often been hungry all day long, indeed so hungry that I felt sick, and still I could not screw my courage up to the point of eating rats. But today after getting a few mouthfuls of beef and bread, and having been hard at work most of the day on kitchen detail I was constrained to try a mess of rats. My friend, Jones (not the renowned Bill Jones), had been very lucky and had captured a sufficient number of rats to make a big stew and invited me to try them, and it would have done a hungry man's soul good just to have seen me eat them. I cannot say that I am particularly fond of them, but rather than go hungry I will eat them when I can get them, though they have become the fashion to such an extent that from twenty five to a hundred are killed every night at each Block and they are already getting scarce. They taste very much like a young squirrel and would be good enough if called by any other name.

20th. Out of curiosity, I this morning weighed myself and find that under the new regime I am falling off about one half pound per day, weighing 127 pounds today against 148 about six weeks ago. I cannot afford to have this continue long.

21st. Yankees terribly frightened at the discovery of a plot to capture the Michigan (Gun Boat) and release the prisoners confined here. The rebs and their sympathizers captured two steam boats up near the Canada shore but unfortunately for us the plot was exposed and the authorities put on their guard. It was a well laid plan, and would have succeeded had they kept it secret; I hope they may try again.[65] Received news of a heavy battle in the Shenandoah Valley in which the Yankees claim to have captured three thousand

65. In the fall of 1863 the Confederate plan to seize the steamer "Michigan" and use its guns to free the prisoners on Johnson's Island had failed (see above p. 144 n. 36). The Federal warship, nevertheless, remained a tempting prize and in July, 1864, Confederate authorities ordered Captain C. H. Cole, C.S.N., to investigate the possibility of capturing her. By September a plan had been formulated. While Cole dined with the "Michigan's" captain, whose acquaintance he had cultivated, John Y. Beall "who had learned to seize ships on Chesapeake Bay, was to capture the passenger steamer "Philo Parsons" and use it against the "Michigan."

On September 19 Beall and a trained crew disguised as civilians seized the "Philo Parsons" and then captured another steamer, the "Island Queen." They put the passengers of both ships ashore, sank the "Island Queen," and proceeded toward Johnson's Island in the darkness. Signal rockets that were to be fired from the "Michigan" did not appear, so it was evident that something had gone wrong. The "Philo Parsons" then turned around and steamed to the Canadian side of the lake where she was burned. Meanwhile, Cole, who had made arrangements to give an elaborate dinner aboard the "Michigan" that evening, had been arrested at his hotel in Sandusky. An informer had revealed the details of the plot to Federal authorities. Thus the whole scheme came to nothing. Downer, "Johnson's Island," pp. 212–13; Stern, *Secret Missions,* pp. 202–3.

prisoners, several pieces of artillery and stands of colors, and to have driven our army twelve miles. They report Gen'ls. Rhodes & Gordon killed. I think this doubtful however.[66]

Attended meeting of G.A.S.F. this morning at nine o'clock, prayer meeting at ten o'clock. Wrote a letter to Miss Sallie and received a letter from Miss Tena C—, spent nine dollars in tobacco and stationery, read a letter from Jim Crow to Major Foster of the Cavalry.

Sept. 22nd. News from the valley worse than yesterday. They claim to have captured five thousand prisoners and to have killed and wounded seven of our Generals, and driven Early twenty miles.[67] I think a good part of this is for political effect. We will have to wait a few days until we see "Malcolm's" account of it before we know the truth of the matter. "The Island Queen" (one of the boats captured by the rebs) is reported again on the high seas,[68] this time with a ship under him which carries forty guns and three hundred men.[69] If this is true, look out Yankee merchants, and look Bro. Winslow and don't show yourself with the "Kearsarge."[70]

Sept. 24th. Last night about eight o'clock after I had retired to my "virtuous couch," a violent storm arose, and I began to feel a little uneasy, knowing that this frail tenement could not stand such wind. I raised up in bed and asked Mitchell which direction the

66. General Philip H. Sheridan decisively defeated Early at Winchester on September 19, 1864. General Robert E. Rodes (not Rhodes) was killed in this engagement. The report that General John Brown Gordon had been killed, however, was false.

67. The news was not as bad as Patterson feared. Still, Confederate losses approached four thousand, and in addition to Rodes, Early lost two brigade commanders. Also Generals Fitz Lee and Zubulon York were seriously wounded.

68. The "Island Queen" had been sunk immediately after she was seized by the Confederates (see above p. 195 n. 65).

69. Evidently Patterson is making reference in this garbled phrase to Admiral Raphael Semmes who commanded the famous Confederate raider "Alabama" until she was sunk in June, 1864.

70. Captain John A. Winslow commanded the U.S.S. "Kearsarge." In an engagement off Cherbourge, France, on June 19, 1864, the "Kearsarge" sank the C.S.S. "Alabama."

wind was from; his reply reassured me, viz. that it was coming from the direction of the big gate. I thought that as long as the wind was only coming against the end of the building we would be perfectly safe. I had just crawled into bed again when I heard the most awful roaring that I have ever listened to, and in another instant the tornado struck us. I heard the crash from Block 4, and felt this old shell rocking like a ship at sea, and the cry, "Out of the Blocks for your lives," could be heard above the tempest; then followed such a scene as has seldom if ever been witnessed.

I think I touched the floor once between my bunk and the door and the next jump I landed outside amid the flying timbers of Block 4, the whole roof of which was taken up and wrenched into a thousand pieces, which could be seen whirling and spinning around in the air as flash after flash of the most vivid lightening succeeded each other, casting a lurid glare over all. Some of the rafters came end foremost as though pitched by some unseen giant, plowing up the ground and cutting through this block as if it had been so much paper. Everybody seemed to believe that this block would be twisted into atoms; men from the upper story, not having time to get to the door, jumped through the windows, smashing sash, glass and everything before them. Others were blown from the platform at the top of the steps. We were right in the path of the whirlwind, and as I struck the ground outside the wind shrieked and howled like a thousand demons, taking the roof from our block as it would a sheet of tissue paper, and after whirling it around a few times, pitched it about fifty yards, the corner of it going through the long dining hall and playing smash generally with my tinware and rations, and at the time the roof left us the whole building moved a few inches.

It must be supposed that I noticed all these things as they were taking place for I was more frightened than I have ever been before during my life, and more than I ever expect to be again. The yard was crowded with men who could be seen by the lightning's flash rolling and tumbling over each other, picked up and tossed about by the wind at its pleasure. For myself, I was blown about twenty feet and happened to land on that part of the body "where mothers smite their young" and took a rather unpleasant ride for some distance until I landed on "all fours" in a gutter where I was pelted with hail stones, shingles, mud and sand until I was utterly demoralized, while the tail of my "nether garment," released from confinement during my undignified ride, fluttered in the breeze as a sign of distress. By the time the wind had abated its violence so that I could stand on my feet, I had partly recovered my senses and was so cold that I was in danger of shaking myself to pieces. St. Vitus' dance is nothing to the way I hopped around.

The men now commenced making their way back into the buildings and the Yankees commenced firing into the yard, so badly frightened that they were firing at random, one shot going through the hospital, one through our block, and several men made narrow escapes. After getting into my room I was surprised to find that I had not one serious bruise. I rubbed myself with a coarse towel for about ten minutes, put on some dry underclothes, and wrapped in my blanket, and after a while succeeded in getting to sleep in spite of the rain.

This morning I found that only a portion of the hospital roof was blown off. Block 4, 9, and 5 (mine) are the only ones entirely unroofed. Only four or five men from our block were hurt and only one dangerously, he having his thigh broken and a large portion of the flesh from his thigh torn off by a rafter from Block four striking him as he went out the door. I cannot see this morning how we escaped as we did, running out as we did right among the falling timbers. It is nothing less than a miracle that no one was killed. Quite a number of the boys have very sore feet at the present having stepped on nails in returning to the Block over the torn roofs. I think I would prefer fighting a battle every morning before breakfast rather than experience a repetition of last night's work. I can hardly write sensibly about it now, as I have not entirely recovered from the demoralizing influence it had on me.

Sept. 26. Ever since the storm the Yankees have kept guards stationed around the yard to prevent the boys from stealing the lumber. We need it to fix our bunks and to make partitions of, as a room two hundred feet long is rather a cold place to remain in during the winter. It is quite amusing to see how we manage to steal the plank, almost from under the sentinel's nose. The plan generally adopted is as follows: Jones or Elkins or myself, or any one who pleases steps up to a fine looking plank and picks it up and starts off with it. The sentinel's attention is of course called to him, and he orders him to "let it alone." Of course the reb objects and has an unlimited number of reasons why he should be allowed to keep it, and finally when compelled to drop it, goes up to the sentinel and engages him in conversation as long as possible. All this time the remainder of the crowd are quietly slipping plank away from behind the sentinel and passing it into the house, where a portion of the floor is raised and our booty deposited under the floor till a safe opportunity offers for working it up. We frequently create diversions in each other's favor. Last night the sentinels were taken out and those on the wall instructed to let no one take lumber or shingles. They could see us if we picked up the plank, but Jones hit upon a happy expedient. He took the long clothes line and one of us would take it and loop it around the end of the plank and then all returning to the house, we would haul in the load. We brought in enough that way last night to build a nice room besides putting a partition through the large hall, all of which we had arranged nicely by roll call in the morning with the assistance of pocket knives and a little saw made of a case knife. I think if we had a few more tools we could build a gunboat. Received a letter today from Mrs. Brown. She writes that all my friends in Florence Ala. are well and offers to send me anything I need.

27th. The Yankees have just fired a hundred guns in honor of Sheridan's victory in the valley.[71] Guards have been removed from the inside simply because we have left them nothing to guard. We have hardly left a piece of shingle large enough for a tooth pick. I don't know who of the Yankee sentinels that have been on post

71. Early was decisively defeated by Sheridan in the Battle of Fisher's Hill, September 22, 1864.

they will hold responsible and I don't care. Received a letter from "Aunt Lydia Rawlings" in Baltimore, offering to supply my wants.

30th. Sept. I notice by the papers today that the officers who left this place a week or two since have arrived at Richmond. Col. L. M. Lewis, who used to preach for us and who was my Bible class teacher, was among the number and is now Senator for the Northern district of Mo. in Congress.[72] He is a very able man and a good man, and will use his influence to get us out of this place. No man has ever left the prison so much admired and loved by every one as Col. Lewis, and he is missed very much.

The Yankees are getting along very slowly with our house, and I am afraid that it will be several days yet before 'tis completed. Association met today in Block 13; no business of importance transacted except to appoint a committee to confer with the authorities outside in reference to building a church in the prison. If they will only give their permission, we can very soon raise the funds with which to build it. If we do not get one built, we will have no place at all for worship this winter as all the blocks will be closed up, partition[ed] off into small rooms.

October 1st. Lts. Jones, Elkins, Mobley, Morre, Seward and myself have concluded to build a small room in the corner of our big block; we have nothing to work with except pocket knives and a little saw made of a case knife. We have already stowed away a sufficient quantity of lumber.

2nd. The Yankees work very slowly on the roof of our house, putting on about three or four courses of shingles per day, and we have rain almost every night; consequently we have to take it as it

72. W. B. Yearns in his work on the Confederate Congress has this to say about Lewis: "The Confederate Missouri legislature was unable to meet after 1862 and [Confederate Governor T. C.] Reynolds filled senatorial vacancies when they occurred. . . . John B. Clark had annoyed the President by his personal conduct and his talk of a counter revolution, and at the end of Clark's two-year term Reynolds appointed L. M. Lewis, a Methodist preacher and an early secessionist. Lewis, however, preferred army life, and for the last months of Congress Reynolds promoted George G. Vest from House to the Senate. Yearns, *Congress,* pp. 57–58.

comes. We have our partition wall up, and have stolen nearly enough lumber from the Yankees to make our bedsteads.

Oct. 5th. I have been very busy for the last few days, and in fact have done more work than all I have done before for a year would amount to. Yesterday was a good day for us; we managed to get a window, and an excellent stove, and cut a door at the side of the block. So now we have as nice a room as any one in the penitentiary. I moved in on yesterday and have arranged my wardrobe.

Oct. 6th. Once more there is a prospect that the gates of this prison house of woe will open and we can get a glimpse beyond. Hope is not yet extinguished, though for a long time it has glimmered but feebly. Today the authorities are preparing to send off fifty of the sick, to go on exchange. Oh, for a spell of sickness. I shall send by my friends, Capt. S—and Maj. Moore for eatables and tobacco. I go to bed and get up hungry, and go hungry through the day, and at night dream of something to eat. Men go about looking so cadaverous, with their sunken cheeks and thin blue lips, that it is fearful to look at them. I have not been in a single room of the prison without hearing the same subject of something to eat talked of. It is a sin and a shame. I would freely give the shirt off my back and wrap up in a blanket, for one good meal of substantial food. I have just written a letter to my cousin, Miss M. L. K. for something to eat, and if I can get my letter approved by the surgeon, will get the articles I send for without delay.

Received a good letter today from Inglewood. Date Sept. 10th. I wish I was situated so that I could get a box from them, I would be all right. I am still at work, "tinkering around my room" and I make some beautiful looking work, fitting up bookshelves and window and door casings. I find it impossible to saw two pieces of planks so that they . . . .

[Here the page is torn away and the portion of the diary up to March 14, 1865, is missing.]

· XI ·

"Blessed day in the calendar"

March 14, 1865, to April 9, 1865

March 14th 1865. Blessed day in the calendar, for on this day we a happy three hundred left our prison home for Dixie. We were called outside the prison walls, and after having examined our baggage, we were marched down to the wharf and went aboard a little steamer, which was waiting to carry us across the bay to Sandusky City, we were some time in crossing on account of the thickness of the ice, through which the boat had to break its way, but arrived safely in the city at 4 o'clock P.M.

"Hoarse sounding billows of the white capped lake,
That against barriers of our hated prison break,
Farewell—farewell with joy, thou inland sea.
Thou too, subscribs't the ends of tyranny.
Girding this isle, waking its lonely shore,
With moaning echoes of thy melancholy roar.
Farewell thou lake. Farewell inhospitable land,

Thou hast the curses of this patriot band.
All save that spot, the holy sacred bed,
Where rest in peace our Southern warriors dead.
Thou! Sunny land, I turn to you,
With blessing and with prayer,
Where man is brave and woman true,
And free as mountain air.
Long may our flag in triumph wave
Against the world combined,
And friends a welcome, foes a grave,
Within our borders find."

Left Sandusky at 5 P.M. and reached Newark[1] after dark. Through the kindness of Col. G. Troupe Maxwell, Capt. Mosely and Peeler, I fared sumptiously. The Col.'s bottle passed around occasionally during the night and this morning, and was a great blessing for we all needed something to stimulate.

March 15th. Remained at Newark until nearly noon. Col. Maxwell, Col. Green, Capt. Mosely, Oglesby and myself went up town to make some purchases. I exhausted my financial resources in the purchase of a pocket knife. My friends, who were in a better condition supplied themselves with boots and hats.

Passed through the State of Ohio, crossed the river at Belle-air four miles below Wheeling. Took the 4 A.M. train on the B. & O. R.R. and landed in Baltimore on Wednesday evening at sun down having been delayed one night on the Alleghaney Mountains by a snow storm, and also being delayed one night at Cumberland Md. on account of high water. Marched from the depot to the landing and immediately went on board the U.S. Transport, "General Morris" and set out for "Aikens Landing," "on the James." At Baltimore the officer in charge of us (Lieut. Ladlow) was placed in arrest on charges made by the Lt. Col. of the 193rd O.V.I. The charges were "Leniency, Drunkenness, and Sympathy with the Rebellion."

1. Newark, Ohio.

Monday Night, March 21st. Here we are at Aikens Landing and within hearing of our own guns once more. Yesterday was my birthday and passed almost without my thinking of it. Oh, that tomorrow would but come.

Richmond Va. March 22nd, '65. Night has again thrown her "Leaden mantle over a slumbering world," and silence reigns over the city, unbroken except by the foot-fall of some solitary soldier as he paces slowly to and fro on his "beat." The rattling of some army wagon over the rough streets, and the dull roaring of the river over its rocky bed. I am weary tonight yet sleep will not visit me. Too many conflicting emotions fill my soul. Thronging memories of the past are coming over me, while my spirits would fain examine the present, and lift the veil that shrouds the future, and see what is yet in store for me. I cannot analyze my feelings tonight. There is a certain indefinable sadness, and indescribable longing for something, I know not what, which fills me and thrills me with a kind of mysterious dread or presentiment of something yet to come,—but perhaps it is the effect of a state of high nervous excitement caused by the conflicting hopes and fears of the past few days. This morning we were transferred to Col. Marnford's boat, "The New York" where we took breakfast. About ten o'clock preceeded by Col. Marnford who was on horseback and bearing a white flag, we marched across the neck of land formed by the bend of the river to where our lines meet the enemy's. We sat on the bank of the river and soon saw our boat coming down the river, the triple barred banner of the Confederacy waving over it, and a band of music to welcome us.

As the boat rounded the point, and came nearer, the excitement became intense. Old men and young men tossed their hats in the air, and cheered and shouted until their throats were sore. I was [so] perfectly crazy that I was almost ready to rush in to the water and meet the boat as it approached the shore. As the boat slowly swung around, the cheers of our party were almost deafening. But as the boat touched the landing, the band struck up in a low sweet tone, "Home Sweet Home." Never have I seen such a change before, everything became hushed and still, and as the echoes died away in the distance up and down the river, every eye was moistened with tears. Old gray headed fathers sat down, bowed their heads and wept like children, and many an involuntary "Thank God" escaped the lips as it rose from the heart. Yes, home at last. We thought not of the suffering of the past, of the long weary months of cold and hunger, nor of the dangers that might await us in the future, we only thought and felt that we were again in our own land, among friends and comrades and were for the time perfectly happy. We reached Richmond at three o'clock this evening, marched up Main Street to the "Spotswood," then separated, each to amuse himself as best pleased him. On tomorrow we have to report to the commander of the district, but I must sleep. Goodnight "everybody."

March 23rd. This morning bright and early, I went around and drew a year's salary, and received a thirty days leave of absence, then came here to see Mrs. Quarles and family. Of course, nothing would do but I must leave the hotel and make this my home.

I find them all well and as kind as when they cared for me so tenderly in the summer of 1862. I find that since that time, Miss "Mary Lew" has married and is now the mother of a fine baby boy. He will do well, if he makes as good a man as his mother is a woman.

26th. Yesterday morning I took the Petersburg train and went to see my regiment, found them camped near the "Howlett" House," supporting the "Howlett House Battery."[2] Oh, how changed since I last saw them. I miss so many faces that used to greet me. A mere handful remains of the little band; they have been wasted by the storms of battle and by disease, and even the few remaining look weary and worn. How I love them and how dear the cause for which they contend, made a thousand times

2. The Confederate position across Bermuda Neck (located between Richmond and Petersburg along the James and Appomattox rivers) was known as the Howlett Line after the Howlett family who had two homes near the Confederate defenses.

dearer by the sacrafice it has cost and is costing us. Father of heaven and earth grant that the struggle may soon end, and end in victory. I find our ranks so thinned that when in line of battle along the works, the boys are scattered eight feet apart. Hardly a skirmish line, yet when the battle comes, they will have to meet solid lines. My dear Ansel is still here, so is Jim Crow, but Chandler, poor fellow, he is gone, gave up his life in the charge that retook the "crater." I returned to the city this evening, and wish to look up Cousin Frank tomorrow.

27th. This morning I walked out to the camps of Kershaw's division [3] and have been spending the day with Frank. He seems to be quite pleasantly situated, and I wish that I could be with him.

29th. Came out to the regiment this morning and brought with me some little articles for the boys. I find that communication is cut off between this point and Alabama so I think I'll spend my furlough, or at least such part of it as I enjoy, before I am exchanged, in Virginia.

30th. Came to the city this morning and Ansel follows me on the evening train, armed with an order from the Quarter Master General for him to proceed to Gordonsville to collect some stores left there some time ago. What a time we will have. I want to get away from the army, for fear that through some accident, I might again fall into the hands of the Yankees, and if found with the army with my parole in my pocket, my neck might be in danger.

"Inglewood" Sunday Night, April 2nd. Back again to the scenes of many happy hours, and some sad ones too, for once I watched with Ansel here when I thought his days were numbered. Ansel and I left Richmond last Friday morning, but came by the cars no farther than "Little River." Sheridan I suppose must have thought the R.R. in the wrong place as he has torn it up from that point to this place, a distance of nearly fifty miles. I did not mind

3. Joseph B. Kershaw.

that though, for we walked it in a little over a day and a half and arrived soon this morning. Stopped at Belle Monte and went from there to church after which we came here. All are well, and all gave us the same old fashioned Virginia welcome. Besides the family I find Miss Pattie Anderson, Alice Hunter, Anna Hopkins, and Cornelia C. . . . here. Of course I will enjoy myself.

4th. News from Gordonsville tells us that no news is coming over the wires from Richmond, that they cannot get a dispatch there. Something must have happened. No railroad communication either. I feel cut off from the world.

Sunday 9th. We are to be off tomorrow morning for the army. I can't see any peace here as matters are now. All kinds of strange rumors afloat about the army and its position. Rumor says that a great battle has been fought at Richmond and Petersburg and that our forces have been defeated, and that they are falling back. Some say by the way of Lynchburg, going to East Tennessee. Some say to unite with Gen. Johnson in North Carolina.[4] I feel sad at leaving here, for I fear it is never to return. I intend to go around the armies if possible, and cross the James River, some where near Lynchburg and join our command. I fear there is terrible fighting in store for us this summer, but the Almighty may care for us as He has in the past.

END

4. Lee had hoped to join forces with Joseph E. Johnston in North Carolina. In February, 1865, Johnston had been ordered to take command in the Carolinas and to stop Sherman's march north from Savannah. At Bentonville in eastern North Carolina (March 19–21) he managed to slow but not to halt the Federal advance. When he learned of Lee's surrender at Appomattox, Johnston decided it would be futile to continue the fight. He surrendered his small army on April 26 to General Sherman at James Bennitt's farmhouse a few miles west of Durham. "Bennitt" (not Bennett) is the spelling that was used by the owner of the house in which the Johnston-Sherman surrender took place. Ethel S. Arnett, *Confederate Guns Were Stocked at Greensboro, North Carolina* (Greensboro: Piedmont Press, 1965), p. 54.

INDEX

Index